A FINE NIGHT FOR TANKS

Tanks at night. (IWM, B7446)

A FINE NIGHT FOR TANKS

The Road to Falaise

KEN TOUT

SUTTON PUBLISHING

First published in 1998 by Sutton Publishing Limited
Phoenix Mill · Thrupp · Stroud · Gloucestershire GL5 2BU

Reprinted 1998

British Library Cataloguing in Publication Data
A catalogue record for this book is available from the British Library

ISBN 0 7509 1730 X

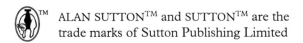 ALAN SUTTON™ and SUTTON™ are the
trade marks of Sutton Publishing Limited

Typeset in 10/12pt Plantin Light.
Typesetting and origination by
Sutton Publishing Limited.
Printed and bound in Great Britain by
WBC Limited, Bridgend, Mid-Glamorgan.

CONTENTS

1 The Night is Not for Sleeping   1

2 The Unassailable Fortress   21

3 Canadian Wizardry   35

4 The Left Hook   50

5 The Straight Right   69

6 Counterpunch at Saint-Aignan   86

7 A Points Victory   104

8 The Opponent's Corner   123

9 The Champion Dethroned   139

10 The Verdict   156

Notes & References   170

Bibliography   175

Acknowledgements   177

Index   179

Tanks raising the dust. (Tank Museum, photo 5463/A1)

Chapter One

The Night is Not for Sleeping

'At about the last watch, with enough of the night remaining for them to be able to cross the plain under cover of darkness, they got up when the signal was given and marched towards the mountain, which they reached at dawn.'
(Xenophon, 400 BC)

It could have been a lovely night. It had been a beautiful day of hot sunshine and green fields. August Bank Holiday, 1944.

Then, at midnight, the fields had been invaded by dust, smoke, death, confusion, darkness, dazzle, deafening noise. The men riding tanks across those fields suffered a constant bludgeoning motion. They travelled aghast at the menace of the green and red death-dealing flashes, the stench of long putrifying or recently charred flesh and the sight of those blazing, tree-high pyres where comrades were being cremated, not after a week of decent mourning or even a tropical day of grief, but instantly, in full view.

August Bank Holiday, traditional day of high summer jollity for the British masses, singing in their charabancs on the way to the beach or, for the better-off family, risking 30 miles an hour on a motorbike and sidecar across the moors. Percy Sumner[1] might have been taking his Sunday School class for a day's outing beyond the smoke stacks of Sheffield, perhaps on a tram, but not in a tank. Certainly not on a 'Churchill Tour' of Normandy!

August Bank Holiday, 1944. Bill Higham remembered that it was his father's birthday. What double rejoicings they would have had by the seaside at Blackpool or New Brighton. Waiting at the start line his crew had switched their wireless net illicitly, as many tank crews did, to the American Forces Network, and the band was playing:

> This is a lovely way to spend an evening,
> Can't think of anything I'd rather do.

Bill and crew had let out hearty guffaws, with that rough humour that so easily disguises fear – 'I sure can think of something effing better to do' – and had switched back to the official net where crackling silence portended horrific messages to come.

As the wireless came alive with messages Bill Deeming, over to the right with 148 RAC, felt overwhelmed. Each tank crew member could hear the external messages filtered through into the i/c (intercom) system. In a leading tank Bill's wireless was picking up the series of bleeps which was intended to keep a tank column on target. It was like an aircraft control system, dashes if the vehicle went too far left and dots if it veered right. A steady stream of green tracer shells from Bofors guns firing overhead also indicated the direction of the target. Added to the dots and dashes in Bill's headphones was the babble of voices, made more irritating for him because the Canadians seemed to be using a different wireless procedure from the British. Or perhaps no procedure at all. It made the head buzz while the eyes were wearied from incessant flashes in many colours.

Using this type of radio tracking beam a single tank, or a tank with two, five or ten tanks behind it, and on a level plain without obstacles, might have been able to keep a straight path. But now there were 1,400 armoured vehicles abroad, in columns of four, on a narrow front, in the alternating brilliant, blinding light and the utter retina-seared darkness. Almost within sight of one another, had it been daylight, there rumbled seven jostling columns of four 30-ton tanks and clumsy mine-sweeping flails, a yard or two apart. And the thick hedges, the sunken roads, the vast bomb craters, the railway embankment, and a desperate enemy, frantically firing into the thundering noise which bore down upon and rolled over him.

August Bank Holiday night, 1944. Canadian general Guy Simonds' master plan to march his tanks at night up the slopes where 400 tanks and thousands of men had perished recently in daylight. Bourguebus Ridge, Verrieres Ridge, the Saint-Aignan heights, if not the strongest German defence line of the entire Second World War, perhaps the one which they most needed to defend with all the professionalism and fanatical fatalism of which élite SS Panzers were capable. Otherwise Patton's Americans coming up from the south might make a junction with Simonds' corps, trapping an entire German army in a defeat worse than Stalingrad.

French historian, Eddy Florentin, captured the mysteries of that night when he wrote:

> Strange green lights to the south and red to the north suddenly marked point by point the Caen-Falaise plateau. The Germans in their trenches saw the glow, and the Canadians, too, in their tanks saw these green fires burning, yet consuming nothing. Thus Fontenay-le-Marmion emerged from the shadows and May-sur-Orne was outlined in the darkness. The Scots also saw Secqueville-la-Campagne loom up green. All these villages sentenced to death by the target-indicator shells, to receive the bombs of Operation Totalize.[2]

The first action of the Night March had been the arrival of the first of over a thousand RAF bombers, attempting to bomb at night, closer than ever before to the ground troops. To the left of the Northamptonshire Yeomanry the woods blazed under the weight of RAF bombs, not one of which landed in the massed columns of the Yeomen only 1,000 yd away – a mere hair's-breadth away in air bombing terms. Tpr E.H. Roberts with another Yeomanry, the Lothian & Border (supporting the Canadians) felt 'spirits

The author in Northants Yeomanry uniform, 1944.

rising but from what I can see the formation is too packed and the lights make it like a Victory Parade. One wonders if Jerry can see us?'[3]

Trying to command the 144 RAC column in that light, Lt-Col Jolly called it 'the blind leading the blind'.[4] For Bill Deeming with 148 RAC, still bemused by the wireless bedlam, it was 'blind man's buff'. With 2,000 yd showing on his yardometer and visibility almost nil, 2/Lt H. Rolland (Lothian & Border) was irritated because the lead tank in front was not showing a red rear light, which was the only guide for most tanks in the column. His irritation changed to consternation when the entire lead troop of tanks executed a 360° turn and hemmed him in on all sides.[5]

The night was terrifying enough for tank crews, trained though they were to grapple with the fear of being trapped inside a travelling incinerator. It was probably even worse for the Lothian & Border and the XXII Dragoons who were driving cumbersome 'Crabs', lumbering tanks festooned with jibs, rotors and weighted chains to flail the ground for mines. These vehicles were difficult to manage and had the same propensity for brewing up in flames as the normal Sherman tank. But it was probably worst for the infantry. Many of them were not walking but had been piled suddenly into open-topped armoured vehicles which would be called Kangaroos and had just been 'invented' by Simonds.[6] There, cramped in groups of ten, they were made to ride through the night, open to overhead shell bursts and also knowing the rapidity with which such vehicles could catch fire.

'All the ingredients of a horror film,' thought Jack Pentelow, near the front of the Northamptonshire Yeomanry column. Stan Hicken could not believe his eyes as the Sherman he was driving brushed shoulders with a Churchill tank. There should have been no Churchills in the Northamptonshire Yeomanry. Down beside Stan in the front compartment of their Sherman, 3 Baker, Rex Jackson watched German tracer flying across their front with what seemed a lazy, dawdling progress until the last moment when it sped with vicious spite at its target.

Lt Ian Hammerton (XXIID) found 'visibility reduced to zero':

> The bombing and shelling had created so much smoke and dust that it was impossible to see even the pin-point red rear lights of the tank in front although our jib and rotor kept bumping into that tank. We proceeded by fits and starts, the radio filled with messages of bewilderment and complaints about the impossibility of seeing anything. Our own gun flashes were blinding in the darkness. Above us, on the underside of the low clouds, shone 'Monty's Moonlight' [reflected searchlights] which cast an eerie glow over everything.[7]

Suddenly, to the tumult of air bombing and thousands of engines, air-borne and land-based, was added the Wagnerian percussion of two army groups of heavy artillery, as awesome to friend as to foe. Not only the jolting allies and the entrenched Germans heard it but, as Florentin recalls:

> the refugees from Caen heard the whole massed British artillery on the heights of the left river bank go into action simultaneously. A barrage of extraordinary intensity was sustained for hours and hours on end. Flames spurted from the mouths of the guns, seeming to touch each other, forming a ring of fire around the town [2 miles behind the rearmost tanks].[8]

The gunners had already made a significant contribution to the Night March, providing the pinpoint accurate markers by which the leading Lancaster bombers could aim their markers. More graphically a Dragoon records:

> The gunners' marker shells whistled towards Lourguichon woods, suddenly painting the skyline with vivid glares of green and carmine light. At once in answer the bombers unloosed their brilliant trails of pink and white target indicators, through whose falling stars there screamed the first salvos of bombs . . . the storm rocked about La Hogue and the woods of Secqueville, its incessant flashes throwing up the silhouettes of motionless trees, of silent tanks, and of ruined farmhouses.[9]

On the left flank the Northamptonshire Yeomanry crews, pounded by the gales of nearby explosions, found that the sight of the air bombardment almost caused the fear of stray bombs to be forgotten:

> Over on our left the other three tanks of our Troop are mis-shapen black beetles swimming in a cauldron of fire . . . great spouts of flame illuminate a long vista of forest . . . in a hurricane of blast the tops of the trees dance against a sky of incandescent orange. The explosions, starting as vermilion pinpricks, bulge into leaping rainbows of light. A huge square object rises lazily above the trees, turns slowly over and over, then drops into the writhing forest.[10]

Grateful as the tank crews were to the RAF bomb-aimers, the massive air intervention was something of a mixed blessing. The two leading tanks of one column fell into a huge crater and could not get out. Ian Hammerton's own Crab suffered the same fate and 'plunged into a giant crater'. His driver, Basil Frost, attempted 'the normal procedure of reversing out, but the loose soil from the bombing so strained the tracks that one broke, and we were stuck in the hole'.[11] Sgt D. Esson, in one of the four Canadian columns, felt his tank lurch into a shellhole or bomb crater and had to reverse to get out, losing touch with the tank in front and causing the crew commander to wireless for more Verey light signals up front to guide them.[12]

The landscape itself, when visible, was enough to cause nightmares for even the hardiest tourist:

> the desolate, pitted lunar landscape of the 'Goodwood' battles. Country fought over and destroyed like the Somme or Passchendaele battlefields of the Great War. Pocked with shellholes. Scarred with slit trenches. Littered with shattered vehicles and the instruments of war. Studded with shredded trees and crumbled houses. Sullied above all by the stench of unburied dead, animal and human. The stench creeps in through the periscope fittings like a live, breathing fog.[13]

Orders had been given that all things walking must be shot. Only the creeping mechanical monsters of the night would be tolerated on those long undulating slopes. So for people like Ian Hammerton and his crew the safe recourse was to dismount their machine-gun and set up a tiny defence post in their bomb crater in the middle of nowhere. According to instructions, they should shoot first and ask questions later of any walking bodies. For other crew the rugged terrain meant less dramatic traumas. In one heavy fall, as his Sherman crashed through a deep ditch, wireless operator John Stenner (Northamptonshire Yeomanry) smashed his nose against the breech block of the big gun in the turret. Feeling like a pummelled boxer, he spent the next five minutes picking up wireless codes, tools and other small items from the rocking turret floor, scrabbling about under the large bag of coarse cloth placed to receive the 'empties' from the 75 mm gun.

The infantry of the 51st Highland Division were just as uncomfortable in their rather crudely adapted Kangaroos. Out of the black void a German hand grenade dropped at the feet of Pte Jarvis, a Headquarters signaller of the Argylls. Jarvis promptly threw the grenade back in the approximate direction from which it had come. Stan Whitehouse (Black Watch) was glad of the protection which the awkward carriers provided, although

> It was a nightmare journey as we cowered down while shrapnel and bullets pinged off the armoured vehicle's sides. We had to pee in our empty food tins and throw the contents over the sides. I did notice a number of dead Germans lying along our route, and a Kangaroo just ahead was hit, whereupon the squaddies aboard baled out, only to disappear in two simultaneous explosions of dirt and smoke.[14]

Meanwhile, what of the Germans submerged under the barrage from heaven and earth? Karl Heinz Decker and his mortar crew were making their usual night-time dash from one anonymous hole to another unknown pit, behind hedges or under trees or within shattered buildings. Every night they had to change position furtively for during the day the domination of the air by the Allied air forces was such that a moving German uniform was as vulnerable as a scurrying rabbit sighted by a flock of hawks.

At the centre of the deadly tumult 1/Lt Willy Scheuermann had been hoping to get a good night's sleep after commanding the advance guard of a relieving infantry division. Hitler himself had order the 12th SS Panzer Division, the implacable Hitlerjugend (Hitler Youth), to move south towards the advancing Americans. They were replaced by the 89th Infantry Division which had been hurriedly brought down from the fjords of Norway. The contrast between the scarred Normandy battlefields, under a torrid sun amid the smell of death, and the temperate, unspoiled, scented countryside of Norway was depressing and ominous. The 89th 'Horseshoe' Division needed a good rest, quiet induction and plenty of horseshoe luck in that situation. They would be afforded none of those as the shattering bombardment spoiled their first good night of sleep in Normandy.[15]

Not far behind them Georg Isecke, adjutant of 12 Panzer Regiment, fretted over the problem which his corps was pondering. Hitler had ordered a move far south of where the Hitlerjugend waited near Cintheaux. Their own commander and his immediate superiors had forecast a major offensive in the next few hours against the unprepared 89th Infantry Division. The Hitlerjugend were, as it might be phrased, 'hanging about', not quite in defiance of the Führer's orders, to see when the northern storm of Canadians, British and Poles would break upon them.[16]

One person who was sleeping was Guy Simonds. For almost two weeks he had been working up to twenty hours a day, planning Totalize. Now all the plans had been prepared and approved, all the preparations had been made, all the columns were lined up for the Night March and commanders had been designated for the two wings of the advance. There was nothing left for the corps commander to do. Simonds could catch a brief sleep before it was time to consider and order responses to reports filtering back from the sites of night action.[17]

A German soldier snatching some fitful sleep, 3 miles up the Caen to Falaise main road, was Michael Wittmann, the highest-scoring tank ace of any war. As the Northamptonshire Yeomanry's navigating officer, Captain Tom Boardman, was to say, 'If we had known he was just up the road we would have been even more concerned than we already were'. But for most of the German troops in the Night March area it was a night of bombardment so graphically described by a young German soldier of the SS Leibstandarte Division:

A furious bombardment intended to finish us off . . . with thousands of shells hitting us all at once . . . the one remaining wall of the house behind which we were sheltering collapsed on top of our tank, and we had to dig it out. One of the tanks of 4 Platoon was badly hit. Some of the armour plating landed on the driver's lap, slicing off both his legs. He begged his comrades to put him out of his misery. All around us were craters so big they could hold an entire tank. We really thought our end had come . . . the tactic of unbroken artillery barrages was gruesome mental and physical torture.[18]

But it was not only the Germans who were beginning to suffer. Lothian & Border troop leader, Lt P.S. Newman, was astonished when 'a machine gun on our left opened up from about 15 yards away, also several groups of men [German] running about somewhat aimlessly'.[19] In that frantic confusion the enemy bullets and anti-tank shot still hit Canadian targets. Tpr E.H. Roberts saw a flash but could not trace the exact source.

Tpr. Spencer has gun layed on target and is awaiting next flash. Have counted ten tanks on fire around us (all Canadians). Next tank to us blows up and turns night into day. We can't fire as our own tanks in way. We have been joined by Tprs. Holton and Sutherland who say their tank has been shot up and caught fire. Nobody seems to know how the attack has gone.[20]

Every tank crew member had either seen a Sherman tank erupt into instant 50 ft high flames, or had prowled around a knocked-out vehicle and studied at close hand the fate which awaited. Les 'Spud' Taylor (Northamptonshire Yeomanry) prowled around a knocked-out tank and never forgot the experience:

The A.P. [armour-piercing shot] had penetrated the left side of the turret . . . only a matter of inches on target . . . the driver's and co-driver's compartment hatches were open and the seats empty. I climbed up to have a look inside the turret . . . the stench was indescribable . . . I saw the loader-operator, his hands frozen in the act of feeding a belt of ammo into his machine-gun, his head resting sideways on his arm. The regimental badge on his beret was clearly visible . . . the appalling thing was, the body was as black as coal . . . from an advanced state of decay. The gunner was just a shapeless mass of decomposition on the turret floor, but the most horrific sight of all was the crew commander . . . the projectile upon entry had decapitated the poor man. His body . . . lay on the floor but . . . the head, as if on display, rested upside down on a ledge, the lower jaw shot away . . . overcome with nausea, I scrambled down from that chamber of death and corruption, and lit a cigarette . . . and vowed never again to look inside a k.o'd tank.[21]

What Les Taylor does not say is that, having finished his cigarette, he then climbed into a similar tank, which drove off directly towards the guns that could wreak such destruction. Another author, also prowling, had a similar experience with similar regrets:

It was only curiosity which induced us to explore the burned-out German tank near Creully. We did not expect to intrude on the privacy of the crew still seated inside, charred to the size of wizened monkeys and to the consistency of burned sausages. The roasting of human flesh and the combustion of ammunition and the defecation of a million voracious flies created an aura of such sense-assaulting horror that we recoiled from it.[22]

With good reason tank crews were both fearful and cautious. The hatches through which they must escape were narrow and the turret hatch could be totally jammed by the dead body of the commander. If the big gun was traversed in certain directions the driver and co-driver could not raise their hatches and had to drop through an escape hatch in the floor. If the tank had grounded in soft soil or on furrowed earth the escape hatch might not detach, in which case the front two crew must squeeze through the turret cage and squirm up through the turret and get out that way. And the Sherman, dubbed the 'Tommy Cooker' by the Germans, was called a 'Ronson' by its own slaves because it took fire in a steep flame with the promptness of a Ronson cigarette lighter. Just a flick and then . . . So it was important for drivers to keep the escape hatch working swiftly. Sometimes the blundering, rocking movement of the tank caused the escape hatch to fall off altogether.

Les Taylor also observes that exit from what he calls the 'mobile crematorium' was not the end of the matter: 'On rough ground the exit through a floor panel depended on there being enough clearance to allow for a way out. Having been fortunate enough to bale out, the lucky crew man then had to run the gauntlet of snipers, small arms fire and all the other lethal stuff flying about.' It must be remembered that at times tanks were sent into positions which would have been suicidal for walking soldiers, but when a crew member baled out he became a vulnerable infantryman.

Rex Jackson and Stan Hicken were having trouble with their escape hatch, having lost the cover during practice runs for the Night March. The empty hole would certainly expedite exit if necessary, but, in this throng of hundreds of vehicles in column, their hatch was blowing up thick clouds of Normandy dust, smoke and other detritus. Stan was almost blinded within his niche, as he was when he put his head out into the open air. Rex looked around the tiny forward hutch which they occupied and noticed a cardboard ration box. He quickly ripped up the tough box by main force, shaped it roughly to the size of the hole and rammed it down, to give Stan some relief for eyes and nostrils. Brian Carpenter (also Northamptonshire Yeomanry) had himself lost an escape hatch – it seemed a frequent problem – on the practice runs but had been lucky enough to find a fitter with a moment to spare to replace the panel.

Fear, in a tank, was an almost tangible thing, evidenced in thirst, sweat, involuntary urination and worse. The crew knew that a German 88 mm shot could flame the tank at a range of 2,000 m, while a Sherman had to be within about 200 yd to be sure of inflicting significant damage on a Tiger (that is, a Sherman mounting the normal 75 mm gun). Then the crew member knew that if the tank ran over an anti-tank mine the thin bottom plating might not prevent serious maiming of the driver or co-driver. If no 88 mm guns or mines were available, the average German infantryman could appear with a portable, throwaway, one shot, bassoon-like *Panzerfaust* which could launch a projectile able to knock out the Sherman from 50 yd or so.

> These messages lie coiled, compressed within the brain, like snakes dozing in the sun. Then, like the unseen, striking snake, they unwhip and flash across the mind within a second, biting their poison into the brain – bleak, glaring ideas against a lurid background of remembered incidents and unremembered dreams and present events. At that point, fear emerges in all its symptoms – the clutching feeling at the heart, piercing sensation in the throat, ice-cold prickles up the nape of the neck and under the ears, burning fire behind the eyes, within the cheeks and across the eybrows. . . . Silence is the worst time. . . . Pray for noise.[23]

Silence in battle? Brian 'Shorty' Coleman's tank had halted out on the left flank. They were alone. The crew emerged for a moment, looking and listening in disbelief. There was an eerie silence. Back in the tank the headphones were filled with urgent messages and fatal announcements. Outside it seemed as though the world had come to an end, only Shorty and crew remaining! Thousands of vehicles gone, vanished into thin air. The silence was ghostly. They quickly clambered back into the tank, started up again, moved off, looking for a faint red rear light to which they could attach themselves.

Shorty and Co. were not imagining things. Also out on the left flank, the troop leader of 1 Troop, 'C' Squadron of the Northants, Lt Tony Faulkner, had halted his tank because the tank in front had halted. It was a strict follow-my-leader procession. Many tank commanders, when halted, ordered their drivers to switch off the thundering engine so that they could listen. This gave them another sense to detect furtive enemy movements which would be lost in the din of the engines. Tony Faulkner ordered driver Sutch to switch off.

Having been travelling in mass columns they were almost assaulted by the sudden silence, like a still tableau. After a moment the silence was broken by the squeaking, grinding sound of a ground anti-tank gun being traversed on its mounting. Intermittent flashes revealed an enemy gun slowly traversing towards Tony's tank at a range of about 30 ft! But the German crew were staring petrified at the Sherman looming 9 ft high, 30 tons of armoured steel, right over

Flail tanks with chains for beating mines. (IWM, B8844)

them. For a moment the British commander was equally paralysed. Then the tank in front moved off, its tiny rear light winking in the mist, and immediately, instinctively, Sutch started up, accelerated and moved into the mists which then hid the German anti-tank crew, still gazing open-mouthed. In silence! It may be that the mists and dust clouds had blanketed and muted much of the noise.

Other people noted the same phenomenon. Far over to the right, another troop leader of a 'C' Squadron, Lt A.R. Burn, with the Lothian & Border, found himself suddenly at the head of a Canadian column in his flail tank:

> We hit a very bad patch of mist . . . and a bad patch of ground which was not on our route, owing to the obscuring of the Bofors [tracer] and the moon and stars. I halted as I was now in the lead with no directional. Visibility was nil and I could see none behind me until someone came in on my off-side and got underneath my jib with his own. This jam sorted itself out and the other vehicle disappeared into the mist. I switched off my engine to listen to the general direction of the advance. Also switched on my lights hoping these would show me up to someone behind. Visibility was so bad that no one saw me switching on and off. In the silence I heard German voices at this period. So I switched off everything and listened.[24]

Of course, the air bombing had now ceased and the RAF had gone home, but they had not escaped unscathed. Ten bombers had been lost, whether from anti-aircraft fire or from collisions. While the RAF enjoyed total ownership of the skies over the Caen area, there was always danger from ground fire coming from the massed troops below. RAF navigator, W.R. 'Bill' Morris, would never forget the tension of the bombing run.

On raids when the Pathfinder force were due to mark the target some minutes before we were due to bomb, those last few minutes as we approached the target were minutes of high tension. Would the marker go down directly before us, indicating that my navigation had been spot on? Or would the markers be well to port or starboard, forcing us to change course violently, and almost certainly bring about a hurried, unsatisfactory bombing run? My Group had a special radar bombing device, G.H., and experienced navigators using this 'led' other aircraft to the target, and these aircraft bombed when the leading aircraft bombed.

Unfortunately, when bombing using G.H., the aircraft could not take evasive action on the bombing run as the navigator had to instruct the pilot while watching the radar screen. I found this three or four minute straight run distinctly gut-loosening as I called out gentle alterations of course, at the same time praying fervently that the German anti-aircraft fire would not be too accurate nor their fighters enjoy our non-evasive approach.

Down on earth the mists persisted, the awakened 89th Infantry Division defenders loosed off a massive smokescreen, the thousand and more vehicles continued to grind up an ever larger cumulus of dust as rear vehicles crunched over soil loosened by forward vehicles. Sunken roads proved those few inches deeper than convenient for clumsy flail tanks. Bomb craters had linked together into multiple pits which were not easily bypassed. Ruins of buildings thrust up their decayed teeth profile. The artificial moonlight reflecting off the clouds was sometimes more confusing than helpful as the cloudbanks themselves made their own Night March. Nothing improved for the navigators as the vital hours ticked by.

W.R. 'Ray' Birt says appositely, 'no connected story is possible of this nightmare operation. Sooner or later every tank commander was left to fight a lone battle to survive.' Remembering the experience of XXII Dragoons, he writes:

A copper-coloured moon had risen over the battlefield, and the air cleared temporarily to show the enemy gunners something of a target. Both forward navigating tanks [of 144 RAC] were hit, and the leaping flames which consumed them lit up the rest of the attacking force – now bunched tight against the [railway] embankment – as if it had suddenly come under the dazzle of a spotlight. To the right a burning house added its steady torch of illumination.[25]

Birt goes on to tell the fantastic story of Dragoon Capt Wheway, finding himself temporarily in command of his lane up front with all 144 RAC's forward commanders *hors de combat*. Seeing a figure appear out of the darkness Wheway drew his revolver and made to shoot. A plaintive voice called, 'Don't shoot, sir. It's Gillard. Lieutenant Boal is sunk in a crater.' Wheway went to investigate and 'found Lieutenant Boal sharing an enormous hole with three tanks that had fallen in one on top of the other'.

Equally astonished, Dragoon 'B' Squadron Cpl Welsh spotted a tank driver apparently sitting in the middle of another crater. Welsh gave the night's password, 'Harry Lauder', eliciting the reply, 'The devil with Harry Lauder! Can't you see my tank's ditched?' The driver was patiently sitting on top of his tank turret, with the whole tank 'turret down' in a multiple bomb hole.

The headphones continued to crackle and babble, with the added problem of foreign voices in the distance. Bill Deeming thought 'the Jerries have broken into our wireless net'. The Polish Armoured Division was also on air, moving up from Bayeux. In the middle of the melée the wireless cacophony was cut out, when a nearby control station began to transmit. Each regimental network then heard the message, 'The Supreme Commander is most anxious you do your best to push on at all speed'. Known responses varied from the dubious to the profane. The reactions from Lt Boal's crater or from the 'turret down' 144 driver have not been recorded. In spite of Gen Montgomery's acclaimed popularity with the troops, most tended to assume, probably correctly, that he would be asleep in his caravan at that hour. Simonds' nocturnal silence would have been more to the taste of frantically busy front-line troops.

While out on the far left the 1st Northamptonshire Yeomanry were booming along, unaware that they were skirting a minefield at a few yards distance, in the Canadian columns mines were causing some disturbance of the formations. 1st Lothian & Border Yeomanry's 'B' Squadron, 4 Troop Leader, 2/Lt John Melville found that 'after about half an hour a mist came on and practially everyone got lost. I blew two mines with my left track and Cpl. Coates blew two also, but neither of our tanks was damaged.' These were possibly anti-personnel mines. Melville's colleague, Lt W.J. Boreham was not so lucky. His flail tank blew up on a Teller mine. It is instructive to know what damage such a mine could do. Boreham, happily intact himself, reported the impact on his heavily armour-plated flail:

> One bogie smashed. Leading off suspension damaged. Jib supports smashed. Hydraulic cylinder and piston torn off. Near-side track cracked. Hole in co-driver's plates. Three remaining tanks flailed past. Cpl. Bradford also blew up – off-side track smashed. Off leading suspension damaged. Both crews retired 150 yards behind their tanks and dug in with ground-mounted .30 Brownings.[26]

Normally flail tanks would not be expected to act as normal fighting tanks in close gun action with the enemy. Ian Hammerton points out that there were technical difficulties with the jibs and rotors and massive chains terminating in flat sheets or balls to pound the earth and set off mines. 'We could not fire forward through the flogging chains, besides the dust or mud flung up filled up the barrel and obliterated the gunner's vision through his periscope sight, in spite of a periscope shield.' And the normal dust raised by one flail tank flogging the earth was compounded by the hundreds of vehicles milling around in the Night March. However, when Capt Wheway or another flail commander found himself right up front he had to contrive to fire his big gun or be destroyed by close enemy fire. In a daylight action there would have been fighting Shermans near enough, and with clear sights, to take up the shooting role.

Another often unsung role was that of the artillery, whose contribution may have been the most vital factor in two world wars. In battle the artillery was evidenced by huge tornados of flame and noise erupting just ahead of our own troops. Its minions, especially the heavy regiments, were way back from the front line marked on the map. In the first barrage of the Night March the crews of 360 Royal Artillery and Canadian Royal Artillery guns were beginning to work their way through a mountain of 205,000 rounds of ammunition. It is difficult to imagine what such an effort would mean in terms of sweat, muscle power, professional skills and danger of German counter-barrages.

Meanwhile the night hours seemed endless to Pte Stan Whitehouse of 1st Black Watch, squatting down inside his Kangaroo, squashed between his pals and his PIAT anti-tank projector. While still wary of air-bursts of shrapnel, 'it felt reassuring and was quite spectacular to peep over the brim and see all the armour'. Spectacular or not, for Stan cramp was the main sensation of those hours.

While Stan and many others in the seven tank columns travelled in comparative safety in the innovative Kangaroos, there were also walking infantry abroad. The gunning Shermans and threshing Crabs and cramping Kangaroos were intended to drive between the fortified villages of the German front line, follow a course across pathless country slopes and form armed camps well beyond the main troops of 89th Infantry Division. The walking infantry would come up behind the columns and hope that the enemy had been scared enough to run or surrender. Did nobody know that there were German troops in the enemy front line? Many front line troopers and privates suspected that it would not be so easy to scare even a fairly green Wehrmacht division.

The then Lt-Col G.L.W. 'Geordie' Andrews commanded the 2nd Seaforths of 51st Highland Division, the battalion which might be said to have drawn the short straw among the British battle tasks. Their walking target was Tilly-la-Campagne which the Canadians had five times tried to liberate. There were not enough Kangaroos to ferry the rear troops, so Lt-Col Andrews walked with his men to their start line:

> I hoped that the noise of armour on our flanks would hide our own movement and therefore chose a 'silent' attack without prior artillery preparation. . . . At 23.50 hours 'D' Company . . . crossed the Start Line, followed by 'A', who were to pass round their left, and then by 'B' who were to go right. For a while there was no sound as we advanced, except the clatter of armour on our flanks, but as 'D' approached the railway Spandau fire broke out and soon afterwards the German artillery defensive fire came down, heavy and accurate – a nasty experience in the open.
>
> The No. 18 manpack radio with me was soon put out of action by a splinter and we had to send the operator back for a replacement. Meanwhile the only contact with the companies was by runner and in the dark it was difficult to discover what was going on. By 01.30 'D' reported being on their objective and while 'B' did so soon afterwards

Lt Wyn Griffith-Jones (back row, sixth from the left) with his 2 Troop, 'A', 1st Northamptonshire Regiment.

they had strayed off to their right . . . 'A' were held up short of the orchard and reported heavy casualties. It looked as if we were getting stuck and I ordered 'C' to come forward. . . . My rear link radio to Brigade had also packed up by now.[27]

Also in considerable trouble were crews on opposite flanks of the continuing advance as 'continuing volcanoes of fire, punctuated by the brief blackness of original night . . . revealed us as clumsy, blind dinosaurs stumbling across a primeval landscape against a background of bleeding skies'.[28] The crews in trouble were those of Lt A.R. Burn, in the Canadian right lane, and Lt W. Griffith-Jones in the British left lane. Wyn Griffith-Jones, aided by his driver Jimmy Kerr, remembers the occasion all too clearly. He was wont to say in jest, 'Don't worry, mother!' Suddenly he was saying, 'Mother, start worrying now!'

No. 2 Troop ['A', Northamptonshire Yeomanry] lined up at the head of their column (behind navigator and flails) with Corporal Howard in the lead followed by myself, then Sergeant Burnett and Corporal Ferrier. Right from the start navigation was difficult because of the dust that the columns had disturbed. The noise of engines, gunfire, and bombs was terrific. As the column advanced the smoke from objects set alight by gunfire and bombs became more of a problem. I asked the leader (Capt. Boardman) to send up a Verey light to ensure that contact was not lost. He did so at great risk to giving away his own location. Shortly after this I took my tank into the lead (of the Troop) and ploughed through a hedge into a potato field. We were later to find out that the German armour were using this field as a laager for the night. There was a green flash to my left as a German tank opened fire from about 50 yards away.

The first shot missed my tank but the second shot hit Cpl. Howard's tank as he came through the gap in the hedge made by my tank. It brewed up immediately. I stopped and my gunner, L/Cpl. Symes, traversed his gun over the tail of the tank and put two shots into the German tank which also brewed up. Little did I realise in the darkness that 25 yards ahead of me was a second German tank which fired twice, and hit my tank, once in the transmission and the other time in the front shield between the driver (Cpl. Kerr) and the co-driver (Tpr. Grint). A third shot from an unknown tank on my left flank hit the engine compartment, and the whole tank became engulfed in flames. The flames went up 50 to 60 feet in the air. We all bailed out and sought shelter in the rows of potatoes. As these were well grown by August 8th they provided excellent cover.

As the tank had been immobilized with the gun over the tail it was not possible for the drivers to get out via the normal route, so they had to resort to escaping through the hatch in the floor. A very tight squeeze. Cpl. Kerr used both feet to push Grint out. A real panic situation with the tank in flames and the hatch small and difficult to release. In the meantime Sgt. Burnett had engaged the tank in front of me and set it alight. By now the field resembled a floodlit soccer field and a German tank in the darkness easily picked off and destroyed the tank which Cpl. Ferrier was commanding, in addition to other personnel carriers.

I raced over to Sgt. Burnett and asked him to follow the column. I then returned to a safe distance from my burning tank in which the ammunition was causing repeated explosions. I could not find my crew. They had in fact been picked up by a Canadian Armoured Personnel Carrier and were later deposited at a first aid centre. I then resolved to hide in the potatoes near my burning tank, hoping that no Germans would venture near.

That was not the end of 'Grif's' adventures but subsequent scenes belong to a later chapter. On the opposite flank, Lt Burn had noticed that the wind was blowing from the south east, that is from Griffith-Jones' column, so that Burn and his neighbours were fielding the dust and smoke from six other columns to their east. After stopping and listening, as mentioned earlier, Burn started off again, meeting up with his fellow Troop Leader, Lt Pelly. They headed towards a disused airfield which was their objective. Before they could reach it there was an orchard in which 'a tremendous melee' took place as a German anti-tank gun under the trees was firing point-blank into the column and every vehicle in the column was trying to take evasive action, hampered by loaded apple trees and other vehicles, to say nothing of the flickering light. Burn saw a Sherman and a carrier hit on either side of him and only feet away. Enjoying luck for the moment Burn and Pelly pushed on with their tanks firing almost continuously, without clear targets, into woods and hedges.

Just before the objective Burn saw another anti-tank gun fire at the column. The shots passed about 10 yd away from him but he could not fire back because of the closeness of other vehicles. The two Shermans ahead turned right and left respectively and halted. As he passed between them, Burn's tank was hit twice head-on by the anti-tank fire, virtually at point-blank range. Burn ordered 'Bale out' and everyone in the turret evacuated rapidly. Tpr Scully, the gunner, was slightly wounded but able to attend to himself so Burn left him behind the tank and went to look for the drivers. They managed to get Tpr Whelan, the co-driver, out of the tank in order to attend to his leg injuries. But the plight of the driver was far worse. The driver's hatch had been bent and the turret was jammed. The driver himself was helpless and stuck between his levers and other equipment.

The column had now halted on or near the objective, so Lt Pelly and Capt Bousfield also joined the attempts to smash a way into the driver's compartment and make space to lift the driver out. They laboured for over an hour before they managed to bring L/Cpl Boyd through the turret and down on to the ground. To their disappointment and grief he died almost immediately afterwards.

In the Canadian centre lane Lt Melville found that things did not always go according to plan. As he had been instructed, and as subsequent war maps indicated, the centre column route was a straight line from Start Line to objective. All one had to do was keep driving straight ahead. Or so they said. Lt Melville must have thought he had been re-routed to some kind of obstacle course on which it was necessary constantly to be bearing back 20 yd this way or that way to maintain the straight line.

> I came to a thick hedge but was unable to see what the ground was like on the other side. I knew there was a quarry near our course. I could tell there was a drop, but how much I did not know. There was too much small arms fire to get out. So I elevated my jib and went forward. The drop was only three feet or so. It was my worst moment. I found myself confronted by a high stone wall with large trees beyond. To my left high wire entanglements. I told my driver to turn right running parallel with the wall. A gun pit appeared on my right. I lobbed over a hand grenade and pushed on. Suddenly a handful of Huns emerged from a hole in the wall, rifles in hand, not five yards away. I gave them another grenade . . . eventually I found myself in trees and realized it was an orchard.[29]

Many tank crews and carrier-borne infantry saw little of the excitement described. Brian Carpenter's tank was in the rearguard troop ('B', Northamptonshire Yeomanry) and the most remarkable thing he saw was that the infantry in front had white tape crosses on their packs so that they would not get fired upon from behind in the confusion. Joe Crittenden found the march 'as much audible as visual'. He was gunner in a 'Firefly', a Sherman fitted with a 'secret weapon', the new 17-pdr gun capable of taking on the 88 mm on equal terms. 'A Firefly gunner had only his telescopic sight for viewing whereas the more usual 75 mm Sherman gunner had his gun-sight incorporated in a wider view periscope. In consequence one had to rely on information coming from the wireless and commander, and one's own interpretation of the battle noises.' He observes that the orders were quite simple. Today they may seem rather trite, but at that time they were tinged with a certain amount of drama: 'Follow the Bofors tracer – don't stop – bash on regardless!'

The British units in the Night March formed part of the Canadian 2nd Corps for the time being. The actual Canadian troops taking part had very mixed fortunes. One of the infantry battalions, the South Saskatchewans under their commander, Lt-Col F.A. Clift, followed the artillery barrage closely, in spite of the dust clouds and the danger from 'friendly fire'. Rushing into their target village, Rocquancourt, they found that the defenders were still sheltering from the barrage. By the very early time of 00.45 hours the South Saskatchewans had occupied the village. On the other hand, Les Fusiliers and the Cameron Highlanders of Canada were at a great disadvantage because the RAF had had to cancel a third of their bombing programme because of the impossible visibility and the danger posed to their own troops of continuing to bomb virtually blind. Les Fusiliers and the Camerons just happened to advance into the least bombed areas.

One company of Les Fusiliers was cut off, although they eventually achieved their goal later on. The Camerons in front of Fontenay-le-Marmion, lost their Commanding Officer, Lt-Col John Runcie. The brigade major took over, Maj. C.W. Ferguson. He was fatally wounded. German tanks, left behind in the wake of the Allied columns, hit the Camerons from behind. Much bravery was displayed. CSM Abram Arbour took over command of 'B' Company when it was left without officers. He led it with such distinction that he was awarded the most unusual decoration, normally given only to officers, the Military Cross. The commander of the Essex Scottish column, Lt-Col T.S. Jones, went missing, badly wounded. There was no place of rear safety or immunity for higher rank on the Night March. A major-general would also be severely wounded in the overall operation.[30]

The question of enemy response would continue to be something of a lottery until the end of the night. For 2nd Seaforths and some of the Canadian Highlanders the travail would continue well into daylight hours. In other places the phenomenon of silence still occurred from time to time. When it is considered that the barrage was only about 2.3 miles wide (4,050 yd) and that about 1,400 vehicles were hemmed in that space, not to mention the firepower of other battalions of walking soldiers, the strange silences did indeed constitute a phenomenon of war. The Northants navigating officer, Capt Tom Boardman, who, on a curving route, had managed to avoid going astray, ran out of Verey light signal cartridges, which were fired from a hand pistol. As tank commanders further back down the column constantly called for Verey signals to keep them on course, Boardman stopped his tank in an oasis of calm, quickly jumped down and went back to Capt Ken Todd in the second navigator's tank behind. On the way he was astonished to see several German soldiers in a slit trench looking up at him in a kind of chilled suspension of conscious action. He thought it best not to rouse them and went on his way, collected more cartridges from Ken Todd, and then hastened back to the relative security of the lead Sherman. The Germans were still staring upwards, immobilized, no doubt by the recent bombing and gun punishment.

Military histories must in the main concentrate on the generals. Books like this one may find room to mention lower-rank officers and the occasional exceptional 'other rank', such as CSM Arbour MC, but the vast majority never achieve a mention. So perhaps it is appropriate to look inside Capt Tom Boardman's lead tank and give a mention to the crew as representatives of so many young soldiers in their early twenties or late teens who bore the main brunt of physical action and constituted the main mass of casualty rolls. They were Tprs Buck, Ager, Walker and Rutledge, the last being the gunner. Buck and Ager shared the front driving compartment.

For at least some minutes of the Night March Buck and Ager were the first two soldiers in that host of at least 20,000 men who were pressing forward in the seven columns. Their left flank was nakedly exposed to whatever forces the enemy might be able to assemble and activate. There was some security in the efficacy of the RAF bombing parallel with their route but they were frightfully exposed. In the event the stupefying impact on the enemy of the massed apparition of overwhelming forces was such that a number of lead tanks and flails passed through unscathed. Less fortunate vehicles further back in the columns caught the blast of reaction as the defenders at last roused themselves to fire their guns, although often uncomprehendingly and at random. An anti-tank gun fired at random at 50 yd range can cause greater damage than an aimed shot at the more usual 500 yd range.

Ray Ager remembers that they had gone off to 'a HQ somewhere' where Capt Boardman was briefed. Then the four troopers had been allowed to visit a NAAFI canteen for a 'cuppa'. On return operator Walker found a strange wireless set had been installed in the turret, 'the one that receives the dot dash dots'. Also there was a new compass. Ager and Buck found different lights fixed on the rear of the Sherman. Before the Night March set off they were assembled with others in front of a blackboard and the route and formation were explained to them. In the not unlikely event of the commander being knocked out they would 'need to know'. So they were well aware of the implications of their post, right at the extreme finest point of the arrowhead which the war artists like to plot on their maps. However, in all the excitement, Ager's main impression was 'the creeping barrage of artillery' flashing just ahead and 'the smell of grass and dust'.

Danger was not only from the front. In the centre of the seven lanes, with the 8th Canadian Reconnaissance Regiment, Sgt D. Esson was driving a tank called 'Black Agnes'. Sundry flashes came diagonally from the front.

> I could see that our armament was traversed to the right and as we started to move back in reverse I expected our crew to open fire. There was a bump and, as I thought we had started firing, I looked through my periscope in an effort to see the target. When I glanced back I saw the gunner baling out. Looking into the turret I could see a red glow and much smoke. As quickly as I could I got out and dived into a shell hole with the others, less one gunner who was in a hole the other side of the tank. The crew commander left us and ran to the leading flail tank . . .

Highlanders watch a Sherman tank entering a Normandy village street. (Tank Museum, photo 2995/F1)

came back with the news that it was a Canadian gun which had knocked Black Agnes out . . . we buried what codes we had taken with us and brought some colour back into our cheeks with a cigarette.[31]

In the 144 RAC column the two navigating tanks had plunged into deep craters. Lt-Col Jolly had needed to take the lead himself and soon discovered that there was danger from the rear up front ! 'After about twenty minutes there came a shot from behind us and another of those now all too familiar showers of sparks as one of our tanks brewed up. All the crew except one were killed but we never discovered the origin of the shot.'[32] Anything could happen. After another 'loose scrum' at a dimly perceived obstacle, Brian Carpenter's tank, which had been in the last row of the Northamptonshire Yeomanry rearguard, suddenly found itself halfway up the regimental column.

It was almost with disbelief that units arrived at the objective. Tom Boardman, on time and only 50 yd off his objective, called up his own colonel, Doug Forster, and the infantry colonel to confirm their position. Never quite convinced of the feasibility of the operation, Black Watch CO, Lt-Col John Hopwood, barked 'Fuck me! We've arrived!' Maj R. de C. Vigors (Lothian & Border) had to convince his Canadian tank colleague that they had indeed landed on their objective and was amused by the sight of some infantry in their novel Kangaroos 'sitting there with the fatuous expressions peculiar to those who are out of their element'. With similar pithy words Vigors saw his column now as somewhat 'less diagramatic'.[33]

Lt J. McAnaly had suffered serious damage to his jib in a collision with an unidentified Sherman, and had halted to discard the clumsy flail apparatus.

He was pleased to see Troop Cpl Anderson driving back with 'four prisoners sitting quite contentedly on the back of his tank'. Some would never be coming back. Others were hoping to make their way back but had perils to face before daylight brought some relief. Lt Boreham and Cpl Bradford were still dug in with their crews, 150 yd behind their still-smouldering tanks, watching for the enemy, waiting for daylight.[34]

Ian Hammerton and crew were also down in their bomb crater as the incredible procession passed them by and the night hours ticked away:

> Gradually the sound of battle died away, and the flickering flames from burning tanks died down. The Kangaroos passed us by, and shortly afterwards were followed by infantry on foot . . . we passed the time of day or night with them and they continued on their mopping up tasks. The night became uncomfortably quiet. . . . The sky lightened almost imperceptibly and the ground mist rose and fell. Our eyes began to see shapes which one moment appeared stationary and the next moving before disappearing and re-appearing again.[35]

Still worrying about his crew, but with no hope of finding them in the darkness, Griffith-Jones continued to lie as still as cramp would allow him. He too had been bypassed by his entire column:

> For about three hours I remained alone lying in the furrow of the potatoes. In between explosions from the burning vehicles and machine gun fire I could hear German soldiers' voices. It was not safe to move or stand up. My binoculars seemed an encumbrance and so I buried them in the soil. On my return to the scene two days later I was able to locate and recover them. On one occasion I raised my head above the potatoes and saw a German with a machine gun going past. He clearly saw me. I lay flat again and I expected a burst of machine gun fire or at least a challenge. After a few tense minutes I raised my head again, but the soldier had gone. He was probably as frightened as I was. He may have thought I had companions alongside me.
>
> Towards dawn human activity ceased and I got bolder and walked about. On the edge of the potato field were trenches and in them wounded soldiers had been deposited by their fit comrades before they continued towards their objective. At the briefing for the operation it had been emphasized that all fit men and vehicles must keep going at all costs to reach Saint-Aignan. The injured soldiers were infantry of the 51st Highland Division, with one exception, my own Corporal Ferrier. I was so pleased, not only to find him, but to see that he was unscathed after fleeing his destroyed tank.

What Lt Griffith-Jones did not yet know was that L/Cpl Dursley had not been so fortunate. He had been taken prisoner in the potato field. And what L/Cpl Dursley himself did not yet know was that he was to become the object of one of those cunning tricks which the gods of war play on mere humans.

Chapter Two

The Unassailable Fortress

'Look at the mountains. See how impassable they are in every direction. This one road, which you see, is a steep one, and you can see that there are men on it, a great crowd, who have occupied the pass and are on guard there.'
(Xenophon, 400 BC)

The Night March was an extraordinary solution to an extraordinary problem. Given the code name Operation Totalize, it had something of the cavalry charge element implied in the horseracing association with the betting Totalizator, and it was also an attempt to give total effect to the efforts which the Allies had been making since D-Day.

Every day after D-Day was marked as D plus something or other. Each new operation was given its own little D-Day date. So D-Day for Operation Totalize would be 'D + 62', the sixty-second day after the Normandy landings. In that time progress had been disappointing for many people who had hoped to see a rapid breakout from the beaches towards Paris and Brittany and the vital channel ports from Le Havre northwards. A number of massive attacks had foundered upon the rock of disciplined and clever German resistance. Some observers, not only in the American army, were beginning to have doubts about Montgomery's strategy and his ability to defeat the Germans in Normandy. And now the Canadian army was gazing up a long slope, defended in great force, where three weeks previously three British armoured divisions had lost over 400 tanks in two days of vain attack.

The troops on the ground saw the situation clearly and in simple terms. Reg Spittles (2 Northamptonshire Yeomanry) summed it up:

> We were on a sticky wicket in open country. Jerry was holding the Bourguebus Ridge ahead; it was not much of a ridge if you were there for a holiday, but we were not there for a holiday, and it was a devastating situation. It meant that the Germans with their 88 mm guns could hit us long before we could even see them, let alone shoot back at them. Previously (in the Bocage country) we had got as close as 30 yards without being aware of each other, sometimes so close they couldn't shoot you.

So why take the risk of driving up that ridge in such unfavourable circumstances? Again using very simple terms – which were Montgomery's own – the Caen area, from which the Bourguebus Ridge swept upwards, was the hinge of the enemy door which he was trying to break down. Away to the right as one stood on the beaches, that is to the west, the Americans

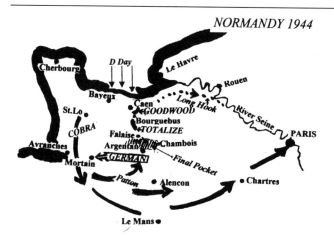

NORMANDY 1944

Map of Normandy,
June–August 1944.

were swinging wide in an arc, like the outside edge of the door. The German army there was being forced back. Now Montgomery wished to smash in the hinge. It might then be possible for the hingebusters to sweep in a left-hand arc and meet the Americans, sealing a pocket in which an entire German army might be surrounded. There has been some debate as to whether this was the original D-Day concept or whether it was an idea emerging from what looked suspiciously like stalemate, just a very few miles in from the beaches of sixty-two days ago.

The Head of Montgomery's Operations and Planning Staff, David Belchem, had no doubts on that score:

> The battle was fought as planned before we left London in June although, inevitably, some delays and setbacks were imposed on the Allies by the changing course of the operations and, even more so, by the incidence of adverse weather conditions in June and July. . . . Throughout the Normandy campaign the strategy was to attract and retain the main enemy strength on our eastern flank (British and Canadian) to facilitate a break-out on the western flank, and there to exploit the American competence in extremely rapid mobility in order to encircle the enemy forces.[1]

This strategy, which was quite evident to the enemy, had two main effects by D + 62, namely that they would take every advantage of terrain offered by the continuing ridges beyond Bourguebus and that they would fight with redoubled energy, professionalism and fanaticism to stop or delay an early collapse of the entire Third Reich. The advantages of the site were exceptional, given the Germans superiority in long-range armoured gunnery, including use of anti-aircraft '88s' for anti-tank work.

One writer has graphically reported the astonishment felt by Allied soldiers as they eventually forced their way up the Caen to Falaise main road and through its adjacent villages – even though the situation was easily discerned by elementary map reading of the crowded contours lying like snake's coils on the local ordnance survey:

Time after time, as they advanced up one hill and then another on the road to Falaise, Canadian war diarists commented with awe on the observation the Germans enjoyed of the Canadian front or line of attack. Their knowledge of the ground also gave them advantages. The protection which a slit trench offered against both bombing and artillery was remarkable on those slopes.[2]

The extent of the defender's view can easily be illustrated by a quick look at the contours along the main road from la Dronniere, between Ifs and Bras – where some of the attacking troops started – to Cintheaux, one of the objectives. Reading off the contours, kilometre by kilometre, the picture is:

La Dronniere		height 45 m approx (148 ft approx)	
Kilometre 1		52	
2		58	
3		72	
4		81	
5		86	
6	(Lorguichon)	100	
7		118	
8	(D80 road)	126	
9	(Gaumesnil)	117	
10	(Cintheaux)	126	(413 ft approx)

The Northamptonshire Yeomanry column would climb from 30 m (98 ft) at Cormelles to 108 m (354 ft) beyond Saint-Aignan.

Canadian 2nd Corps commander, Guy Simonds' biographer, Dominick Graham, described the strength of the German position and offered no excuses for the failure of previous attempts to penetrate it:

After the Germans were pushed out of the industrial suburbs of Caen . . . the pivot of their position was the twin villages of Saint-Andre-sur-Orne and Saint-Martin-de-Fontenay on their left, with May-sur-Orne as the back-up. That triangle of villages was the strongest part of the German line. Its left flank was covered from German positions on high ground (up to 87 meters) above the west bank of the Orne. As well, the Germans could infiltrate back into their positions after they were overrun, through mine shafts with exit behind the British forward positions. Major General Foulkes's operations were dominated by his Second (Canadian) Division's failure to take this position as an anchor for the corps' right wing on the Orne . . . in the centre of Foulkes's front an open convex swelling – Verrieres Ridge, with the village of that name on its eastern side – invited a British armoured thrust, but its western flanks were covered from the 'German triangle'.[3]

Canadian troops endeavoured to improve on this position in Operation Spring in early August with sparse results for a tragic letting of blood.

Perhaps commentators have laid too much emphasis on command failures (which there probably were) and not enough on the continuing ferocious German resistance, with which the Canadians had been having to cope since soon after D-Day. Canadian troops already in action were tired and depleted while other Canadian units coming up were as yet untried in battle.

Montgomery had written that 'the eastern flank (Caen area) is a bastion on which the whole future of the campaign in N.W. Europe depends; it must remain a firm bastion; if it became unstable the operations on the western flank would cease'.[4] That was written from the Allied point of view. By D + 62 it was even more true for the Germans. Patton's mobile host of Americans were surging hard and wide far to the south but if the Germans could hold the bastion of the Caen–Falaise area the Americans on their own would not close the Falaise pocket. And there was always the chance that, in his unceasing quest for more and more territory, Patton might run out of supplies to continue without additional port facilities.

The Polish General, Stanislaw Maczek, estimated that there were 4 km of first-line defences to be penetrated by the Night March, but after that there were tank obstacles and pillboxes at Soignolles and in Quesnay Woods, up to 8 and 10 km behind the front line.[5] A Canadian military historian stated that their 'forces would be confronted by three major defence lines before they reached Falaise. Further, the numerous small villages and farms, many of which had been denied to the Canadians during SPRING, had always been fortified, many with anti-tank weapons.'[6] It was worrying to think that a fifth attack on the fortified village of Tilly-la-Campagne had been beaten off on 5 August.[7]

The Canadian official historian sums up the problem, drawing from Simonds' own appreciation of the situation before him (the three points below carry the original item numbers from Simonds' paper):

4. The ground is ideally suited to full exploitation by the enemy of the characteristics of his weapons. It is open, giving little cover to either infantry or tanks, and the long range of his anti-tank guns and mortars, firing from carefully concealed poisitions, provides a very strong defence in depth. The defence will be most handicapped in bad visibility – smoke, fog or darkness, when the advantage of long range is minimised. . . .

6. If all available air support is used for the first 'break in' there will be nothing for the second except diminished gun support, unless a long pause is made with resultant loss of speed. If, on the other hand, the first 'break in' is based on limited air support with all available gun support and novelty of method, the heavy day bombers and medium bombers will be available for the second 'break in', at a time that gun support begins to decrease. . . .

7. In essence, the problem is how to get armour through the enemy gun screen to sufficient depth to disrupt the German anti-tank gun and mortar defence, in country highly suited to the tactics of the latter combination.[8]

Analysis of the German preparations for the Goodwood attack reveals how tough was the task of those attackers. It also illustrates the depth of defences which would continue to be met in the area:

> Panzer Group West had disposed the forces of 1 SS Panzer Corps and LXXXVI Corps in four defensive belts nearly ten miles deep, with a fifth as the reserve. Within the axis of the Goodwood advance there were two infantry divisions in the first belt and two panzer grenadier regiments of 21st Panzer Division in the second. The third belt was a series of villages heavily fortified with anti-tank guns and infantry and some 270 *Nebelwerfers* – the six-barrelled heavy mortar known as the 'Moaning Minnie' – whose fire was used to support the second belt. . . . The fifth belt, well out of range of the British guns . . . held some sixty to eighty tanks as his mobile reserve.[10]

Keith Jones, commanding his tank and wondering why British attacks were launched on such a narrow front compared with Russian attacks, did not know until later that the German defence at Goodwood 'was two and a half times as thick as what they were opposing at that time to the Red Army'. In the Goodwood action, he estimated that, on the first evening, his squadron, spread wide on a flank, 'must have been the only one in the division [11th Armoured] to remain complete and unscathed'. By the evening of the second day his regiment, 2nd Northamptonshire Yeomanry, 'from its usual sixty-one, was down to twenty-three tanks'.[11] Three full armoured divisions had been launched towards the Bourguebus Ridge and, in two days, over 400 tanks had been lost. Only one of the first day objectives had been gained and the hoped-for breakout was still far in the future.

> The British were attacking across more open country than in any battle of the campaign thus far. So much has been said about the difficulties of fighting amid the hedges of the *Bocage*, that it seems worth emphasizing the equal difficulties of advancing against powerful defences over an unbroken field of fire. . . . Here, perhaps, more than in any other battle in northwest Europe the British paid the price for their lack of a survivable battle tank; armour of the weight of the German Tigers and Panthers might have battered a path up Bourguebus Ridge.[9]

British tanks had thus tasted the bitter agony of trying to attack in daylight across this type of countryside, although traditionally the Salisbury Plain type of terrain, much used for tank training, had been regarded as 'typical tank country'. When fighting in the dense Bocage many tank crews had been encouraged to think that the 'typical tank country' beyond Caen would be almost a 'Sunday afternoon tea on the lawn' experience. Goodwood was the reality. And the minor gains made then, affording a foothold on the ridges beyond Caen, would make the defenders even more determined to defend to the death, while other Panzer divisions moved away south in an attempt to cut off Patton's army, as he appeared to be 'sticking his neck out' too far for safety, or so Hitler thought.

The forces defending the ridges were relatively few but very formidable. Although Hitler was insisting on moving tanks away from the area, the Canadian historian, Roy, states that 'there was no lessening on the front of either anti-tank battalions or German 88 mm anti-tank guns':

> An estimated sixty to seventy of these dual-purpose guns were in the area to be attacked, most of them situated where the two armoured divisions were to begin operations in the second phase. These formidable weapons were to take a deadly toll. . . . The German 101st Heavy Tank battalion . . . was attached to Kurt Meyer's 12th SS Panzer Division with ten tanks in operation. Experienced crews in these 54 ton monsters with their thick armour and 88 mm guns could take on Sherman tanks with impunity.[12]

Reynolds adds that Meyer also had available thirty-nine of the smaller, older Mark IV tanks, which were still able to repel Shermans in a situation of advantage as defenders. In addition there were the eight 'combat ready' Tigers. Other troops included:

> twenty-seven Jagdpanzer IVs, Waldmuller's 1st SS Panzer-Grenadier battalion, the Corps and Division Escort Companies, the 12th SS Panzer Artillery Regiment . . . of three battalions, less the Wespe battery . . . and the 12th SS Flak battalion. In addition parts of the III Luftwaffe Flak Corps and the 83rd Werfer Regiment . . . Chester Wilmost estimated that there were some one hundred 88 mm and 75 mm anti-tank capable weapons facing Simonds' Corps, and Kraemer confirmed that there were two 75 mm anti-tank battalions and 100 howitzers.[13]

A German author, Patrick Agte, confirmed that Michael Wittmann, the ace commander of 101st Heavy, had only eight battleworthy tanks immediately available, but another five Tigers of the unit were in combat against an Allied attack only 5 miles away. Agte describes the defenders as 'exhausted and inadequate forces',[14] but Operation Goodwood had shown what a group of four or five 88 mm guns could do against massed opponents.

The actual front line opposite the Canadian 2nd Corps had only just been taken over by 89th Infantry Division, relieving Hitlerjugend. These were fresh troops, which might also have proved to be 'green'. An officer who fought with the division later in the campaign verified that almost 64 per cent of the division were aged nineteen or younger, and the unit was, under the German system, 'qualified for defence but not for attack'.[15] The adjutant of one of the SS Panzer regiments confirmed that the 89th division 'had no tanks and only a few anti-tank guns'.[16] However, the redoubtable Hitlerjugend had a similar age profile and had been 'green' at D-Day, as had several British and Canadian Divisions which had fought well from the start.

> The German troops of the 89th Infantry Division had not yet seen action; they had been bathing in the Norwegian fjords. Suddenly everything changed: ordered to drop everything and pack up, the unfortunate soldiers

were hustled into trains for the Baltic, transhipped across Holland and Belgium in convoys and were now . . . in France. . . . From the destroyed villages, which became more frequent as their trucks approached the Caen-Falaise road, the men of the 89th realized that their hour had come.[17]

Granted that the 89th was not one of the élite SS Panzer divisions, it was never safe to underestimate any German troops. Montgomery's close aide, David Belchem was under no delusions about the quality of German troops, observing that 'German forces at divisional and lower levels fought with great skill and tenacity. This would be expected in the case of élite troops of the SS formations, but in fact it applied to virtually all the Panzer and infantry divisions. . . . Our soldiers were faced by high-calibre troops'.[18] Those sentiments were echoed by others, including the then Lt-Col Geordie Andrews, whose 2nd Seaforths were about to be locked in the most bitter of battles with unyielding German troops, none other than the 'green' 89th.

The defenders were also helped and inspired by a superiority in weapons of most front-line land categories. The German tanks were widely feared but other arms also merited mention. Hastings has written at some length about this material superiority:

> the Germans possessed the supreme weapons in their MG 34 and 42 machine guns – invariably known among the Allies as Spandaus – with their fabulous rate of fire . . . the MG 42's tearing, rasping 1,200 rounds a minute, against the bren's 500 . . . the handle on the German 'potato masher' hand grenade enabled it to be thrown far further than its British or American counterparts . . . their mortar 'stonks' . . . grated the nerves of every British and American unit in Normandy . . . all German small arms enjoyed a significant advantage . . . in using ammunition which produced less flash and smoke. The Germans . . . were equipped in Normandy with the excellent *Panzerfaust*, the finest infantry anti-tank weapon of the war.[19]

As to the tanks available, the Allies relied much on the Sherman which was available in vast numbers but was out-gunned by the 88 mm cannon of the Panther and Tiger. The Mark IV, up-gunned with a longer 75 mm barrel, was at least on a par with the Sherman. Only when the 'Firefly' – a Sherman with a 17-pdr gun – began to appear a few weeks before D-Day did the Allies have an equivalent cannon, but still on a tank with thinner armour. The Cromwell had good features but was not intended as a main static battle tank, although Cromwells were used in that role in Operation Goodwood. The Churchill originally had too small a gun but served in many 'funny' capacities such as flails and flame-throwers.

A comparison of weight and thickness of main armour is interesting:

Panther	Thickest armour: 4.72 in	Weight: 99,868 lb
Tiger	Thickest armour: 4.33 in	Weight: 125,441 lb
Sherman	Thickest armour: 3.00 in	Weight: 71,175 lb
Churchill	Thickest armour: 4.10 in	Weight: 87,360 lb

In terms of mobility the Tiger's top speed was about 23 mph, and the Panther's 28.4 mph. In contrast the Normandy Shermans would normally achieve 30 mph, although sometimes quoted, as for earlier models, at 24 mph. The Churchill was rated at 15.5 mph because of an underpowered engine. There was a significance different in height. The Sherman, at 11 ft 3 in to the top of the turret, towered over the Tiger at 9 ft 6 in, the Panther at 9 ft 10 in, and the Mark IV at 8 ft 6 in. This difference of 2 ft 9 in became quite crucial on 8 August when Mark IVs were able to use a gully to great advantage. The Sherman was always more difficult to place in a turret-down position, while in those Normandy apple orchards at harvest time commanders were liable to see nothing but branches loaded with cider apples.[20]

The Sherman's better mobility could not always be put to good use in situations where the enemy was liable to score a brewing-up hit with the first unannounced shot. In a direct shoot-out it was 'no game'. At 1,000 yd the Sherman gun could penetrate 60 mm of armour compared with the Tiger's 102 mm penetration. And the Sherman frontal armour was only 76 mm, and its side armour 51 mm. Easy meat for a Tiger at 1,000 yd! Reversing the picture, at 100 yd the Sherman could penetrate 74 mm, but the Tiger had front armour of 100 mm and side armour of 80 mm. Hardly worth firing the gun, the Sherman gunner might have thought!

Such data must be considered with some caution because in battle there were often freak circumstances. A low-powered shot might land on a weak joint or lodge in an enemy gun barrel and defy all known data. For instance, the Sherman was rated as having only a 2 ft clearance of vertical obstacles. If Sherman commanders had heeded that statistic when putting their steeds at the giant Bocage hedges, often mounted on banks 3–4 ft high, they would never have passed from field to field as they often did. On 8 August Sherman 75 mm gunners were able to force Tiger commanders to close down into their cramped turrets with poor visibility if periscopes were knocked out. Then the Firefly had time to move into a killing position. But, to use a totally inappropriate modern phrase, 'on a level playing field' the 88 mm was a terrifying sight. The Polish General Maczek and one of his front-line soldiers, Witold Deimel of 10th (Polish) Dragoons, both recount the story of how an 88 mm shot from a confirmed 2 km distance bored right through both turret walls of a Sherman and continued out the other side.[21]

It is therefore no surprise to learn that, while the Germans on the ridges were outnumbered, they were ready to accept exceptional 'odds against' in the operations which the British had so quaintly named after horseracing courses and traditions – Epsom, Goodwood, Totalize. That the attacker may need a three to one advantage is a factor often accepted in warfare. Although the front-line enemy were expected to be of poor quality, the Allies in the 1991 Gulf War planned for such a ratio.[22] Florentin says of 1944 that 'there was an accepted loss of four Shermans for the loss of one German tank' (i.e. including Mark IVs).[23] And Estes comments, 'Military doctrine generally holds that an offensive superiority of at least three to one is required. . . . In Normandy the Germans found they could accept a ratio of nearly five to one.'[24] During the critical period early in Goodwood, four

The *Hummel* (Bumblebee) self-propelled gun, like the one which knocked out Wyn Griffith-Jones' Sherman during the Night March.

anti-aircraft 88 mm guns lowered their sights and knocked out sixteen British tanks in a few minutes. At Villers Bocage the famous Wittmann troop of Tigers scored twenty-five for four of their own lost.

Although faced with overwhelming odds, the morale of the German troops manning the bastion was generally high. They had given the Tommies a bloody nose and still had a low opinion of the Yanks. As might be expected, morale was especially high in SS Panzer units. One young soldier, Jan Munk, had no doubts about his loyalty:

> All I can say is that we believed in what Hitler said, and I myself was convinced that Germany would win the war right up to March 1945. I only really knew the war was lost for sure when we heard that Hitler was dead. As far as Hitler was concerned we regarded him as a true man. He was only a corporal when he earned the Iron Cross First Class in World War I. . . . When he spoke at meetings . . . he was able to get us in a mood where we believed everything he said and we left fired with enthusiasm.[25]

Karl-Heinz Decker and his mortar crew of six were already beginning to notice shortages of military supplies and food, and they found the Allied daylight bombing raids terrorizing. But as they made their stealthy way by night from one hideaway to another they had no idea of surrender. In fact their resolve to fight to the bitter end was strengthened because rumours were rife among the troops that the Canadians had committed atrocities against SS soldiers earlier in the Normandy battles, and they knew they were facing the Canadian army. It was a sobering thought that if you were captured you would be put up against a wall and shot immediately. NCOs like Karl-Heinz had no way of checking out the rumours. The safe policy was to assume they might be true.[26]

If the German morale was sound, and possibly deliberately reinforced by stories of the atrocities which awaited those who surrendered, there were some flaws in the Allied psychological state. Both Canadians and British had suffered heavily in separate battles and might be somewhat reticent to expose themselves to the German guns. That the Allies would now win the war was more or less self-evident and Allied soldiers were generally confident of victory, but that in itself provided a negative factor. The obvious willingness of the Russian command to sacrifice millions of soldiers, and the equally obvious ability of the Americans to produce more and more tanks, ships and aeroplanes, and the RAF and Royal Navy command of their spheres of influence, could induce in the ordinary Normandy 'squaddie' the thought, 'Why should I stick my blinking neck out and get killed when the effing war may be over before Christmas?'

No doubt the average Allied soldier believed that Nazism must be defeated, but some of the worst features of the Nazi reign, such as the concentration camps, were not revealed to ordinary foot soldiers until they themselves drew the task of marching into Belsen or Buchenwald. One 1944 trooper, reflecting in the cold light of hindsight, was not sure that his commitment in the Normandy campaign was what has been assumed in later days by both serious historians and media hype:

> Was I highly motivated? I would have packed it all in from the day I joined, so much did I hate the Army. I don't think I had much time to think of the major issues. . . . My father was one who survived the Somme. My reading has told me that the generals of those days were little short of butchers. Haig and Kitchener looked at the working classes as gun fodder. . . . Fortunately for us, our generals, like Montgomery, sent us into battle reluctantly and wanted as few casualties as possible. Consequently we didn't win our first battles. But all this is mature reflection.[27]

According to Simonds' biographer he was also 'ill served by army intelligence, which was confused by the frequent moves of German divisions and their reduction to fighting groups of a single division appearing simultaneously on different fronts. As a result, Simonds overestimated German capacity.'[28] Although much has been said of the ingenuity of Allied deception methods, in relation to the Normandy campaign it is sometimes forgotten that the Germans too were adept at deceiving their opponents. For instance, Max Wunsche, commanding a Panzer battle group, had, five days before Totalize, erected more than sixty dummy tanks a mile or so east of Saint-Aignan, that is to say, perilously close to the open left flank of the left-hand column of the Night March.

Simonds was also concerned about the lack of infantry available. This consideration had weighed heavily with the British generals in deciding to set up Goodwood as, in the first phase, an armoured attack with very little infantry support. While numbers of tanks were lost in Normandy the ratio of tank crew casualties was much lower than infantry losses. Hastings states that in the month of Totalize only 56 per cent of British troops in Normandy were classified as 'fighting troops'. Only 14 per cent were infantry, compared to 18 per cent gunners, 13 per cent engineers and 6 per cent tank crews.[29] It was, of course, the infantry who suffered most casualties. In the Goodwood battle 12.33 per cent of infantry officers were casualties, followed by 9.69 per cent of tank officers (remembering that these were armoured divisions with a high ratio of tank crews, and that many infantry had been left behind because of traffic blocks). Of infantry Other Ranks 8.83 per cent had become casualties, compared to 4.31 per cent of ranker tank crews and lesser percentages of other arms. So all Allied generals were most concerned by the shortage and inevitable wastage of prime infantry. Only in recent times have commentators noted that, in fact, the numbers of trained infantry being held in the UK was about equal to those actually engaged in battle in Normandy.[30] The reasons for that strange situation pertained to politics and higher strategy, and Simonds was also constrained by the fact that Canadian reinforcements were limited.

A further impediment to clear strategy decisions was the apparent tendency of those running the war at a higher level to put self-interest on a level with, or even above, commitment to the war effort. Montgomery's own attitude to other commanders and his promotion of his own image had caused much resentment. While it can be held that his general strategy was achieving its purpose, his actions and statements along the way had roused serious criticism. There was even a move towards sacking him, although such a decision would not easily have been forced upon Churchill. The animosity was not always Britisher against American or Canadian. Montgomery's immediate superior was Eisenhower. Eisenhower's deputy was the British airman Tedder. The latter was among the leading critics of his compatriot general. It is likely that Tedder was trying to persuade his chief 'that if Eisenhower should want to rid himself of this tedious ground commander for failing to "go places" [during Goodwood] with his muscular three-armoured-division offensive, he would not run into trouble higher up', which might not have been good advice.[31]

At this time Montgomery appeared to be suffering from 'anti-American resentment. . . . It did not escape him that now the Americans had achieved their great breakthrough, the part that his strategy and determination had played in it was being overlooked'.[32] Eisenhower was becoming impatient and wrote Montgomery three letters within a week implying that 'he felt that the British and Canadians were not pulling their weight' and that 'we must go forward shoulder to shoulder with honors and sacrifices equally shared'. The last phrase of that statement implied not too subtly that the sacrifices were not being equally shared.[33]

There is clear evidence that Montgomery had a low estimation of the capabilities of Crerar, Simonds' immediate commander, through whom

Montgomery needed to communicate his requirements. Montgomery could be scathing, as when he commented to the CIGS, Gen Brooke, about Crerar, 'I fear he thinks he is a great soldier, and he was determined to show it the moment he took over command at 1200 on 23 July. He made his first mistake at 1205 and his second after lunch'.[34] When the British I Corps was placed under the command of the 1st Canadian Army, Crerar had a serious quarrel with the I Corps commander, Crocker, and tried to get him ousted. While relations between the American and British commanders were normally no worse than could be expected in the stresses and traumas of war, one or two high-profile Americans added fuel to the flames of disenchantment. One such instance was when Patton made his remark, which became widely known and quoted, 'Let me go on to Falaise and we'll drive the British back into the sea for another Dunkirk'.

For his part Simonds also had problems relating more to his lack of confidence in some of his divisional and brigade commanders: 'Simonds was of two minds whether to sack Foulkes for the way he handled his division.' Dempsey and Crocker were 'already unimpressed with' another divisional commander, Keller. Simonds would later, very reluctantly, relieve another major-general, Kitching. Brigade commander, Ben Cunningham, had already gone home at the end of July, together with battalion commanders Petch and Christiansen. Another complaint about a general was that 'he drank too much and made an objectionable fool of himself on social occasions'. Simonds 'recognized that the tasks he had given them were difficult'. In reports to higher command he pointed out that 'losses among junior leaders have been heavy'. With one division having suffered 5,500 casualties in June and July 'the men hardly know one another, or the junior leaders their men and men their leaders . . . unit commanders and brigadiers are apprehensive . . . because they feel their units are unfitted in their present state of training'.[35] And much of the damage which the Canadian formations had suffered was due to the fanaticism of the Hitlerjugend, which now waited somewhere up along the ridges.

Obviously the Germans had their problems, in addition to being outnumbered. It has been said that 'our principal "ally" was Hitler'. Our problems would have been immeasurably greater if he had not interfered in the direction of his forces, in spite of the advice and opinions of the German generals who were for the most part professionally competent.'[36] One of Stacey's sub-chapters in the official version of Totalize is headed 'The Fuehrer intervenes'. It tells how Hitler decided to withdraw SS Panzers from in front of Caen in order to try to cut off Patton's looping advance further south. On the map Patton did looked precariously poised, his forces like a spreading flower on the end of a long stem. The stem passed between the hills of Normandy and the sea and looked vulnerable. However, the reading of the German generals was that, firstly, Patton was too strong to be broken in that way and, secondly, the move would weaken the vital Caen–Falaise bastion. Stacey records the conversation of the generals involved, Warlimont being the envoy of Hitler's supreme headquarters:

Dietrich: If the SS divisions are pulled out south of Caen the enemy will attack there and break through.
Warlimont: However, the SS divisions are not in their proper place

there; they are employed in an immobile role and not at the focal point of the enemy's effort.

Eberbach: . . . the SS divisions must be held ready in the rear to support the [Caen] front. The main question remains how the front can be held in the long run against an enemy so far superior in material.

The Germans were also disadvantaged by the loss of the wounded Rommel and the sacked von Runstedt, two men with impressive records.

Von Runstedt had paid the price for stating that the war was virtually lost, with widely reported words, 'Make peace, you fools', to Keitel at Hitler's OKW headquarters.[37] He was replaced by Hans von Kluge, a man of 'vacillating character and weak-minded opportunism', who was constantly torn between his own military expertise and his desire to toady to Hitler. In Russia he had been severely criticized by two of Germany's best generals, Guderian and Hoth. He retaliated by intriguing to get Guderian, the 'tank expert', sacked. No fool, nicknamed 'der kluge Hans' (Clever Hans), he was not precisely the type of commander needed at this dire emergency for the Reich. Indeed, within comparatively few days he had (at a time of plots against Hitler, at which he connived) vacillated himself into committing suicide, leaving a letter asking for Hitler's understanding.[38]

The main weakness of the Germans' last citadel in Normandy was the lack of air support. Von Kluge himself was witness to this fatal flaw, observing in a letter to Hitler on 21 July that 'there is no way by which, in the face of the enemy Air Forces' complete command of the air, we can discover a form of strategy which will counterbalance its annihilating effects unless we withdraw from the battlefield'.[39] Another writer has very succinctly shown both the advantage and disadvantage of heavy air support for ground forces. 'There was no doubt about the effectiveness of the attacks: they subjected the German troops to a profoundly terrifying experience and in nearly every case made possible an advance. However, the broken roads and villages prevented the rapid bringing up of supplies and the allied ground forces could not sustain their momentum.'[40]

In 1944 the use of air power to support ground troops was not as simple as might be imagined. There were problems of coordination. A Canadian commentator outlined the normal routine:

A unit being hit had to inform Brigade Headquarters; they would tell Divisional Headquarters; Divisional Headquarters would pass the message on to Corps Headquarters; and Corps Headquarters would pass it on to Army Headquarters. The message would be given to the Senior Air Staff Officer who would relay it to the appropriate authorities in Bomber Command. Meanwhile the bombers were flying at about 250 miles an hour, Squadron after Squadron, dumping their bombs on friendly troops.[41]

An RAF OBOE ground operator who was directing raids at the time is content to have his opinion included here. He sees the 'Canadian Disaster' as 'one that was waiting to happen':

due to the confused and confusing command structure. Who designed it, I don't know; but there seemed to be far too many air force 'chiefs' (many of them of questionable competence), with fingers (and tongues) in the pie, and little or no detailed coordination of the activities of the various air forces and commanders. Low marks for that to Ike, and lower still for Tedder, who should have known better.[42]

With all these factors to consider, Simonds would have little more than a week in which to conceive, refine, organize and set in motion totally revolutionary concepts and techniques, to attempt to conquer with less than desirable forces what had so far proved to be an unassailable fortress. In Phase 1 of Operation Totalize he would score an astonishing victory, which the victors would forget.

Chapter Three

Canadian Wizardry

'What city, then, will produce the general to take the right steps ? . . . I propose
that we should form up with the companies in column . . . each officer will lead by
the easiest route . . . if any company is in difficulties, the nearest one will give
support. . . . This plan was agreed upon, and they formed the companies into
columns.' (Xenophon, 400 BC)

On 5 August, 1944 Charlie Robertson of 7th Black Watch, 51st Highland
Division, went with other company commanders and specialist platoon
commanders to see a sand-tray display. They were astounded by what they
learned there. Within an hour or two they were hustled away to a practice
ride in a strange-looking vehicle, like a tank with the turret chopped off.
After a cramped, bumpy ride, they were told they would be riding again at
night, in total darkness.

The news was working its way down. On 4 July Lt-Col A. Jolly,
commanding 144 RAC, had gone with his peers to a higher-level briefing.
They too were astonished. Jolly confided, 'No lecture I had attended had ever
dealt with the possibility of squeezing through a defence system like this. But
when you find that, according to the rules of the game, the enemy has the
better of you, you seek a loophole in those rules.'[1] On 3 July even higher
commanders had been equally amazed. Elliot Rodger, who was there, recalled
Simonds' 'O Group before Totalize when the several divisional commanders
sat in a circle under the pine trees (all being much older than GGS and some
with desert sand in their ears) to whom he opened, "Gentlemen, we will do
this attack at night with armour". Their jaws dropped noticeably . . . but the
whole plan poured forth complete and crystal clear.'[2]

Who then was this wizard, waving a magic wand of tactical ingenuity and
able to produce out of the hat rabbits of surprise invention? Guy Granville
Simonds was born on 24 April 1903, which made him a youthful lieutenant-
general of 41 at the time of Totalize. He was born in England but educated
in Canada, graduating top of his class at the Royal Military College in 1925.
When the war commenced in 1939 he was made a major on the
Headquarters of 1st Canadian Infantry Division.

He soon achieved regimental command as a lieutenant-colonel and by 1943
was a brigadier observer of Montgomery's assault on the Mareth Line in North
Africa. Returning to England he took command of the 1st Canadian Infantry
Division, leading it into Sicily in July 1943 and then in Italy. When the 5th
Canadian Armoured Division arrived as a reinforcement in Italy he took over
that unit until recalled again to England in January 1944. His meteoric rise now

Lt-Gen G.G. Simonds with Churchill, Montgomery and (at the back) Dempsey. (IWM, B7879)

continued with his posting to command the 2nd Canadian Corps in the rank of lieutenant-general, with responsibility for the Canadian share of the D-Day landings. He had taken particular note of a New Zealand attack in North Africa when smoke and dust were used effectively to storm exceptionally strong enemy defences across open ground at el Hamma in 1943.[3]

Simonds now produced a simple plan of two 'break-ins' (into the heart of German defences), one of them at night, and one 'break-out' into clear country beyond the established defences. The first 'break-in' with most risk would be undertaken at night.

The official historian claimed to find 'two features of marked originality' in the plan: 'One was the intervention of heavy bombers in the ground battle during the hours of darkness. . . . The other innovation was the use of what have since come to be called armoured personnel carriers'.[4] From his point of view with the British XXII Dragoons Birt saw that Simonds' plan was even more extraordinary than the Canadian claim:

The plan was remarkable for its innovations. It was the first to run the risk of using close-support bombing for ground troops at night. It was the first in which armour was required to move direct into an enemy-held line in darkness. It was the introduction into north-west Europe of the use of Bofors fire to guide assaulting troops to their objectives; of the use of searchlights to give additional illumination to troops on the ground; and of the use of armour converted to act as tracked carriers for the infantry.[5]

Hastings further cites the employment of 'a sophisticated range of electronics and illuminants to guide his men to their objectives through the night' – sophisticated in 1944 terms, that is.[6]

More than one writer has referred to the hope that the unparalleled air and ground bombardment, coupled with the literal overrunning of the German infantry by masses of armour, would cause panic and flight behind the armoured columns once they had passed by. Not only was this an insult to the morale of the average German soldier (although a few did retreat in disorder), it also overlooked the fact that the German infantry actually trained men to remain behind and attack the enemy from the rear once they had advanced. Montgomery certainly felt that there was a tendency in some quarters to underestimate the German response. He accused Crerar of having 'gained the idea that all you want is a good initial fire plan and then the Germans all run away'.[7]

Simonds was not of that way of thinking for he made elaborate plans to send sufficient infantry into the areas behind the advancing armour in order to clear out the German resistance which would occur in some places if not all. Yet there may have been a little too much of hope and not enough of rational thinking, to suppose that the isolated enemy posts would yield at a rate convenient to the second wave of armour and the echelons.

The author of this ingenious plan was the first to recognize the risks. For instance, not one of the mass of Sherman tanks had a night sight, so firing would be at random and at an enemy whose muzzle flashes were smaller than the Allied muzzle flashes. Birt again remarked that soldiers at ground level recognized the risks: 'men of our battle groups prepared for the action in the sober fashion of those who did not expect to survive it. To drive tanks against a strongly held position by night – and flails, unwieldy by day, were dreadfully difficult to handle in darkness – was a task which required us to be prepared for heavy sacrifices.'[8] It is doubtful if the average tank crew would have phrased their apprehension quite like that – it would have sounded too heroic – but Birt doubtless described what was in the back of many minds, especially the commanders who would take responsibility for the casualties.

With the seed of an idea now germinating in Simonds' mind, events suddenly moved into a giddy round of suggestion and accomplishment as the following diary format will illustrate:[9]

29 July 1944 Canadian army commander, Gen Crerar, instructs Lt-Gen Simonds to prepare a plan to break through the German defences along the Caen-Falaise road.
30 July Simonds responds with general comments, stating that another infantry division, another armoured division and total air support will be needed for the proposed action.
31 July Simonds presents outline plan to Crerar verbally, and commits it to writing the next day, 1 August.

2 August Simonds gives first warning to divisional commanders and has staff preparing various innovatory techniques in anticipation of approval of his plan.

3 August Montgomery approves plan and and requires it actioned for a D-Day of 8 August latest. Simonds wants more time (preferably a week) for training in unaccustomed tactics and adaptation of the necessary mechanical items for which no precedent exists. Simonds told that the 51st Highland Division, 33rd (British) Armoured Brigade and 1st Polish Armoured Division will be available to him. 51st Highland Division comes under Canadian command at midnight.

4 August Regimental colonels briefed. 1st Polish Armoured Division comes under command while still moving up after landing in Normandy (effective, 06.00 hours, 5 August).

5 August Crerar addresses senior aides. At noon 2nd Canadian Corps issue full plan instructions. By 18.45 hours tanks of 33rd Armoured Brigade are rehearsing north of Caen.

6 August After disagreement on the practicality of bombing plans a trial RAF bombing run takes place in darkness. Plan O.K'd. Right flank support attack launched over River Orne, securing that base of the proposed advance. KG (Battle Group) Wunsche with some Tigers is drawn off from ridges to oppose River Orne crossing.

7 August 23.00 hours, RAF bombing commences. 23.30 hours, armoured columns move off.

That diary requires perhaps two brief general notes. The attack across the Orne was mounted by 59th Division of 12 Corps. Nearby 43rd (Wessex) Division had just completed the heroic clearance of Mount Pincon which dominated the Normandy landscape for miles around and on which the defenders had long held out in one of the most ferocious battles, even by Normandy standards.[10] These divisions were not under Canadian command, of course, but offered a threat to the German's western flank.

The other note concerns Montgomery's insistence on 8 August as the latest date for the Night March. In his initial appreciation Simonds had stressed that possible delays might be 'avoided if the first zone is penetrated by infiltration at night but this can only be attempted with careful preparation by troops who are to do the operation'. Given the doubts which existed about the battle-worthiness of some of the troops to be used, it is difficult to understand how Montgomery could have expected such unusual tactics and novel material to be put into operation between his agreement on 3 August and D-Day on 7–8 August. It has been pointed out that 8 August was the anniversary of the Canadians' great victory at Amiens in 1918. This may have been of interest to professional officers, war historians and the media, but would not have had much meaning to an *ad hoc* corps of temporary soldiers, many of them conscripts and non-Canadians. An extra two days of training might have served them better.

There have been suggestions that at this stage of the Normandy campaign Montgomery was to some extent affected by the political and international pressures mentioned earlier. Hastings considers that this is not possible to

Sgt Wilkins explains the plan of the Night March to the crew of 3 Able, 'C', 1st Northamptonshire Yeomanry. Left to right: Tpr Boorman, Tpr Milner, L/Cpl Pryde, Tpr Thorn. (IWM, B8794)

prove[11] but it may well have been a factor. The Americans were storming up from the south, the British public was wondering why the arrowheads on the newspaper maps were not shooting south faster on the British and Canadian front and even Churchill was being urged to stimulate more action, unfair though these attitudes may have been in view of the real problems encountered in the Caen sector. Simonds had to accept the final decision of higher command but would be blamed if things went awry.

If the overall plan was hectic, there was no better example of technical ingenuity in moments of extreme urgency than the Kangaroos. There is some debate about the origin of the term, and some writers like the concept of the Kangaroo as a marsupial, a creature which carries its young in its pouch. The Kangaroo carried its infantrymen in a contrived pouch inside safe armour (safe compared to the PBI's normal walking lot). Other commentators suggest that 'Kangaroo' was simply a random code name. The name Kangaroo was a popular choice. Fortunately, the headquarters baptismal department did not select 'Marsupial' which might have elicited from some Highland foot-sloggers the reaction 'Phit the Hell's a bluidy "Ma's-soup-ial"?'

For the previous exposure of infantry along these ridges during Goodwood, Lt-Gen Sir Richard O'Connor (Corps Commander) had wanted to ferry infantry in self-propelled gun carriers of the artillery. 'There were predictable howls of outrage at this temerity to violate the hidebound organizational structure of the army' and Dempsey, O'Connor's superior, vetoed the idea. When he saw the casualty figures after Goodwood, O'Connor regretted that he had let the matter drop there.[12] In fact the tactic had a pedigree. As far back as 1917 Britain designed the Mark IX tank 'to meet a requirement for carrying infantry . . . in an enclosed armoured vehicle'. The Americans had used sleds towed by tanks at Anzio well before D-Day in Normandy.[13] Simonds himself used towed knocked-out armoured vehicles to carry infantry in Italy. So the time was ripe to produce a permanent and satisfactory vehicle in Normandy, with one week to do it in!

Taking into account the fact that Montgomery did not approve the plan until 3 August, and could well have vetoed it, and remembering O'Connor's experience with his superior, Simonds had considerable temerity in giving his instructions for 'Kangaroo' on 31 July. By that time he had gone directly to the Americans to borrow some disused guns from D-Day. These were US M7 105 mm SP guns, known as Priests, which had been used in the assault landings and were now being withdrawn from service. The 105 mm gun was, of course, larger than the 75 mm Sherman gun, so that the hole left by removing the Priest gun would give a fair amount of space into which up to ten infantry bodies might be inserted. Inevitably the adapted Priests acquired the affectionate names of 'Unfrocked Priests' or 'Holy Rollers'. War was not without its moments of grim humour which kept many people sane.

So on 31 July the DDME (Mechanical Engineer) of the Canadian army, Brig M.C. Grant was told to take over seventy-two Priests and convert them to Armoured Personnel Carriers by 6 August. This was on the familiar military basis of, 'Don't ask "How?" Do it!' Grant did. The task was complicated because it might be necessary at a later date to restore the guns, so damage would have to be minimal. It was found that the gun, mounting and mantlet could be removed, leaving only a relatively small gap in the steel shield. Having been withdrawn from service all seventy-two vehicles also needed full engine overhaul.

Grant took over fields outside Bayeux as 'AWD Kangaroo'. He sought skilled personnel from fourteen British and Canadian REME units, all of whom were already busy with their own battle tasks. He especially requested welding equipment and welders. REME units thus approached released a total of 250 personnel to 'AWD Kangaroo' for start of work on 2 August. Four days to go! The breakers and welders were put on a fifteen-hour day which included two hours for meal breaks. One of them just laughed, 'We took no notice of that. We worked all day and all night if necessary, to finish the job'.

Maj Wiggin was later awarded the MBE for his 'make do and mend' initiatives. Although the main base of protection was there in the body of the vehicle, there was still a need for a considerable amount of armour-plating for covering gaps and building up further protection. No adequate supplies of armour-plating were available. Maj Wiggin sent people down to the

D-Day beaches to cannibalize suitable steel from wrecked tanks. A test was made with metal from wrecked landing craft but this was not tough enough. Wiggin came up with the idea of 'sandwiches'. Gaps in the armour-plate would be covered inside and outside by thin skins of ex-naval metal welded to the hulk of the Priest. The two metal plates were then filled with sand, resulting in a reasonably well-armoured plaque.

At the same time, 123 LAD, the 'Kangaroo LAD', was formed as a repair unit, under the command of Capt G. Duncan. As tests were run, both in the Kangaroo fields and with actual infantry on board, minor adjustments were immediately seen to be necessary. Accidents happened and the normal range of repairs and maintenance came under the Kangaroo LAD. Initially this LAD was intended to serve only the thirty-six Kangaroos which would carry Canadian infantry but exigencies of the service meant that it also took on the work of the other thirty-six, which would carry Scottish troops. The LAD was kept busy during Totalize as Kangaroos were put out of action by enemy fire or mines.

Canadian tank drivers were allocated to drive the tanks, and eventually this hurriedly contrived formation became the permanent and satisfactory solution required. On 24 October 1944 Simonds' seed of an idea, and the technical nous of people like Grant and Wiggin, gave birth to the 1st Canadian Armoured Carrier Regiment.[14]

Meanwhile other staff and technicians were developing what Hastings called the 'sophisticated' devices. One such was the radio directional beam, similar to the air traffic control concept of two radio lanes within which the craft must travel. Of course, there was no such machine for tank purposes. Technicians fitted wireless 33 sets with windscreen wipers working on a differential basis to send out dots and dashes to the unfamiliar turret sets which Ray Ager and his mates found already installed when they came back from their NAAFI break. On a less delicate but equally difficult vast administrative scale, echelons were required to move 80,000 tons of supplies – ammunition, spare parts, water, petrol, food, crosses for graves and so on – in less than two days, through pitted roads and over rough country already thronged with one of the biggest traffic jams in history. The mass of armour had to be crammed into relatively narrow folds in the ridges outside Caen, in order to escape constant observation and strafing from the German artillery posts so conveniently located on the higher slopes.

In that blockage of traffic, as D-Day approached, one of the minor problems was that encountered by gunners of the immensely long Firefly 17-pdr gun. The gun sights needed to be tested and set. This was done by sighting an object about 1,500 yd away and using it as an aiming mark at the gun's optimum range. Joe Crittenden found great difficulty in locating a target because of the press of vehicles which screened off almost any object 1,500 yd away and also made traversing of the turret with its long gun a hazard both to the gun and its neighbours. The Firefly itself was something of a 'sophisticated' element very recently introduced. Joe Ekins, lining up on his sighting mark, had only fired the gun once in England, it being a 'secret weapon' and not available in mass numbers. He had been astonished by the

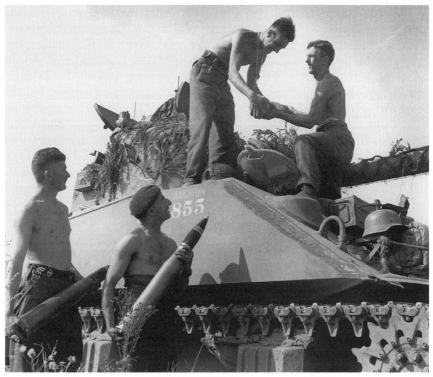

Firefly 'Hanging Houghton' ('C', 1st Northamptonshire Yeomanry) loads up for the Night March. Left to right: Sgt Ginns, Tpr Capocci, L/Cpl McKenzie, Tpr Reid. (IWM, B8793)

muzzle flash, which almost wrapped itself around the turret and virtually blinded gunner and commander. Combined with the dense smoke produced, observation of fall of shot was difficult until gunner and commander learned to keep their eyes shut for the fraction of a second while the gun fired. Since landing in Normandy in June, Joe's tank had not been required to fire a shot – such chances occur in the vagaries of tank warfare. So he was preparing to go into a crucial action with only one firing practice on his record. Some other Firefly gunners had not yet fired a round. The Canadians, allocated four Firefly tanks per squadron, had commenced by forming a Firefly Troop, but now had dispersed these so that a troop had one Firefly and three 75 mm Shermans, as did British regiments.

While all these technical preparations were taking place, Simonds had finalized his tactical plans. He had at his disposition, as constituting the specially reinforced 2nd Canadian Corps, the following units:

2nd Canadian Infantry Division (Maj-Gen Foulkes)
3rd Canadian Infantry Division (Keller)
4th Canadian Armoured Division (Kitching)
1st Polish Armoured Division (Maczek)

51st (Scottish) Highland Division (Rennie)
33rd (British) Armoured Brigade (Scott)
Units of 79th (British) Armoured Division (Hobart).

The 79th was, of course, the specialist division which had developed flail tanks, flame-throwers, Royal Engineer Assault Units with bulldozers, bridging facilities and so on. Two corps groups of artillery were available with a total of 720 guns, of which 360 would fire the first barrage. For this purpose each field gun would have a stack of 650 shells, or 8 tons of ammunition[13], all of which was delivered in a 36-hour stint by artillery drivers and crews.

Operation Totalize would be divided into three phases:

PHASE 1: armoured columns to drive by night from the Ifs, Bras and Cormelles assembly areas, through the enemy first lines and on to the line of Saint-Aignan through Cramesnil to Gaumesnil and Caillouet, a distance varying according to the assembly area but generally about 5 miles. The columns would then establish armed camps behind the German line. At the same time 'walking infantry' would move forward slowly from the old front line and clear the areas through which the armour had passed. Those areas would include fortified villages from which, in daylight, the anti-tank guns would have treated the tanks to another Goodwood-style reception.

PHASE 2: About midday on 8 August two further armoured groups, the 4th Canadian and 1st Polish armoured divisions would pass through the Phase 1 troops and would drive into the last prepared line of German defences which would have been softened up by daylight bombing.

PHASE 3: As soon as Phase 2 had been accomplished, Canadian and Polish troops would rush towards Falaise virtually unimpeded and close the Falaise trap by joining up with the Americans advancing towards them. The three phases were due to take place from 23.00 hours air bombing from 7 August until 9 August. Success depended to a large extent on free access for follow-up troops and echelons through the Phase 1 area and a prompt launching of Phase 2. It also depended, in the event, on fairly minimal resistance by the German troops in the Phase 1 area and an inability to be able to organize an effective counter-stroke in the Phase 2 area.

The Caen to Falaise main road, ruler straight, would be the centre line of the advance, with Canadian armour on the right of it and British armour on the left. The Poles would move through the Highland Division on the left. The Phase 1 advance would be in columns. There has been some confusion about the actual number of columns taking part and this may result from misunderstanding of the word 'column'. To confuse things further, there were seven columns, each of four columns! Here 'column' is used in the first place to denote a single battle group advancing along its prescribed lane towards an objective. But each of those battle groups were advancing 'in columns', that is in four files line ahead, like the First World War formation of an infantry unit on the march. So, to confuse the issue even further it could be said that, in fact, there were twenty-eight columns.

To speak therefore of 'battle groups', there were seven armoured battle groups in Phase 1. In 1944 the British army had not yet evolved a standard permanent formation of battle groups. In the German army, and to an increasing extent in the American army, the battle group was a mixed formation of armour, infantry and support services, able to undertake a battle action on its own. In the British army, armour and infantry normally belonged to separate battalions or regiments and were split up according to the needs of the moment. After Totalize, for example, the 51st Highland Division would demand the support of the 33rd Armoured Brigade on a permanent basis and disparate units would come to know each other. In fact, on 7 August officers of those two formations had a brief social get-together so that there would be harmonious cooperation.

So, on the right of the Caen to Falaise road there would be four columns, alias battle groups, three of them aiming straight across country southwards. The fourth, formed on the 8th Canadian Reconnaissance Regiment, would go parallel with the others until the last few hundred metres when it would cross the main road to occupy the crucial height at Lorguichon. Behind them the Canadian 'walking infantry' would clear the villages, and behind them would be a 'firm base' reserve of troops. The flail and mobile engineer functions would be carried out by troops of the 79th Armoured Division, including the Scottish 1st Lothian and Border Yeomanry and the 79th Assault Regiment of Royal Engineers. The whole Canadian wing would be under the command of a Canadian armoured brigade officer, Brig Wyman.

On the left of and nearest to the road would march the 144 RAC with the 7th Argylls in their four files, alias columns of armoured vehicles. Following on in the tracks of 144 RAC would be 148 RAC with 7th Black Watch in Kangaroos and other suitable vehicles. Before the 144 RAC objective, 148 RAC would branch off to attack another village. On the extreme left flank would travel the 1st Northamptonshire Yeomanry with 1st Black Watch in carriers. These '51st HD' and 33rd Armoured Brigade units would be joined by the flails of XXII Dragoons and also the 80th REs. This eastern wing would be commanded by armour Brig H.B. Scott. The armoured colonels would command their respective columns until the Phase 1 objectives were in reach, at which point the infantry colonels would come forward and direct the assault (if necessary) on and formation around the objective villages. Two of the generals, Canadians Simonds and Foulkes, would be behind the right flank columns at Ifs, and Highland Division's Rennie would be at Bras. The REs would light the routes as far as the No Man's Land area while the much maligned military police would be doing a dangerous job of lining up the columns in proper order – dangerous because in that kind of major battle the MPs' pistols and batons would not be much protection, as it was always their lot to stand out in the open at junctions which were prime enemy artillery targets, and trying to direct thundering 30-ton Sherman tanks and blundering flails with their overhanging jibs could be an almost suicidal task.

If the above details seem rather less than charming, a little humanity crept in with the choice of code names for various localities en route. The right boundary of the entire corps was named Barrymore and the left boundary was Eddy (for popular film stars Lionel Barrymore and Nelson Eddy). The interdivisional boundary down that vital main road was Flynn, after that great star of the Hollywood epic adventures, Errol of that ilk. The Phase 1 objectives report line was (Charles) Laughton. Also coded along the way were screen lovers, Carol Lombard and Rudolf Valentino.

Was someone on the baptismal department exercising grim foresight when he named objectives which eventually proved to be tragically unattainable as Opium, Heroin and Aspirin? And, perhaps the most tragic report line of 8 August evening, Cauvicourt to Robertmesnil, was 'Alarm'. Naturally the Poles had their own code names, which may have added to the wireless confusion mentioned by Bill Deeming and others. In place of Lombard, Valentino and Opium, the Poles were moving from Markiza (Bras) to Semafor (Saint-Aignan) and aiming for Ygrek (Saint-Sylvain) on their left flank and from Markiza to Cewka (Cramesnil), aiming for Lina (Gaumesnil).

Perhaps brief words here would clarify the armour's wireless system. (Never say 'radio', command the operators in their memoirs. We never had a 'radio'. It was a 'wireless'!) A Sherman tank had an intercom system on its wireless set, by which crew members could converse and not be heard outside the tank. They could, however, hear outside broadcasts filter through into 'i.c.' To speak outside the tank the commander or operator would switch to 'A' set, when all that was spoken within the tank could be heard throughout the regiment. Uncomplimentary references were often leaked in that way, to the squadron leader's profound ire. There was also a 'B' set, which was a mystery to most troopers, but which fed back on a kind of restricted circuit to headquarters.

The tank would be part of a four-tank troop, normally Troop Leader, Troop Sergeant, Troop Corporal and Firefly. Normality was not always present in battle or for days afterwards. Each troop would use its number on air. The squadron consisted of four troops, plus a fighting headquarters troop (HQ/F) with a major squadron leader, captain 2 i/c, and a rear link or spare or 'squadron captain'. Each squadron would have a letter reference in battle. 'A' squadron might be W, pronounced William; 'B' squadron could be A, pronounced Able, and 'C' squadron F, pronounced Fox. 'C' squadron's 1 troop leader would then be Fox 1. In 1 troop the sergeant would be Fox 1 Able, the corporal Fox 1 Baker, and the Firefly Fox 1 Charlie. The system of avoiding confusion between B, C, D, G and so on when speaking on wireless or phone had been extended in the First World War to using syllables such as ack-ack and pip-emma. For tanks in 1944 this had been updated and formalized into an alphabet of words:

Able, Baker, Charlie, Dog, Easy, Fox, George, Howe, Item, Jig, King, Love, Mike, Nan, Oboe, Peter, Queen, Roger, Sugar, Tare, Uncle, Victor, William, Xray, Yoke, Zebra.

The only numbers likely to be confused on air were 5 and 9, so these were pronounced simply as 'Fife' and 'Niner'. This may all seem irrelevant, but from Simonds' headquarters down, wireless officers were working hard to rationalize the hullabaloo of multiple broadcasts, allocating codes to avoid confusion on the Allied side and to encourage confusion on the enemy side. Somewhere at a distance deception troops were sending out fictitious broadcasts which the very efficient German listening stations would pick up and need to consider seriously.

A major element of Simonds' plan was the air support to be given by the RAF at night and the American air forces by day, plus ground attack planes like the tank-destroying, rocket-firing Typhoons of the RAF. Simonds issued his air programme, well aware of the problems of inter-service cooperation. He may not have been too surprised that his neat programme almost foundered on the huge, immovable rock called Sir Arthur Harris, formidable head of the RAF Bomber Command.

One requirement of the air programme would have caused tremendous laughter among tank crews had they known about it at the time. It read, 'Troops are to be provided with ear plugs to avoid the danger of blast deafness'. Simonds was not to know that the common disability of British tank crews fifty years later would be blast deafness because ear plugs were not in common usage among the lower ranks. But it was a nice thought.

The air programme covered two phases:

PHASE 1: Heavy night bombers with high explosive. 'Cratering has been accepted with a view to isolating the corridor through which the armoured infantry are to advance.'
PHASE 2: Heavy day bombers with fragmentation bombs. 'Cratering had not been accepted' because the armour would have to roll over the bombed area. 83 Group RAF and 9th USAAF to carry out armoured recce at first light south of the line Urville-Bretteville-Estrees, attacking enemy movement. Recce to report groups of/in excess of 100 infantry, 10 tanks, 25 mechanized transport. 1 VCP each for 2nd Canadian Division and 51st Highland Division to keep a listening watch (Sherman tank with VCP wireless).[15]

On 4 August a high-level conference took place between Crerar, Simonds and Crocker for the army and senior air commanders, Leigh-Mallory, Coningham, Broadhurst (83 Group) and Brown (84 Group). The Chief of Staff to Crerar, Brig Mann was appointed to fly to England the next day for detailed conferences. He went assuming that the 4 August conference had approved the night bombing plan. However, in England he discovered that not only were there reservations about details, but that the 'great man' himself, Air Chief Marshal Sir Arthur Harris, had been consulted and was set to veto the idea. He stated that he was 'not prepared to bomb at night as planned . . . and that there was no question of deviating from this policy'. The implications of the veto at such a late stage were so alarming that Mann asked Harris to phone Montgomery. Harris refused.

Harris may have acquired a certain reputation for a brutal attitude to the victims of bombing, but he had served in the trenches in the First World War and could visualize the suffering of his own troops caught under a rain of heavy high-explosive RAF bombs at night. He considered the margin of 1,000 yd to the nearest tanks to be too narrow. Brig Mann then asked if it would be possible to stage a trial with artillery markers used in the dark. This would have to take place on 6 August, leaving only twenty-four hours before the H-Hour of D-Day. Harris conceded a trial. Mann's colleague, Brig Richardson phoned the headquarters in Normandy, requesting the artillery to set up a test with 25-pdr guns firing red and green marker shells on to the limits of the RAF target areas. Pathfinder master bombers would fly overhead and then report back to Harris as to whether they could guarantee to bomb within the marked limits. The trial was a success. The air programme would go ahead as timed.[16]

This would be the third massive heavy bombing operation around Caen. On the eve of the battle to enter Caen city the RAF deployed 467 heavy bombers in close formation. For the Goodwood attack there were 863 American aircraft and 1,056 from Bomber Command. This time there would be 1,019 Bomber Command heavies with 491 American day bombers to follow, plus ground support Typhoons, fighters and recce planes.[17]

Harris was not alone in his qualms about dangers to ground troops. Hastings has commented:

> It was a dangerous business using heavy bombers with a mean aiming accuracy of three miles to support ground operations. . . . Until the end of the war many airmen and some thoughtful soldiers argued that it was counter-productive to send in Bomber Command, for the devastation caused serious problems for advancing armour and bombing was not accurate enough to pin-point German positions.[17]

One ground controller of that time, already quoted in a criticism of air staff work, was dubious about accuracy, although he worked on the successful OBOE system:

> Until the advent of the 'smart', laser-guided bomb, the odds were against the bomb-aimer, by day and night. . . . The snags were that bombs were not precision made; so that the ballistics were subject to error. Minor error in most cases, but not if the bombs were our much-used 'cookies' or 'blockbusters', which looked like outsize dustbins packed with HE, and lacked any pretension to streamlining. When you dropped one of them it seemed to stop, wobble, look around – turn around, even – and then go on its own way. Fine, if the target was as big as Krupps factory, or an oil refinery; but not for use close to our own troops! On such occasions the bombloads were generally streamlined 1,000 pounders which went, within reason, where they were aimed. OBOE . . . was a very accurate system. . . . In practice, using the Mark 2 equipment available in mid-1944, target indicators (or bombs) usually landed within about 200 yards of the target . . . then, of course, the lads in the main force had to bomb the target markers. Those were very high-powered green, or red, or red and green pyrotechnics in 250 lb bomb cases, and burned for about five minutes . . . another safety measure was taken on 'close support' targets; a Master Bomber checked the positions of the target markers and radioed any necessary corrections to the Main Force. His, or 'backer-up' aircraft, also re-marked targets with 'puff' bombs of colours different from the main markers, whenever necessary.[18]

The same OBOE controller has some sympathy for the American airmen whose bombs dropped on ungrateful friendly troops:

> The Americans were in a much less favourable position. Except on a few rare occasions they did not have OBOE markings. . . . So all of their equipment and training was for high altitude (25,000 to 30,000 feet) daylight work, out of range of ack ack, in large formations designed to best concentrate their gunfire against fighters. Their navigation to the target was by a Lead Navigator; and their bomb-aiming controlled by the Lead Bombardier. When he bombed, the other Bombardiers dropped their loads as soon as they saw the Leader's bombs leave his aircraft. That wasn't exactly 'pickle barrel' accurate . . . and the constant small changes in direction and height needed to fly in close formation made absolute precision, and concentrated bombing, impossible. I hate to say that, for I think the Fortress and Liberator crews were the bravest of brave men . . . the odds against them were so great.[19]

Other brave airmen had flown the skies above the Totalize target areas in order to take photographs which would help the ground forces plan their advance. Unfortunately air photos, 1944 version, had limited clarity of detail. Just south of Saint-Aignan-de-Cramesnil there is an infamous gully, le Petit Ravin or le Val to the locals, using which German tanks were able to knock out a number of British and Polish tanks with a sad tally of fatalities. On the air photos from 4 August le Petit Ravin shows up as simply another cross-country track on the level with others. In fact at one point its bottom is 9 m (28 ft) lower than the fields within 20 m on each side.[20]

It has been said that Simonds was ill served by army intelligence.[21] Fortunately, Hitler's system of forcibly conscripting non-German nationals from occupied countries often caused negative results. On the night of 6/7 August a Yugoslav conscript deserted to the Canadians with the news that the 89th Infantry Divison from Norway had taken over the front line from the fearsome Hitlerjugend. It was known that 272 Infantry Division linked to the 89th on the Totalize left flank. The Hitlerjugend would be somewhere nearby, available for counter-attack. But the kaleidoscopic German formation movement and the dummy tanks at Billy and Conteville all served to confuse the issue.

The Polish general, Maczek, had doubts about the plan. He pointed to 'The open terrain, with wide horizons extending to more than 2 kilometers, assured the Germans of superiority in the duel between our Shermans and Cromwells on one hand and their Tigers and Panthers with the incomparable 88 mm on the other.'[22] Both Maczek and the Canadian divisional commander, Kitching, also had reservations about the plans to send them in on a very narrow front, having to await the outcome of American bombing around midday on 8 August. On the other hand, knowing that these were untried formations, Simonds was seeking safety first in giving them a very straightforward plan with maximum air support.

Maczek says also that the Allied battle order (*l'ordre de l'armée*

Canadienne) had fallen into the hands of the Germans on the eve of the action, revealing to them all the detail of the attack and its execution. He says that the plans were found in the destroyed car of a dead staff officer.[23] Be that as it may, the immense preparations left the Germans in no doubt. Hitlerjugend formally advised 89th Infantry that an attack was due up the main road and left liaison officers there.

In spite of all the doubts about unprecedented tactics to be carried out by 'green' or tired troops, there was morale uplift for lower ranks in the massed vehicles and unusual proceedings. Something was happening at last. Crerar himself gave voice to this sentiment, echoing Montgomery's reference to the great Canadian victory of the First World War at Amiens: 'I have no doubt that we shall make the 8th of August 1944 an even blacker day for the German Armies than is recorded against that same date twenty-six years ago.' Had he perhaps forgotten one word – 'Hitlerjugend'?

Chapter Four

The Left Hook

'So for that night they . . . lit a number of beacons on the mountains all around them as signals to each other. At the first sign of dawn, they formed up and marched against the enemy. As there was a mist they got up close without being noticed, and made an assault on the ridge.' (Xenophon, 400 BC)

It was not too pleasant, that August Bank Holiday, waiting for the start. The sun did indeeed shine, August Bank Holiday fashion. There were green fields in Normandy, but not here at the 51st Highland Division's assembly area at Cormelles:

> It was a scene of dreadful desolation; a landscape of grey-white craters dominated by the tattered skeletons of the factories, crushed and tossed about by weeks of every sort of bombardment. And still the shells fell among the wreckage, except that now they came from the south (from the Germans) and not the north.[1]

Over on the Canadian wing 'the hot clear weather, together with the movement of both tracked and wheeled vehicles, had produced a fine layer of dust that covered almost everything and everybody in the vicinity. . . . "It will sure be a relief", wrote the war diarist of the Calgary Highlanders, "to break out of the sardine can . . . the concentration of troops and armour within the small area of Ifs is a sight to behold."'[2]

The full details of the plan were still seeping down to troopers and privates. Rex Jackson and Stan Hicken on 3 Baker were still wondering about it. 'Like, I'm sure, a lot of others, I was puzzled when we started to train for the Night March – lining up with Troops in file and then Squadrons, all chugging across the fields. We assumed the Troop Leaders were in the know but it didn't come down to us then,' declared Rex. Of course, many troopers like Brian Carpenter made a good guess when the rum ration came up: 'a sure sign of a tough time ahead!'

Troop leaders and specialist platoon leaders like Charlie Robertson did have a good idea of what was to happen because they had seen it graphically demonstrated on the sand model. Capt Tom Boardman knew even more about it, because his squadron leader, Gray Skelton, had told him to report back to the brigade commander, 'Black Harry'. There the brigadier briefed the three officers who would be the lead navigators of the 33rd Armoured Brigade's 'battle groups', advancing through the night towards three objectives marked on the map. The first part of the Night March would be over territory

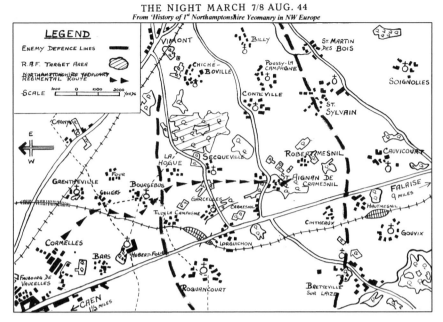

THE NIGHT MARCH 7/8 AUG. 44
From 'History of 1ˢᵗ Northamptonshire Yeomanry in NW Europe

The Night March (1st Northamptonshire Yeomanry).

already occupied by British troops but which, for much of the distance, could still be viewed by the Germans higher up. Then, crossing the No Man's Land between the two armies, the advancing columns would strike straight for those beckoning Xs on the maps, not stopping to fight the German front-line troops but 'pushing on regardless'. Capt Boardman was to go out and survey the route which 1st Northamptonshire Yeomanry (in which he was second in command, 'A' Squadron) must take, checking for tank obstacles as far as he could go towards the enemy line. He was also advised about the changes being made to his tank turret. A special compass and radio directional device would be fitted. In particular he was instructed not to allow his turret to be traversed as this would affect the compass. This meant that he would not be able to fire his big gun unless a target obligingly presented itself directly ahead at zero degrees. It was going to be a naked enough feeling out there in front on one's own without the knowledge that one could not fire the gun.

To Ken Quail fell the none-too-welcome task of driving his captain up as near as possible to the German front line in the dusk. Ken certainly felt that it was a time to use one of the meanings of his name and 'quail' at the prospect. But it would be worse for the captain when dismounted, for he would have to crawl around with a small hand torch, trying to work out tank routes. They halted behind a railway embankment and the officer said to the trooper, 'Wait twenty minutes. If I'm not back go straight to RHQ and report. Twenty minutes. No longer. That's an order, Quail.'[3]

The railway which ran diagonally across the Totalize front had been a salient feature in the Goodwood operation. It provided some cover on the down side of the slope, from which the Allies were advancing, but the up side was a prime hunting zone for efficient German binoculars and 88 mm gun sights. Perhaps even more risky for tanks in the night were the sunken roads, of which there were a number in the area. Tom Boardman was soon assessing gaps which were too narrow for ordinary Shermans and even more so for flails with their apparatus stuck out like iron crinoline skirts. The doughty Highland engineers would have to come out and blow bigger gaps in the embankments and he would then have to return in daylight to check the resulting breaches. There was a great deal of flashing and banging which made the night unpleasant, while in the silences German voices could be heard close by.

During one of the brighter flashes, Ken Quail, waiting in the scout car, thought he saw three German soldiers sitting propped up against the embankment. He rubbed his eyes and waited for the next flash. Yes, they were there and they were laughing at him. He thought it better to remain motionless. Perhaps they could not really see him? It was a number of flashes later before he realized that the three soldiers were dead. Meantime there was another worry: Tom Boardman's time limit had elapsed. Ken Quail had never directly disobeyed an order before, but he decided to give it another five minutes. Precisely on the five minutes of extra time his captain came crawling back through a gap. 'Home, quick!' he ordered, and, as if to encourage the driver, the enemy dropped a mortar stonk right where the scout car had been a moment before.

Scouting missions were dangerous, but there was danger too for those who only stood and waited in the assembly area. The unsighted German gunners were sending tentative feelers out, using the massive 210 mm shells. John Cutland, intelligence officer of the 7th Argyll and Sutherland Highlanders, was almost catapulted out of his slit trench when a shell landed only 6 ft away. It did not explode. When John finally decided to explore, he found that the shell had bored a hole as deep as his trench. Cpl McLean and Tpr Mitchell of XXII Dragoons were not so lucky. They were both killed by another 210 mm landing directly in their dug-out shelter.[4]

Last minute preparations were well in hand. Capt John 'Bing' Crosby, signals officer at RHQ of the Northamptonshire Yeomanry, had taken part in the get-to-know-you sessions with his Highland counterparts. He discovered that they had no wireless which would conveniently link into the tanks' net. He asked Lt-Col Doug Forster's permission to lend the Highland Division men a couple of spare 'B' sets which had found their way into his possession, excess to inventory. All the extra equipment needed for Simonds' novel tactics proved impossible to stow into the colonel's command tank, which was a normal Sherman and did not have a dummy gun like some command tanks. So a follow-up radio centre was set up in a van, which the adjutant, 'Lew' Llewellyn would run, leaving the colonel's turret free for firing.

The Highland engineers had been forward and blown more gaps in the embankments and sunken roads. Other engineers were busy marking the route as far as the ultimate point of danger, setting up lamps on 5 ft high pickets. The lamps were green on the right of a lane and amber on the left. The artillery had loaded their guns and were ready to fire.

What kind of troops was Simonds sending up the ridges on his left flank, troops seconded from the British army to a Canadian army which had bled outside Caen at a rate rarely experienced by the Allies in the West? Not a few of the tankies had felt some kind of premonition when they saw that they were going to be welded together with the famous Highland Division, the 'Ladies from Hell', into the army of the fearless Canadians, whose battles with Hitlerjugend around Caen were already almost legendary a week or two later. What could a humble brigade of tankies offer to such a proud formation?

Brig H.B. Scott, DSO, a physical giant and an African veteran, had taken command of the 33rd Armoured Brigade in March 1944. He had needed a light tank to 'swan' around in and noticed that the Northants had acquired a new mark of the fast Stuart, or Honey tank. So he took over not only the new Honey but also two of the Yeomen, Cpl Wilf Mylan – the operator and commander in the brigadier's absence – and driver Johnny Taylor. On their first recce together a sniper's bullet passed between the heads of the brigadier and the corporal with an inch or two to spare. 'Black Harry' was, apparently, unmoved. Wilf Mylan was deeply moved. From that moment he had a great admiration for the 'boss', whom he describes as a 'real pro and good to be with'. The Honey was part of the Tac. HQ, which moved around in a mobile fashion with the brigadier. Tac. HQ was run by Capt Cochrane, with three scout cars, two wireless trucks, two Jeeps, a caravan (captured by the brigadier from an Italian general in the desert) and a Sherman with a dummy gun, which was the 'boss's' working office. He commanded the 1st Northamptonshire Yeomanry, the 144th Regiment of the Royal Armoured Corps (144 RAC) and 148 RAC.

The Northamptonshire Yeomanry had a long but intermittent pedigree. The regiment had been founded in 1794 during the Napoleonic wars by the Earl Spencer of the day, the First Lord of the Admiralty who had promoted Nelson. Early camps and latter-day ceremonial parades were held at Althorp House, the Northamptonshire seat of the Spencers. When there was no state of war the Yeomanry was 'stood down' only to be revived for a new war or an occasion like the visit of Queen Victoria to Kettering. The Northamptonshire Yeomanry had been members of the 'Old Contemptibles' in 1914. In 1939 the recuitment rush was so great that two 'regiments' were formed and the Northamptonshire was the only provincial Yeomanry to provide two tank regiments for the Normandy landings. (Other Yeomanry had two regiments in other roles.) During Goodwood the 2nd Northamptonshire Yeomanry had suffered with the rest of the 11th Armoured Division. Unburied, undiscovered bodies were still lying on the continually blasted Bourguebus slopes, later to be identified by the White Horse of Hanover badge on their berets.

At a time when the British army was critically lacking in numbers of infantry it is surprising to note that both 144 and 148 RAC were infantry battalions retrained for tank service. No. 144 had been formed on 28 November 1941 from the officers and men of 8th Battalion the East Lancashire Regiment. They had very soon become a typical tank regiment with their priorities related to mechanical and professional efficiency rather than the more superfluous external signs of military brilliance. When Tpr E. Howley and his mates of 144 arrived to be brigaded with the

Northamptonshire Yeomanry near Bury St Edmunds before D-Day, they saw the Yeomanry flag, with its white horse, flying from a flagpole surrounded by white stones, their first reaction was 'What a bullshitting shower!' (In fact the Yeomanry were, like 144, what is known as an 'easy' regiment.) After meritorious service in north-west Europe the 144 were to suffer another transformation, this time being welcomed by the highly selective Royal Tank Regiment, to replace the original 4th RTR which was lost at Tobruk.

No. 148 RAC had commenced life as 9th Battalion, The Loyal Regiment, another Lancashire unit, in July 1940, becoming 148 RAC in November 1941. Like the Northamptonshire Yeomanry and 144, the 148 RAC was officially a regiment new to battle in the Second World War. However, they had been 'blooded' in an unusual way long before D-Day, having formed part of the Mersey Garrison during the blitz on Liverpool. Guarding the docks they had one man killed by the Luftwaffe, two by mines washed ashore and three accidentally drowned.[5] They were commanded on the Night March by Lt-Col R.G. Cracroft, while Lt-Col A. Jolly commanded 144.

If those were the armoured regiments, the men were for the most part young conscripts, leavened with older volunteers among the NCOs. Many of them had no previous warlike tendencies or even cadet or similar experience. One young tank gunner, who had no thoughts of becoming a hero, might be taken as fairly typical of his generation of tank crews. Joe Ekins was born in the small Bedfordshire village of Yelden in 1923, making him just twenty-one in Normandy. He left school at fourteen years of age and became a trainee 'clicker', cutting the shapes of shoes out of leather skins, in a shoe factory. He went to night school to study shoe manufacture and, as the war progressed, discovered that he was in a reserved occupation. So it was necessary for him to volunteer for the army, which he did in December 1941. Posted to the 51st Training Regiment, RAC, at the home of the tanks, Bovington Camp, he quickly realized he was not 'cut out' to be a soldier.

He was trained as a gunner on 75 mm guns but just before D-Day was sent to fire a 17-pdr. On the first time of firing he was 'shocked when the massive flash shot right around the turret'. He now sat in his Firefly, ready to go, but having fired the massive weapon only once.

Riding with the 33rd Armoured Brigade would be the 154 Infantry Brigade, of the Highland Division, the lucky ones in Kangaroos, the rest in whatever other armoured vehicles could be found. Brigadier Oliver commanded the brigade from a Tac. HQ at Hubert Folie. The other Highland brigades, 152 and 153, would have walking roles. The Highland Division, a very potent force in the desert, had been criticized for being somewhat less efficient in the bogged-down conditions of the Normandy bridgehead. One Black Watch officer, Charlie Robertson, expressed this clearly:

> It was basically a return to offensive action after the weeks we spent in the woods across the Orne protecting the left flank of the bridgehead. Morale and performance – it is widely accepted – reached a low level during this period, and people were saying the HD was a spent force, bomb happy after too much fighting in Africa and Sicily – so really it was 'Totalize' that

put us back on our feet again! The Battalion felt it was getting back to its old form . . . which would be equally true of the whole Highland Division.

Criticism with the benefit of hindsight is often unkind and it might be argued that, given the terrain and quality of enemy encountered and the orders imposed, the Highland Division had done no worse than a number of other units, some of whom had suffered disasters of greater magnitude. Be that as it may, the recently appointed Highland Division commander, Maj-Gen T.G. Rennie had no time to publish an in-depth analysis and contented himself with a brief rallying message: 'In Africa we fought side by side with Australians and New Zealanders. Now we are with Canadians, and it is a coincidence that during the closing stages of the Great War we were fighting beside a Canadian corps.'[6] Montgomery had also pointed out that 8 August was a historic date. What Rennie did not mention was that in a First World War action similar to Simonds' battle in its innovative factors, the Highland Division had fought alongside the first massed tanks, at Cambrai.

According to plan, the air bombers would arrive at 23.00 hours on 7 August, the armoured columns would cross the start line at 23.30, and the great artillery bombardment would begin at 23.45. In reality the armoured columns were faced with two 'start lines'. In battle terms the start line of the attack could only be from the point of moving out of friendly into enemy territory. The novel circumstances of prior shelter near Ifs-Bras-Cormelles, the conditions of fire-dazzle darkness and dust 'smog' and the use of cross-country routes across broken terrain meant that the journey from the 'start-off' point had, for some vehicles, as many problems as the 'attack' across the enemy front line. The left flank group had to negotiate no less than 6 km (about 3.7 miles) of this alien country before actually reaching the German defences and tacking on to the rolling artillery barrage.

The tank colonels were to command their respective columns through the Night March as far as the point where the infantry would debus.[7] They were given a certain amount of discretion in the formation of their groups. Northamptonshire Yeomanry went forward with one navigating officer in his Sherman and a reserve navigating officer following in another Sherman. 144 RAC had the navigating officer up front in a light Stuart tank, with two reserve navigators also in Stuarts and 148 formed similarly to the Yeomanry. As very precise details have been recorded on formation distances it is apparent that some columns set out in closer files than others. A wider file ran the risk of losing each other in the dark. A narrower file ran the risk of collisions on uneven ground.

The Northamptonshire Yeomanry with 1st Black Watch (Lt-Col Hopwood) had vehicles in four parallel columns, 10 yd apart left to right and 15 yd apart nose to tail. This gave a block of vehicles roughly 50 yd wide (including four Sherman widths of 8 ft 9 in) and about 800 yd long. Capt Tom Boardman of 'A' Squadron led, followed by Capt Ken Todd of 'C'. They were supported by a row of four Shermans from 1 Troop of 'A', then a row of flails from XXII Dragoons. The second troop of 'A' came next, followed by their squadron leader (Skelton), the rest of 'A' Squadron and the remainder of the twenty flails, commanded by Maj Clifford. 'RHQ' and 'C' Squadron (Bevan) came

Crew of 3 Baker, 'C', 1st Northamptonshire Yeomanry, prepare the 75 mm gun before the Night March. Right to left: Tprs Jackson, Tucker, Hicken, Cpl Snowdon and the author. (IWM, B8795)

next. The second-in-command of Northamptonshire Yeomanry (Wykeham) had his Sherman back alongside the Black Watch CO in the first rank of Kangaroos. Sandwiched in between were useful vehicles of engineers and fitters, including AVREs, bulldozers, the regimental fitters and medical half tracks. The entire procession was guarded at the rear by 'B' Squadron's Shermans (Brassey). At the assembly point the vehicles had been shaped up in a very close nose to tail formation, which then widened out to the scale mentioned as the whole group began to shunt forward.

Lt-Col Jolly of 144 RAC seems to have opted for a tighter formation, which he describes as 20 yd wide by 300 yd long, a matter of 6 yd between vehicles left to right and 6 yd from nose to following nose. There were about fifty rows of four vehicles abreast. Maj Shuter commanded the Dragoons flail contingent. The 7th 'Argylls' were the riding infantry, their CO (Lt-Col Meiklejohn) linking to Maj Tom Lovibond, second in command of 144. The Argylls record that as the 144 group moved off it stretched to about 600 yd long.[8] Jolly had selected Capt Bob Osbourn as lead navigator with Capt Gregson and Capt Pickering as reserves.

The task of 148 RAC navigator was a little different in that the regiment had to follow in the tracks of 144 until it reached a point about 2 km beyond the German front line. There it would perform a sharp left turn and drop its infantry, the 7th Black Watch (Lt-Col Cathcart) to face in to the straggling village of Garcelles-Secqueville where, by that time, the defenders might well have been truly roused by the passage of 144 RAC. Capt Johnny Hukens, second in command of 'C', an 8th Army veteran, was lead tank for 148 RAC, with Lt Seddon, a 'C' Squadron troop leader, following.[9] Owing to a shortage of men, 7th Black Watch was reorganized on a three-company basis, (as also was 1st Black Watch), 'A', 'B' and 'D', all of which were riding behind 148 RAC.[10]

The 'walking' roles, aiming to clear out the bypassed villages, were undertaken by Highland Division's 152 Brigade (Cassells) while 153 Brigade (Murray) formed a firm base against counter-attack. Also included in the firm base were the Highland Division machine-gunners, the Recce Regiment (2nd Derbyshire Yeomanry) and Crocodiles (flame-throwers) of 79th Division Royal Engineers. Forward observation officers of the Royal Artillery accompanied all formations, armoured and walking, riding beside the tank COs in the armoured columns.

Unusually it would not be the artillery voice which would herald the start of the advance but the RAF. Punctually at 23.00 hours the first bombers began to unload their bombs. Some 1,020 bombers took to the air, but, in the words of Harris himself, 'regret lack of wind and accumulating smoke made it unsafe to put down last third of tonnage on each objective but hope two thirds did the trick'. The 'two thirds' totalled 3,462 tons of bombs and again it should be repeated that 'no bombs fell among our troops'[11] – a truly incredible performance with a stated safety range of 1,000 yd and with some left flank tanks drifting within that range as diversions dictated.

More than one account states that only ten aircraft were lost. Some might object to the use of that word 'only'. For ground troops, to watch a friendly aircraft fall flaming from the skies was appalling. Compared with a tank brewing up it took so much longer and the end was somehow more sickening. For accompanying air crew it was a traumatic experience in which they shared. For the few survivors, if any, of that crew there was no question of 'only'.

WO John Torrans, flight engineer of Lancaster bomber, ND 817, code 'S' for Sugar, of 582 PFF Squadron, RAF, remembers:

We left our base, Little Staughton, at 22.30 hours, our duties to act as 'backer-up', i.e., to keep the markers going which the Master Bomber had dropped to mark the target. On our run in to carry out this task our bomb aimer missed the aiming point and we had to go around again and make another run in. As far as I can remember there was very little flak over the target. Our problem started on the way back, coming up to the coast . . . we were attacked by a night fighter. Both our gunners opened fire but during the attack our aircraft was raked with cannon fire and caught fire in the nose and mid fuselage. I went forward to open the nose hatch. . . . I thought the Captain had been hit as he was slumped over the controls. The Navigator then gave me instructions to bale out. The aircraft by this time was just a fire ball. I donned my chute and bailed out. I could see the night fighter still attacking the aircraft. I landed in a field near a canal (in enemy occupied territory).

Torrans later learned from the navigator, Flt Lt Hill, DFC, who had also baled out successfully, that the pilot, Sqn Ldr Wareing, DFC, was in hospital with severe burns and, with the second navigator, King, would become a prisoner of war. Wireless operator Blaydon, DFM, bomb aimer Hawkins and gunners Campbell and Caughran had died in the blazing plane. As the ground Night March gathered pace, Torrans, burned and with a bullet in his right thigh, and Hill, also burned and with a broken ankle, were stranded separately in thick mist somewhere to the north.

Fifteen crews were sent on the raid by 419 'The Moose' Squadron. They appreciated the star shells fired by the artillery as additional markers. Flg Off Bell described them as 'a finger pointing to the target'. Plt Off Hartford's experienced crew said it was 'the best they had ever seen'. One massive explosion was assumed to be an ammunition dump. Only one crew claimed to have seen a stick of bombs overshoot the target area.

Of the 419 Squadron planes 'only' one failed to return: Flg Off B.D. Walker's 'F' for Freddie. During November and December word filtered through that the crew were all prisoners of war. It was not until May of 1945 that news was received that the graves of all seven crew had been identified in Seine Inferieure: Walker, Durrant, Schryer, Merrick, Wilson, Jones and Longmore still together. For Flt Lt Wilson it was the tenth mission of his second tour of duty. None of the crew had undertaken fewer than nine missions. Nobody saw their plane fall.[12]

At 23.45, with the air bombing still in full spate, Brig Richardson gave the order for the artillery to open up along the entire Totalize front. To mortal men in tanks and walking on foot 'it was a terrific din. The guns kept up their thunderous roar and the bombs came crashing down with deadly accuracy, fairly obliterating enemy positions with a sickening thud. While the battalion was on the move, however, the full effect of the noise was lost as the vehicles effectively drowned it.'[13] Some found that, at 100 yd per minute, in lifts of 200 yd, 'the barrage was timed to move too fast for the tanks to be able to keep up with it. The difficulty of getting to the opening line in time made it impossible to get the advantage of starting (close) behind the barrage'.[14]

On the extreme left of the 4,050 yd front, the Northamptonshire Yeomanry had been formed up, as had all armoured columns, by the 'Red Caps', the Corps of Military Police. The colonel of the police strolled up to the lead Yeomanry tank to wish the commander the best of luck. Capt Boardman found himself shaking hands with Col Ferguson, the peacetime Chief Constable of Northamptonshire. Unfortunately Ferguson could not offer an escort of police motor cyclists where the Northants Yeomen were going. The routes of the armoured columns had been planned, as far as possible, to follow straight lines across country, avoiding the fortified villages. On the left flank the proximity of RAF bombing complicated the straight line idea. There was also a problem of railway embankments too high to blow gaps in and ruined No Man's Land villages through which night traffic was impracticable. So the first stage of the Yeomanry's journey had to be on a curving pattern before the 'straight line country' could be reached. This meant that from the factories at Cormelles the group had to run south-east towards Soliers in order to cross the railway. Then it was a south-south-west diversion avoiding both Soliers and Bourguebus on the column's left. Another south-east stint around the latter village brought the tanks to the enemy front line near Le Clos St Denis and on to point 50 in Les Noires Terres. From there it was the straight line almost due south to Saint-Aignan-de-Cramesnil.[15] The route was lit past Bourguebus but this did not simplify the task of manoeuvering huge, clumsy vehicles through sharp bends and over considerable variations in normal ground level, not to mention shell and bomb holes.

While all the columns started off in good order, confusion was the most common factor within a relatively short distance. It is possible that, if the units taking part had experienced Night Marches in actual battle previously, they would have recognized confusion as an inevitable but fairly minor factor which could be ridden through. But this was the first Night March of its kind. The regimental navigator of 144 RAC found, as they started to move, that his beam wireless was not emitting any dots and dashes to guide him within the radio lane. When the barrage started his compass went crazy, swinging from north to south and back again. The Northamptonshire Yeomanry's navigator could hear the dots and dashes but, as these were on a fixed line suited to a motorway, every deviation round a bombhole or passage behind a slope or embankment caused the signal to be lost. He commented that this might be a useful guide for a plane coming in directly to land at 150 mph but the effort necessary to concentrate on frequent dodging back and forward in and out of the radio lane meant that the navigator was distracted from the other more profitable techniques of his onerous role.

On Cpl Ted Bowden's tank with Northamptonshire Yeomanry 'A', Bill Higham, still amused at this being 'a lovely way to spend an evening', was one of many tank crew peering out through periscopes and wondering what was going to happen:

> Off we went, just about seeing the tank in front. We had gone maybe a mile or so, I don't know, when there was a bang and a flash by the side of Sgt Ryan's tank and it came to a halt. We had orders not to stop for anyone. We heard machine gun fire so we gingerly crept forward passing by the side where the flash occurred. We saw nothing but, with baited breath, waiting for the same to happen to us. (Sgt Ryan had been killed.) Someone up there was looking after us.

A few yards from Bowden's tank a flail had corkscrewed across the gaps in a sunken road as it had tried to take a sudden twisting drop into the road. Tanks following on were having to seek other gaps, at the same time watching out for the navigator's green Verey lights and the Bofors tracer firing overhead. Germans were just as confused as British. L/Cpl Neal had halted his 2 Troop tank, named 'Louisiana'. (In the Northants 'A' Squadron tanks were named after Russian cities, 'B' had American names and 'C' stayed with names from the home county.) Neal's tank was stuck at a traffic jam. He got out to investigate. He asked operator, L/Cpl John Bower, to stand guard while he looked for a suitable route. John Bower thought he was dreaming, here at the epicentre of modern warfare, when a horse and cart came clip-clopping out of the night. Was this a ghost from former wars? He was only a little reassured when he perceived that the cart contained two German soldiers, their hands raised high and their lips forming the desperate words, 'Kamerad! Friend!' – words hardly heard in the noise of dozens of low-gear engines looking for gaps. Instantly Bower had another problem, 'What to do with German prisoners in a situation like this?' Just then an infantry carrier came up the queue of vehicles, and the Black Watch knew what to do with prisoners. Bower was unaware of the fact that the enemy division, nicknamed the 'Horseshoe', was still using horse transport.

If Bower's confusion brought a tiny spark of comedy into the proceedings, there were also tiny moments of human tragedy. The mortar platoon of the Argylls could not find room in the few Kangaroos available and so were 'bowling along' in their more customary bren carriers somewhere behind the 144 tanks. Their commander, Capt D.A. Rowan-Hamilton, was 'feeling very naked in comparison with the others', his fragile bren carrier having to be exposed in the same way as the huge Kangaroos and Shermans. Suddenly, out of the dark, a German soldier came running up to the carrier and shouted to Rowan-Hamilton. It could have been a cry of surrender or a plea for medical aid. Rowan-Hamilton never found out. An infantryman behind him, supposing his officer to be under attack, shot the shouting German dead on the spot.

Up front from the mortar platoon, 144 had run into real trouble. Their navigating tank had disappeared into a huge bombhole. Trying to evade the hole and pick up the lead, the next two tanks with their reserve navigators also fell into craters. That their tanks were the smaller, lighter Stuarts might or might not have been a factor. The next vehicles were flails and Dragoon Capt Wheway took up the lead. Flail tanks were not ideal for that kind of purpose, so Lt-Col Jolly himself worked his way up and put his map-reading to the test (which he confessed to be not his strongest point). Meanwhile his second in command, Maj Tom Lovibond, was engaged in a life or death struggle for the possession of the vital railway embankment in that sector.

Maj Robert Reid of 144's 'A' Squadron took the lead of the tanks which were sorting themselves out at the railway embankment. They had at least found their first report point, a railway hut. However, on crossing the railway Reid's tank was hit and brewed up. Two more tanks following were also hit by what must have been infantry-held *Panzerfausts* firing at short range and with none of the vast flash associated with an 88 mm anti-tank gun. Tom Lovibond took the risk of crossing the railway 200 yd further down. If it was an anti-tank gun firing, 200 yd would be no protection. If it was a *Panzerfaust*, perhaps 200 yd would be far enough away. . . . They doused the railway hut with machine-gun fire. Then a wood loomed up. Was this the wood where a mysterious Panzer division was supposed to be lurking? And not where the RAF had been bombing? They turned their hoses of Browning tracer on to the woods. Consternation of a few minutes ago had changed to enthusiasm. Leading tanks yelled over the wireless to their comrades behind them to stop shooting up their vanguard. And now, which way to go? The Bofors tracer was so high that its exact line was difficult to discern. How far had we gone? How shall we know when to stop?

It was about the same time that Wyn Griffith-Jones' tank of the Northamptonshire Yeomanry column was hit. His driver, Jimmy Kerr, had been encouraged to see that the regiment was to be accompanied by the Black Watch. 'As a Scot I felt better having them around,' said Jimmy from Fife. Then:

Suddenly the whole tank seemed to explode. I remember Wyn shouting to Syd Symes (gunner), 'Left, Left !', and Syd firing immediately, and saying 'I've got him, sir'. Not being able to see much, sitting in the front of the tank, it was all a bit bewildering at first. No sooner had Roy Grint (co-driver) and I come to our senses when we were hit by another shot, right between Roy and me. We still seemed to be mobile up to this point. . . . We were then hit by a third shell which scooped a groove in the front armour. (I think it was you, Wyn, who found out later that the only reason it hadn't penetrated was that it hadn't reached its full velocity owing to the fact that the gun was so close!)

This was not our lucky day though, as were hit by a fourth shell in the engine compartment, putting us out of action and setting the tank on fire. 'Bale out!' Our means of escape was the hatch under Roy's seat. He was still blasting away with his machine-gun when I shouted to him to open the escape hatch and get out. This he did with some difficulty and started to squeeze through. Knowing that I was going to be the last man to leave the blazing tank, I asked him to hurry up and, without thinking, planted my army boots in his back. This seemed to do the trick. I squeezed out and crawled from under the tank.

Even though there were tanks busy all around us, it was difficult to get our bearings. All we knew was to get as far away from the tank as possible in case it exploded. We took to our heels and ran straight into a patrol from the Black Watch. The sergeant pulled a Sten gun on us and then said, 'You lucky bastards! I thought you were Krauts!' Then the mortar bombs started to come down. By this time there were half a dozen of us – Roy Grint, Syd Symes, Micky Bannon and two others, I think. We actually buried ourselves in some small hay stacks.

One Yeoman, watching from further back, wrote of the incident:

A louder crash sounds once, twice, thrice. A fan of fire shoots high into the sky, silhouetting a distant Sherman tank. Tiny figures of crewmen come squirming from its turret like maggots out of a ripe Camembert cheese. A new puff of fire lifts the turret into the air. Then there is only a Roman Candle of flame spurting the usual fireworks.[16]

Tank crews did not easily put their emotions into words. The British stiff upper lip was the order of the day. But one crew member watching found the words by putting them into the mouth of an imaginary trooper:

He didn't want to die. . . . He expected to be blasted into eternity at any moment. He didn't know from second to second whether they were in

Maj Tom Boardman, MC (1st Northamptonshire Yeomanry), 1944.

Tom, now Lord Boardman, and (right) Tony Faulkner at the Fiftieth Anniversary of Liberation, Saint-Aignan, 1994.

range and view of the enemy or whether they were temporarily in cover. His religious faith helped him not one whit as he fought desperately in his mind. No loving God could subject men to this hell. . . . As the tank bounced along he could not avoid thoughts of death, mutilation, burning, scorching and the certainty of his end.[17]

Capt Tom Boardman in the lead was being asked by troop leaders behind him to shoot off more Verey lights. These lights provided a good clear guide to following tanks. They also illuminated the lead tank for anyone watching, for a considerable distance. Lt-Col Forster understood the dilemma and gave his subordinate the opportunity to decide whether to fire the revealing rockets or not. When Boardman said he would, the colonel radioed with gentle irony, 'Be it on your own head!'

The forest fires lit by the RAF gave the Northamptonshire Yeomanry navigating officer some kind of landmark and, as a single tank, he had been able to pick his way around obstacles. Back in the ranks of vehicles travelling four abreast it was not always easy to maintain station or find another route with massed vehicles blocking the way in every direction. So the firing of the Verey lights was an important guide. Then Tom Boardman realized that he had shot off his entire store of Verey cartridges. Ken Todd behind had not been using Verey lights. As, for the moment, things seemed quiet, somewhere between Bourguebus and Saint-Aignan, Boardman decided to replenish his stock of cartirdges. Halting the tank, he quickly dismounted and began to walk back towards Ken Todd. He was astonished to see a number of German soldiers looking up at him out of a trench. They were either dead or petrified.

Almost as scared himself, the Capt hastened back to his colleague's tank, grabbed a supply of Vereys and then returned to his own tank at the double. The Germans were still in the trench, more terrified than the Britisher.

The columns of the left flank continued to surge forward, sometimes by dint of brilliant navigation and sometimes by what might be termed 'gifts from the laps of the gods'. After the main columns had passed by, the village of Tilly-la-Campagne was to be the scene of some of the bloodiest fighting on the road from Caen to Falaise. In the early hours of the Night March one tank from 144 RAC, having lost the tail lights of the vehicle ahead, found itself trundling down a village street even though no tank column route was planned along village thoroughfares. In fact the tank commander felt that the village should not be where it was, according to his map. However, he gave the matter further consideration and realized that he had passed right through Tilly-la-Campagne, one of the most feared strongholds in the German line. Unmolested by its occupants, who were perhaps more bemused than he was, he directed his vehicle back into the trackless fields and eventually picked up the welcome sight of the green Bofors tracer pointing out the correct direction of march.[18]

Sgt George Duff, 'C', Northamptonshire Yeomanry, had also lost sight of the rear lights ahead. For a moment he was tempted to panic, but then a welcome red blur appeared ahead. He fastened on to that and drove safely on through the night – until morning revealed that he had enlisted in 144 RAC, who kept him with them for the day. Not to be outdone, a Canadian Firefly, from right across the other side of the main road, also contrived to cross the road and enlist in 144 RAC. It seemed for a while the 144 might end up with more tanks than they had when they started.

Night action could be confusing for a tank commander, 11 ft up in the turret top. It could be equally confusing for an infantryman with his ear literally to the ground. Stan Whitehouse, of the Black Watch, cites an incident involving his pal, Shorty Shorthouse. Like Stan, Shorty was an English reinforcement into the Highland Division – a Normandy phenomenon. Sent out as a runner in the dark, Shorty heard voices. Crawling cautiously nearer he heard a lot of 'ochs' and 'uchs' and 'ichs'. Being new to the Highland Division he thought the voices must be talking Gaelic. However, not wishing to surprise them and perhaps get shot into the bargain, he continued his wary crawl and suddenly realized that the 'ochs' and 'ichs' were the German variety. He reversed promptly.[19]

Crews of 144 RAC were beginning to congratulate themselves as they drew near to their objective at Cramesnil after frustrating delays. The persistent crackle of the wireless cut into a silence as someone commenced to transmit. There is no difference between the silence which precedes glad tidings and that which precedes sad news, yet tank crews often suffer a premonition in the first moments of such a silence. This silence reported that Maj Tom Lovibond, the respected second in command, who had performed prodigies of route-finding during the night, had been killed just short of the objective. The Argylls reported this as the result of 'bazooka' fire from German infantry, the 144 signals officer being killed in the same incident.[20]

At 02.38 hours Capt Boardman halted his tank at a thick hedge, behind which it was planned to debus the infantry, and found that he was within 50 yd of the precise hedge corner marked as his objective. On time, on target, ahead of the rising moon, this was a magnificent feat of navigation. As the Northamptonshire Yeomanry's second navigator, Ken Todd, and the troop leader of 'A' Squadron's 1 Troop, Desmond Coakley, eased their tanks up to the hedge, Tom Boardman wirelessed the news to the colonel. In accordance with the plan, Lt-Col Forster, commanding the armoured column, came forward with the 1st Black Watch CO, John Hopwood, to ensure that Boardman's 'landfall' was indeed correct. As the Black Watch report was to confirm, they had 'debussed at exactly the place that had been arranged on the map, formed up, and launched their attack, all according to plan, and as had been rehearsed and practised beforehand'. Like many battle heat reports this was not absolutely accurate.

Lt Coakley was called over by the two colonels and ordered to do a recce through the hedge. It had been thought that the hedge would protect the infantry while they debussed. It was immediately apparent to Boardman that there were huge gaps in the thick hedge, undoubtedly made by German tanks. Jack Pentelow, driving Coakley's tank, was not entirely thrilled to be chosen as a potential hero to accompany Coakley on foot through the hedge, Jack carrying a very fallible Sten gun with which to confront the assembled SS Panzers. He remembers:

> We walked through the hedge with the imagination working overtime, in the darkness and swirling mist, expecting to meet the Tiger tank responsible for making the gap. The thickness of the hedge was more like a copse – it seemed that hedging tools were not part of Normandy farmers' equipment – our footsteps crushing twigs and cracking branches. We retraced our route and reported having seen no tanks. Our Colonel then ordered our three tanks (we had lost Sgt Buck Ryan's tank on the march) through the hedge with orders to shoot at anything that moved.

What had happened was that the two colonels had decided that, as the hedge was not a totally secure refuge, it would be just as useful to proceed to another hedge 500 yd nearer the village of Saint-Aignan. The infantry would debus there with a much shorter final assault course to cover. At this alternative rendezvous, as the two colonels agreed that it was to be the final debussing point, the infantry colonel took over command from the armoured CO. This again was established in the original plan.

Coakley's troop moved forward to the further rendezvous, followed by another 'A' Squadron troop. Tanks make a lot of noise and it was without warning to the crew that Coakley suddenly collapsed down to the floor of the turret. He had been shot through the head. Jack Pentelow reversed back through the original hedge and found the medics already there. With the crew they managed the difficult task of squirming up through the turret hatch with a body in between them, but it was too late for any aid to be given to the troop leader.

Pentelow reflects on the bond which united many tank officers with their crews and the real sense of loss and mourning which battle death could

'Brewing up'

By Major David Bevan, MC,
Squadron Leader, 'C', 1NY.

Late Night Dining'

generate. Only one casualty among so many, and yet an individual tragedy for those closely concerned: 'Des Coakley was a very quiet, caring man. I never remember him losing his temper, or swearing; the type of person who was brought up to go to Sunday School twice on a Sunday. He and I were the full backs in 'A' Squadron football team at which he was first class. He is buried in the Canadian Cemetery, just south of Saint-Aignan.'

At the final debussing point most of the 1st Black Watch were descending from their cramped positions, in some cases after three hours or more without opportunity to stretch a leg, much less attend to other needs of nature. It was not only the infantry who were suffering from cramp. Peter Smith was a sergeant in charge of 'A' Squadron fitters' half-track with a crew of 'five other craftsmen of various trades'. As the half-track was vulnerable to enemy fire, it was decided that, for the Night March, Sgt Smith with his second fitter, Cpl Frank Booker, and electrician, L/Cpl Gibson, should travel on the ARV (the armoured recovery vehicle which went to the aid of ditched or trackless tanks). The ARV normally held Sgt Jay, with a REME craftsman and a driver. Now its crew had doubled, Sgt Jay was not highly pleased and cramp was endemic.

Less than a mile away from the Yeomanry, in front of Cramesnil, by 04.00 hours, the persevering Lt-Col Jolly was leading 144 RAC, less about eight of its own tanks, to their debussing point, joined by six tanks which had successfully taken a different route led by the ill-fated Tom Lovibond. As 'B' Company of the Argylls were sorting themselves out into attack formation, tragedy struck again:

After about twenty minutes there came a shot from behind us and another of those now all too familiar showers of sparks as one of the tanks 'brewed up'. All the crew except one were killed but we never discovered the origin of the shot. . . . Somewhat to our surprise we found ourselves being congratulated on the complete success of the operation.[21]

The way in which sheer determination to 'push on' overcame the inevitable confusion of night advance is illustrated by the Argylls' report of their subsequent attack on Cramesnil after debussing from 144's column.

> 'B' Company collected itself by degrees and moved off to its objective. . . . 'A' Company, whose objective was forward of 'B' on the right, arrived at the debussing point in driblets. 'D' Company then dribbled in. (Like 1st and 7th Black Watch, 7th Argylls were down to three company formation.) 'A' Company had the stiffest opposition and it was while they were attacking a spandau post that Capt. Andrew McElwee and one other rank were killed. However, by 5 o'clock that morning the battalion had completed its job, with 8 Germans killed and about 35 taken prisoner. 'A' Company quickly made contact with the Canadians on the right, and 'D' Company got in touch with 1st Black Watch on the left.

Following in the track marks of 144 RAC, 148 RAC had ferried the 7th Black Watch to Garcelles-Sequeville, an area behind Cramesnil, but of strategic significance, which the Germans would choose as the objective of their counter-attack when it came. The Scots were dropped precisely on target, and Charlie Robertson remembers the series of impressions so typical of battle:

> we seized the target area with much lighter casualties than anyone dared hoped (mainly because of the first approach in armoured Kangaroos and not on foot) . . . the Anti-tank platoon had its first kill, a Mark IV at 700 yards . . . mopping up machine-gun posts in houses and gardens . . . daylight coming all too soon before we were fully dug-in . . . the ensuing shelling and mortaring . . . 52 casualties in all, but 60 prisoners taken.

Referring to earlier criticism of the Highland Division in Normandy, the battalion felt it was getting back to its old form of the desert and Sicily days, and 'that comment would be equally true of the whole Highland Division – basically a return to offensive action after the weeks we spent in the woods across the Orne. . . . Totalize put us back on our feet again!'

Fractionally forward of the Cramesnil positions, and on a totally exposed left flank, 1st Black Watch were also on the offensive, using their Kangaroos almost up to the menacing stone walls of Saint-Aignan-de-Cramesnil, another village which the Germans had evacuated and turned into a minor fortress. As the infantry approached the villages, 'A' and 'C' Squadrons of the Northants poured a huge volume of fire into a narrow frontage of fortified cottages from some sixty Browning machine-guns and thirty tank cannon firing high explosive. One tank gunner, his foot pressed hard on the machine-gun trigger button, observed:

> My tracer overlaps and merges with the tracer from other tanks. Alien tracer, probably enemy, crosses our front from the right. The multiple lines of fire criss-cross and interconnect like the warp and woof of a brightly coloured oriental carpet . . . large shell flashes mingle with the sparkle of

our tracer. . . . Among the jagged, leafy contours of nature about a dozen houses show as squared, lighter blotches, dancing wildly in the swirling smoke and haze . . . where tracer strikes against a solid wall, a tiny sprinkle of sparks radiates upwards and as quickly falls away. The noise of the bursting barrage slams back at us, still with that irregular barking dog rhythm – whoof-whoof; whoof-whoof-whoof; whoof-whoof . . . [22]

In his more prosaic report the Black Watch CO records that the barrage was codenamed BRIMSTONE. At this point it might be relevant to stop and question the value of inventing exotic codenames for such events as a confined barrage which would terminate within a few minutes and which German intelligence would have no way of countering, even if their listening posts picked up a passing reference to an immediate artillery 'stonk' on point such-and-such? BRIMSTONE certainly encouraged 1st Black Watch as they jumped out of their Kangaroos and ran into Saint-Aignan. 'B' Company had lost two Kangaroos on the Night March when a German SP had appeared out of the mist and marched alongside them for a few yards, before disappearing into the mists as mysteriously as it had appeared.

However, 'B' Company, on the left past Saint-Aignan church, and 'A' Company, on the right past the community hall, exploited the orchards beyond the village. A German infantry patrol of seven men searching the orchards suddenly found themselves face to face with a full company of well-armed Highlanders. Lt-Col Hopwood summed it up:

Motoring over the last 800 yards . . . was entirely successful, owing first to the heavy artillery concentration, and secondly to the magnificent fire support given by the Yeomanry from their 75s and Brownings which plastered every place that could have possibly held an enemy post. . . . Slight confusion was caused by a thick ground mist, which was accentuated by the cordite smoke . . . and the fumes of the tanks and Priests. In spite of this 'A' and 'B' Companies maintained direction and advanced on their respective objectives . . . there were odd spandau posts which held out and had to be mopped up . . . by 05.30 hours the forward Companies were at their objectives.[23]

Thus the left flank of Phase 1 of Operation Totalize had achieved total success somewhat ahead of schedule. A fortified village on the third line of the series of villages had been occupied. The tanks had moved up and formed a tight circle around the village, with the infantry digging in between. Ahead, through orchards already disastrously ravaged by war, the ground sloped gently towards an apparently innocuous hedgerow and then upwards again to the Robertmesnil ridge at the same altitude as Saint-Aignan. To the left Northamptonshire Yeomanry's 1 Troop of 'C' Squadron looked out over a vast landscape of fields which were still the enemy domain. A wide open flank!

The 1st Black Watch CO evidently considered his battalion's losses to be extremely low considering the circumstances. They suffered 11 killed, 43 wounded and 15 missing. They had taken 82 prisoners and captured

4 vehicles, 4 anti-tank guns, mortars and machine-guns and, most appreciated, those excellent German field glasses. However, a non-infantry observer might have felt that the 'butcher's bill' was serious. It underlines the difference in infantry and tank casualties as the Yeomanry, although 'up front' for most of the time had, at this point, lost only two killed. On the other hand it will be seen later that other 'walking' infantry units suffered far more than the carrier-borne troops.

Various commentators have cited varying distances for the Night March advance, probably due to the different stages involved. While distances might be calculated from the 'start line' (No Man's Land) it has been seen that at least two Canadian tanks were destroyed by German guns before reaching that line. Some of the travel problems have already been described. For some vehicles the trek up to the 'start line' from the actual departure areas was more problematic than the 'action advance' through enemy territory. Capt R.F. Neville, with the Yeomanry's 'B' Squadron rearguard, had been held up by the concertina effect of the slow progress up to the start line, but, once into enemy territory, his Sherman completed the last 2 miles at a constant 20 mph. So it is useful to quote distances over the entire night's route and also particular stages of it. While this can be done from the map, one of the Lothian & Border flail commanders recorded a precise total of 8,880 yd on his milometer for his total advance.

The Northamptonshire Yeomanry route, rounded up to the nearest quarter of a kilometre, included 6 km from assembly area to German front line, then 4 km to the revised dawn attack start line, followed by 0.75 km to Saint-Aignan church, and a further 1 km to the farthest point reached by 2 Troop of 'C' across Le Petit Ravin. That makes a total journey of 11.75 km (7.3 miles), of which 10.25 km (6.4 miles) was traversed in the dark, ending 5.75 km (3.57 miles) beyond the point of crossing the enemy front line.

Taking the centre line of the Caen to Falaise road, the distance from La Dronniere (between Bras and Ifs) to Lorguichon (8 CRR objective) direct is 6.5 km with a further 2 km to the D80 La Jalousie report line (Saint-Aignan to Bretteville road), and a final 1 km to Gaumesnil, a total of 9.5 km (5.9 miles) to the ultimate Canadian Phase 1 objective. There were, of course, few absolutely straight lines that night.

One historian comments that although the RAF had well-established marker techniques, 'the Army, however, had little experience to draw upon. No such attack as Simonds planned had ever been attempted and the problem of keeping direction was considerable'.[24] Another comment states that 'in spite of . . . countless complications . . . by a very high standard of leadership on the part of all officers and tank commanders concerned, the operation was a success'.[25] Highlanders, Yeomanry and RAC now sat in an unaccustomed local silence and listened to the sound of the Canadians still 'bashing on' to come up level on the right flank.

Chapter Five

The Straight Right

'When they had had supper and it became dark, the troops detailed for the job set off and seized the mountain height. At daybreak . . . they advanced on the road. As soon as the enemy realised that the heights had been occupied, they were on the look-out. Most of the enemy stood their ground at the pass.' (Xenophon, 400 BC)

The tank crews of the Sherbrooke Fusiliers Regiment were ready to go. Known now by the less emotive name of 27th Canadian Armoured Regiment, they were to be the front force of the Canadian drive down the right side of the Caen to Falaise main road. 'A' Squadron had lined up tight in columns. Their squadron leader, Maj S.V. Radley-Walters, was able to traverse the entire squadron without touching the grass by leaping from one tank's deck to another. He found everything in order but was well aware that the Night March threatened imminent disorder.[1]

It was doubtful whether the planners could ever have imagined the extent of confusion through which the armoured columns would have to find their way. With hindsight one writer described it:

A thousand vehicles raised a cloud of dust in the darkness. . . . At the same moment a smokescreen rose above the lines of the 89th Division of the Wehrmacht. Navigators were blinded. Drivers strained their eyes to make out the faint light of the vehicle ahead. . . . There were some spectacular collisions, lamentable errors of range, tanks firing against friendly tanks, while the blazing hulks provided a magnet for the German guns and mortars.[2]

The prelude to the Night March on the right flank was orderly enough as the Canadians of their 2nd Armoured Brigade and 4th Infantry Brigade lined up at point 044634 south-east of Ifs. There were minor problems, for instance, of reinforcements. Radley-Walters was only able to assemble fifteen Shermans instead of the full nineteen of a squadron's strength. The troops were generally in a good state of morale, now that a really big show was to happen. Sgt Ensor met a Canadian NCO bringing round the password for the operation, 'Present Arms' with the response 'Montreal Canadians'. The Canadian then remarked, 'It's a god-damned job going forward in the dark, then sitting tight and waiting for daylight. But if some Heine or other comes knocking at our door for breakfast, he'll get it!'[3]

At higher levels there was some criticism of the quality of the units involved in Operation Totalize and that criticism would redouble after the action. It had been pointed out that both the Canadian and the Polish Armoured Divisions, which were to mount Phase 2, were 'green' and only recently arrived in Normandy. This was seen to be a disadvantage.[4] Yet other Normandy units had also been untried in battle and had emerged with highly complimentary reputations. The fearsome Hitlerjugend was one such formation as were the British 11th Armoured Division and a number of very successful American units. At the same time the 51st Highland Division, as with other old Middle East formations, was criticized for being too tired and slow to adapt to the very different conditions of Normandy. Over a very brief period before and after Totalize a number of senior Canadian commanders were relieved of their commands. Brig Ben Cunningham and Lt-Col Petch and Lt-Col Christiansen had already gone home, Simonds was not happy about the performance of Maj-Gen Foulkes and Maj-Gen Keller, while Maj-Gen Kitching would return to Canada as a result of Totalize.[5] History may be kinder to some of the above than it was possible to be in the heat of battle, but a certain inadequacy of high command was apparent (taking into account also Montgomery's low opinion of Crerar). So it was not with total confidence that Simonds could launch the available forces under the available command structure.

On the other hand there were some very proud Canadian regiments involved and much of the Canadian army had so far acquitted itself well in the bloody fighting around Caen when it met the Hitlerjugend again and again. The Canadians had an excellent 1914–18 reputation to live up to. Some of their units had a very long history, including militia regiments raised in the 1650s, compared with the 1794 founding of the British Yeomanry. In addition, as distinct from the British army, 'each individual serviceman was invited to decide whether or not he would serve overseas'.[5] So the Canadian soldiers were by no means unwilling conscripts on a foreign soil.

The immediate task of the right flank is well reflected in one squadron leader's report on his mission:

> Speed of advance was to be governed by vehicles going in bottom gear – 'bull low' – barrage speed 100 yards a minute, and our line of advance was down Caen–Falaise road (also our left boundary) to our objective the Cramesnil feature Area 071566 passing Verriers, Roquancourt [*sic*] on the way – enemy was expected on line between Verriers-Tilly. Coy of SS dug in on either side of main road – suspected minefield between Roquancourt and main road. A/Tk guns sited in area of the minehead at 068579. Difficulty expected in crossing railway in 068583 and 068558, the line having strip cutting and embankments.[18]

As on the left flank, flails were in close attendance on the leading Shermans so that 'If mines were located in our lane the leading Troop of the Armoured Regiment would pull over to the left, allowing the flails to draw out to the right and flail a path through the mines. Once clear of mines the leading Armoured Regiment Troop could resume the lead.'

There were many similarities between the experiences of left and right

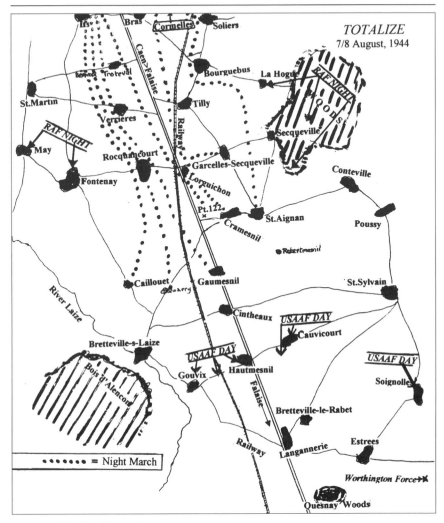

Operation Totalize (Phase 1).

flanks, but Brig Wyman, the Canadian armoured commander, had disposed his columns in a somewhat different way from Brig Scott on the left. The latter had columns consisting of one tank regiment and one infantry battalion working as a single battle group – 1st Northamptonshire Yeomanry with 1st Black Watch, 144 RAC with the Argylls. In contrast the Canadians had one of the armoured regiments disposed across three columns, each of which had a separate infantry battalion, with another armoured regiment as reserve.

The Canadians were to advance along four lanes. At the front of each of their three right-hand lanes were two troops of the 27th Canadian Armoured Regiment (CAR) – the Sherbrooke Fusiliers. These troops would advance four tanks abreast. Behind each group of two troops of Shermans would come two troops of the British Lothian & Border Yeomanry with their flail tanks loaned from 79th Armoured Division. They in turn would be followed by one troop of the Canadian Royal Engineers in AVREs. This entire force of six troops of tanks, six troops of flails and three troops of AVREs was called the 'Gapping Force'. In addition the left-most of the Canadian lanes would be headed by a similar grouping but with Shermans from the 10th CAR (the Fort Garry Horse). Those Shermans, flails and AVREs were also part of the 'Gapping Force'. The 'Sherbrookes' were formed so that 'C' Squadron's Shermans would lead the extreme right-hand lane, with 'B' Squadron next and then 'A'. This entire 'Gapping Force' was commanded by the Sherbrooke's colonel, Mel Gordon.

In the respective Canadian lanes then came an 'Assault Force', this comprising an infantry battalion, followed by the remainder of the Sherman Squadron in that lane, then a troop of the 6th Anti-tank Battalion, a platoon of the Toronto Scottish (machine-gunners) and a section of engineers. The infantry battalion on the extreme right was the Essex Scottish (Lt-Col T.S. Jones). In the second lane the Royal Hamilton Light Infantry (Lt-Col G.M. Maclachlan) supplied the infantry. The third lane was occupied by the Royal Regiment of Canada (Lt-Col J. Anderson). The left-hand Canadian lane had, in place of a normal infantry battalion, the 8th CRR (Canadian Reconnaissance Regiment – Lt-Col B.M. Alway). In each case the 'Assault Force' in a particular lane was under command of the infantry colonel. Finally there came the 'Fortress Force', the remainder of the Fort Garry Horse (that is, less those tanks working with 8CRR), acting as a mobile reserve to be deployed in cases of delay or unforeseen resistance.

While Lt-Col Gordon was in command of the 'Gapping Force', and riding with them, all the tanks of his regiment were on the same wireless net and could be assembled quickly if needed.[7] This was the standard formation but there may have been some slight variations, for one report on the extreme right flank has only one troop of 'C' Squadron of 27 CAR leading two troops of flails, plus the flail squadron HQ, followed by the second troop of 'C', 27 CAR. In any case strict formations would soon disintegrate.

A problem for the Canadians, intending to pass to the right of the village of Verrieres, was the narrow frontage, allowing only about 150 yd between lanes and auguring eventual intermingling of columns. In contrast, 144 RAC and 1st Northamptonshire Yeomanry, also avoiding villages but passing on either side of Tilly, would have at times as much as 1,000 yd between them, making for rather less inter-column commingling.

Although inter-unit cooperation was generally excellent, allowing for sometimes rather frail communications links, the heat of the moment sometimes brought irritation or frustration. One flail commander called to a pre-Night March conference was not too happy. He reported: 'came back to conference. Attempted to put in two comments, one to my mind most important, i.e., crossing of railway. Nobody was interested so gave up trying.' A little later he was still disgruntled: 'Followed Sherman in front with great difficulty as fool kept his rear light off and dust made it difficult to see.' A failure to switch on rear lights was a complaint from more than one following vehicle, even in the dusty move up to the 'start line' from the assembly area.[8]

As with the left flank, once the Canadians had moved from the assembly area they were crossing territory which was ostensibly occupied by their own forward infantry well dug in, but could be viewed by the enemy from the point of their initial move to the start line. And, as with the left flank, the armoured column surge would be preceded by an air attack on the area of two of the most heavily fortified villages, May-sur-Orne and Fontenay-le-Marmion, led by master bomber, Wg Cdr Macmillan.

Australian Syd Johnson, DFC and bar (582 Squadron RAF), was on his twenty-fifth mission on 7 August 1944 when he directed his Lancaster bomber towards the Caen area, noting in his log book, '1050 aircraft on this and four other front line targets – star shell marking – Visual Backer up – DCO – chop alley!' Syd explains that DCO means 'Duty Carried out' and chop alley indicates a lot of enemy fighter activity. He remembers:

> My function that night was that of visual backer up which means that on one of the five aiming points, following the star shells with which the Master Bomber would have marked the target, with, say, red target indicators, I and the other backers up would follow in at intervals, backing up the reds with green target indicators. There would have been about 200 aircraft on this target and on each of the other aiming points. Altogether PFF (Pathfinder Force) had ten Lancaster Squadrons (about 30 aircraft each) and nine Mosquito Squadrons.
>
> One of the features of PFF was its dependence on precision navigation and precision timing, and the crews, each an independent band striving for perfection, were accorded the most responsible jobs according to their demonstrated abilities. Given a special job to do, as in this instance, our crew would be pre-occupied with arriving at the target within seconds of the allotted time and doing what we had to do to the best of our ability. The overall picture of the raid as a whole would be a distraction rather than a material consideration, so I cannot help much with the broad picture.

Syd Johnson's comments[9] again underline the obsession with accuracy which possessed élite RAF bomber crews. For many of them August 1944 was a particularly busy month. Denis Hughes was the flight engineer on Sqn Ldr H.G. Manley's Lancaster, pilot, navigator and wireless operator all being Australians. Their log book reveals ten missions in August compared to five or six in other months. Seven were night raids and three day raids, two over Germany and eight over France. This was during service with 550 Squadron before posting to 582.[10]

Down on earth, the start line ran along the D89 road, approximately from Moulin de Voide through Beauvoir to Troteval. The objectives were, from right to left, the village of Caillouet, the quarry on the old Roman road, the village of Gaumesnil and point 122 on the main Caen to Falaise road near La Jalousie. On the left, 8 CRR would have moved across the main road to link up with 144 RAC on that dominant shoulder of the ridges. The lanes led from assembly areas at about 42–5 m elevation, across start lines at 57–68 m high, with objectives at 85, 101, 118 and 122 m respectively.

A separate radio beam was focussed on the objective for each lane. The dot-dash repetitive signal continued while the leader was on course. If he veered to the right he would hear only the dashes, while a deviation to the left would bring in a series of dots. This system worked well for the first 1,000 yd but then merged into static. The 40 mm Bofors tracer firing red overhead was a more constant signal. The tracer changed to green over the main road, the divisional boundary. The AVREs threw out green and amber markers as they moved and also trailed some 10,000 yd of the white tape normally used for marking minefields.[11]

For the first 1,000 yards things went reasonably well, although 8 CRR column lost two Shermans early to an 88 mm gun, which was in its turn destroyed by other tanks. The defenders had now roused sufficiently to let off a thick smokescreen, which combined with the dust raised by the columns of vehicles. It was pointed out that the south-east wind meant that vehicles on the right, western, flank suffered progressively more obscurity from accumulated dust raised by other columns as well as drifting mist and smoke. So 'C', 27 CAR and the Essex Scottish had the worst of that bargain.

Two major difficulties of transit compounded the poor visibility. A number of sunken roads occur in the Night March area. There was also in 1944 a railway which ran from the east of Caen diagonally across the line of the Night March. This diagonal line meant that 1st Northamptonshire Yeomanry on the left struck the railway earliest in their progress. The line then passed between Hubert-Folie and Bourguebus, on 144 RAC's route. It crossed under the main Caen to Falaise road at point 93 due east of Rocquancourt, just short of Lorguichon. It then seemed to develop an attraction for the main road, running just the other (west) side of La Jalousie, Gaumesnil and Cintheaux. Although the Canadians were not required to cross the line early in their march, it afforded excellent roosting places for enemy anti-tank guns. It complicated 8 CRR's crossing of the main road to attack point 122. It then became a factor in the progress of the next column, 'A', 27 CAR.

The Canadians would also have to contend with a large disused airfield, which would probably afford a good field of fire for anti-tank guns, especially if approached after dawn. In spite of these features the planners' arrows on the going maps looked simple enough as they pointed in three parallel thrusts straight across country to the right (west) of Verrieres. There may have been some confusion in that the plan referred to the three right-hand columns as forming up 'in one lane',[12] whereas tactically they were three separate battle groups with distinct and well-separated objectives. The close formation, as distinct from the distancing of 144 RAC from 1st Northamptonshire Yeomanry, might also mean that if one element of the three columns veered, all might be influenced in that direction.

In the event, veering did take place and became evident when Rocquancourt was reached (perhaps a little before the halfway mark of the distance to be covered through enemy territory to first objectives). All three columns were planned to pass to the right of the village. The 'lefterly' of the three arrived and passed left of Rocquancourt, and the centre group drove straight through the village. The 'C' and Essex did pass to the right but not on the precise route and in some state of disorganization as a result of vehicle losses. Some of the 8 CRR column also began to cross to the 51st Highland Division area but then adjusted and achieved the objective.

There is little evidence of any undue carelessness in navigating and certainly no panic, although individual commanders must have been near to 'panic stations' when they found themselves suddenly alone in a desert of dark open spaces and fluctuating misleading lights. The veering is not explained but could be due to two reasons apart from the configuration of the ground at any point. First there was the massive air bombardment on the right, which left rising flames, more smoke and threats of danger from above (ground crews were not at that point to know of the accuracy of the RAF – air attacks were not always so disciplined). This might cause right-hand vehicles to favour left-inclined options around obstacles. Second, there was the relative comfort of the forces to the left when the extreme right flank was wide open, as was the extreme left of 1st Northamptonshire Yeomanry's march. While red tracer marked the direct Canadian route, green tracer could be seen over the divisional boundary on the main road. The green marked a central point where the massed forces made life seem safer than out on the exposed unmarked right. It would be natural to favour the central security.

Having said that, the mean veering to the left of the entire mass of vehicles was probably no more than about 500 yd, while the centrality of the main road and its green light markings meant that a major deviation by a large body of troops was unlikely. The problems turned out in the end to be relatively minimal and a matter of a very few vehicles transgressing a relatively few yards either way. Obviously, it did not appear that way to the men riding head out of a tank turret or forced perhaps to get out and scout around on foot.

Lt Boreham, who had been worried about the railway crossing, became even more disgruntled when, having been led off course by 'the fool' who would not switch on his red light, his track was blown off by a mine. At 1,000 yd beyond the start line, another troop leader, Lt Melville, ran into considerable confusion:

> We were having great difficulty keeping course and at about 1,000 yards the left column bumped into us. When we emerged from all this the pilot Troop was scattered, all going in different direction. I set my gyro and carried on, checking my position from time to time with the Bofors firing above us. Progress for the next thousand yards was good. Apart from flares and small arms fire there was no opposition.[12]

Lt H. Rolland was one of those who encountered problems at a sunken road. He too was concerned because the vehicle in front was not using a rear light. The leading tank suddenly turned left and then back right to avoid a huge crater. This caused considerable mixing of ranks when only one red light glowed ahead and all tried to follow. He then hit the country road:

> It was not very pleasant not knowing how steep or deep were the banks. My Charlie tank (Cpl Kirkwood) would not take it at first, but after a little

coaxing on the driver's part (Tpr Wilkinson, C.) it came out all right. The tanks in front now halted and, as I ordered my driver to halt, the right flank tank backed into me. We could not see him coming because of the smoke. I felt very annoyed because he had no tail light showing and was on the point of getting out to vent my wrath on him [early day 'road rage'?] when I suddenly changed my mind as two armour-piercing tracers whizzed across our front! Our yardometer read 5,950 yards.[13]

Another troop leader, Lt A.R. Burn, was rolling along in formation, watching the rank of tanks ahead when they hit a very bad patch of mist. He was astounded to see the four vehicles ahead, 'being very confused, divided themselves conveniently to the four winds, N, S, E and W, and were never seen again'. He also observed two flail tanks which had collided, with booms interlinked 'like two fighting elephants with their tusks jammed together'. Unlike Melville, who had only small arms to contend with, Burn was soon knocked out by direct hits, head on, and his driver died.[14]

Tanks lost contact with their leader and then latched on to another guide. Others veered to a flank and were recalled by green Verey lights fired by the commanders who were sure of their location. Some fired at gun flashes in front or to the flank, and prayed that they were the enemy. More than one vehicle suffered from a shot into the engine from the rear, which could have been enemy or friendly fire. Nobody would ever find out. Tank crew with a moment to think realized that the enemy must be even more confused than themselves. The infantry rode patiently in their unaccustomed armour and did not yet know the statistics which would prove how safe they had been compared to the walking infantry. At the moment of worst confusion the Bofors ceased firing tracer overhead, according to plan. A multitude of requests poured in to the squadron leaders and the Bofors were caused to open up again.

One confused and possibly hungry commander, arriving on the outskirts of Rocquancourt, reported that he was at 'Roquefort'. Vehicles arriving at the large disused airfield were able to reorientate themselves easily. Did any of them remember that, before D-Day, a top priority of Allied planning was to seize airfields within a few days? It was now D + 62!

Reflecting on the tortuous path that 'A' Squadron tanks had followed in detours around obstacles, one of Maj Radley-Walters' drivers commented that the route 'was enough to have broken a snake's back'. By persistently bashing on, the squadron had arrived at its first objective near Cramesnil by about 06.00 hours on 8 August. Other groups were shunting into correct locations with time to spare as Phase 2 was timed to commence after midday.

It was 'A' Squadron 27 CAR with the Royal Regiment of Canada which observed the first movement of enemy counter-attack along the main road at about 08.00 hours. A number of German tanks, Panthers and Mark IVs, with infantry, ran into the Canadians, and the tank fire destroyed a number of the lighter carriers belonging to the anti-tank platoon and the machine-gunners of the Toronto Scottish. The Canadian Firefly tanks (as with the British, one 17-pdr Firefly with three 75 mm Shermans formed a troop) gave a good account of themselves. Two Panthers and two Mark IVs were knocked out and the enemy withdrew.

'A' Squadron, 27 CAR mess in Normandy. Right to left: Maj S.V. Radley-Walters, Lt Claire Thompson (killed in action, Verrieres), Capt (Adjutant) Douglas Bradley, Capt Willard Humphrey (Admin.), Lt Nairn Boyd (killed in action, Buron).

Subsequently, Radley-Walters moved his squadron further up towards Gaumesnil. This action no doubt caused the Germans to be wary of their left flank when sending a troop of Tigers down the road. A strong and tenacious Canadian presence on the west side of the road meant that the Tigers approached cautiously, seeking whatever cover they could find on the east side of the road. Their approach did indeed stimulate 'A' Squadron of 27 CAR to open fire while 'A' Squadron of 1st Northamptonshire Yeomanry was hidden to the east of the Tiger's route. The Tiger commanders, concentrating on the western danger, therefore had their backs to the eastern danger. The complementary actions of the two 'A' Squadrons were not prearranged in a master plan but were the logical outcome of the innovative idea of the Night March. This placed the two 'A' Squadrons in primarily defensive positions which, to an extent, reduced the overwhelming advantages of power and armour enjoyed by Tigers and Panthers. The reverse of Goodwood was now happening in miniature. But for 'Rad' Radley-Walters, as for Tom Boardman at the time, 'to us it was just another German tank attack and it wasn't until after the war that I heard about this German ace', Wittmann.[15]

The Canadian Phase 1 troops continued to move forward. The Royal Regiment was moved up to join 'A' Squadron after the tanks had held the Gaumesnil area for some hours. For some time the 27 CAR colonel, Mel Gordon, had been urging higher command to allow his tanks to push even further forward. 'Rad's' squadron had lost only three tanks en route while their Royal Regiment infantry had suffered very light casualties (four killed and thirty wounded) by infantry battalion standards. They felt they could continue to advance against a weakened enemy.

The Essex Scottish had incurred the worst casualties and their CO was missing for a while. The second in command, Maj J.W. Burgess, was riding at the rear of the column and had to make his way up through the throngs of vehicles, only to find his front ranks disorientated. He had to wait for daylight to sort things out and it was 08.45 before he could lead his group on. They reached and occupied their objective village of Caillouet about noon.[16] Although the Essex had suffered casualties they had also 'recruited' along the way. At one time or another they had acquired a platoon of the Royal Regiment of Canada, a platoon of the Royal Hamilton Light Infantry, a section of mortars, a platoon of the Toronto machine-gunners and a squadron of 'Recce'.

The Royal Hamiltons, known as 'The Rileys', had also acquired 'B' Company of the Royal Regiment of Canada on the way. Two of their Kangaroos had fallen into bomb craters and those infantry had hitch-hiked the rest of the way. Their column was further delayed when they landed in the middle of the village of Rocquancourt and found it much more difficult to manouevre there than in the open countryside. By about 03.00 hours they were able to travel across country again. Their objective was a quarry between Caillouet and Gaumesnil, on the old Roman road of conquest. At about 04.00 the Rileys came in view of their target but found the enemy dug in, with tanks and self-propelled guns. They took advantage of the early dawn mist to dig in around the objective. At 08.00 they were able to alert the Sherbrookes to a force of about ten German armoured vehicles advancing in the counter-attack which 'A' Squadron repelled. Typically, one source claimed two Mark IVs and two SPs knocked out while the tank men claimed two Mark IVs and two Panthers. It might be expected that the tank men knew best.

Linking hands with 144 RAC, 8 CRR had established themselves across the main road. It was claimed that the objectives of Phase 1 had been secured, to all intents and purposes, within twelve hours from the ground H-Hour. Certainly midday on 8 August found a strong line of armour and dug-in infantry from the eastern slopes of Saint-Aignan to the western village of Caillouet. However, the tempestuous surge of the Night March columns was only part of the story. The columns had avoided certain villages known to be strongly held. There was no precedent for judging what would be the reaction of defenders in the villages when they found a mass of armour sited behind them. Would they resist and hope for relief? Or would they panic and surrender or retreat? It might have been assumed that, if the Hitlerjugend Division had still been holding the villages, panic and retreat would not have been likely outcomes. But on the eve of Totalize the front line had been taken over by the green troops from Norway. Would they be a 'pushover'?

There had been time for only a limited number of Kangaroos to be prepared, only thirty-six for the Canadian columns and thirty-six loaned to the 51st Highland infantry. These would be used for the Night March columns. The infantry undertaking the shorter routes to the bypassed villages would have to walk in the time-honoured fashion of the PBI. Their mission was an integral and highly important part of the entire operation. On the right side of the main road

Scottish infantry in their newly adapted Kangaroos. (IWM, B8806)

the task fell to the 'Iron Brigade', 6th Canadian Infantry under their commander, Brig H.A. Young. On the left it would be 152 Brigade of Highlanders under Brig Cassells. Theirs would be the toughest fighting of the night.

Coming up behind the armoured columns, the Iron Brigade and Highlanders had to walk the gauntlet of traffic jams, mutilated terrain, sniping and shelling before even reaching their start lines. Brig Young had been given the task of clearing the Rocquancourt area, which included railway sidings, mine buildings and underground mine workings through which the enemy might move. He must also clear the badly bombed villages of May and Fontenay, where the enemy might be demoralized but the going through craters and rubble would be doubly difficult. He was tempted to take the normal course of clearing the objectives one by one, with a battalion in reserve forming a firm base. However, he reacted to the innovations of the night by using an 'all up' approach.

The South Saskatchewan (Lt-Col F.A. Clift) formed up behind Troteval Farm. At least the walkers were not asked, like the armour, to assemble miles back and then do a route march to the start line. The Saskatchewans were directed the 2 miles from start to Rocquancourt village. While the dust and smoke of the armoured columns just ahead were a source of much discomfort to the infantry, they effectively blinded the enemy until the Canadian walkers were almost on the objective. The defenders started a sporadic fire and Lt-Col Clift was himself wounded. The defensive confusion was heightened when, unexpectedly, an armoured column veered and drove right over them. In two hours all company objectives of the South Sas. had been achieved, but the green 89th Infantry Division included some tough soldiers who stayed on fighting as snipers for another six hours. In this village the expected confusion of the Night March had succeeded.

On both sides of the main road, Canadian and British, there were Cameron Highlanders. The Queen's Own Cameron Highlanders of Canada (Lt-Col J. Runcie), in their assault on Fontenay, were not to escape as lightly as their Cameron brothers of the 51st or their South Saskatchewan comrades further east. Fontenay had indeed been bombed, but, because of the incredibly bad visibility already well illustrated, the RAF commanders had wisely called off the raid with a third of their bombs still loaded. This undoubtedly avoided some erratic bombing of ground troops but left Fontenay only partially destroyed.[17]

There were open fields in front of the village and the enemy's defence line was still more or less intact. In the dark the Camerons advanced through machine-gun and mortar fire, keeping station mainly by reference to a track lined with tall poplar trees. The engineers had to be called forward to deal with mines. The CO was badly wounded. The brigade major, C.W. Ferguson, was rushed up to take command. The Germans used defensive fire from well-sited trenches as well as active counter-attack to resist the Camerons.

In the dark groups of attackers became separated from one another. A company commander, another officer and a dozen men were surrounded and invited to surrender. They regrouped themselves and shot a way through into the village. Another platoon commander attacking a quarry found it held by five machine-gun posts. Infantry counter-attacked but could not get close to the Canadians. The Camerons continued to probe and push and suffer casualties and inflict even more than they suffered. The commander of 'B' Company, Maj McManus, having acquired two Polish prisoners, tried to persuade German troops to surrender by sending in an interpreter. The green infantry fresh from the Norwegian fjords continued to resist.

As the Camerons made their slow progress into Fontenay it looked as though the battle might have been won. Maj Ferguson had arrived to take command. He held an Orders Group in a farmyard with his company commanders. He was then fatally wounded when a German shell landed in the farmyard. The commander of HQ Company, the regimental adjutant and the artillery forward observation officer were all wounded by the same shelling. Maj McManus took charge and went the rounds of the unit. He was shot by a sniper. Amid all this the Germans appeared to be massing with some tank support to counter-attack again.

Companies were now being commanded by lieutenants and a sergeant-major (Arbour). Until midday all available artillery fire had been required by the forward columns. But at that point Brig Young was able to obtain use of a squadron of 1st Hussars, 'C'. The South Saskatchewans had completed most of their tasks in Rocquancourt. Two companies of their battalion linked with the Hussars and the battalion's carrier platoon and rushed towards Fontenay. Because of enemy fire over open fields, the force had to hook north, but the ensuing pincer, linked to a last-ditch effort from the Camerons, began to douse the fierce resistance. The South Saskatchewans eventually collected some 250 prisoners. The Camerons' mortar platoon took another 80 prisoners. A few defenders continued to resist in the fields outside the village. Effectively one of the two strongholds which had claimed hundreds of Canadian casualties over the weeks was now safely in Canadian hands. The other stronghold which had resisted successive attacks on the west of the main road was May-sur-Orne.

For two weeks the Germans had been strengthening the fortifications of May against continuing Canadian attacks. Now Les Fusiliers Mont-Royal had been pulled back from their slit trenches so that the RAF bombers could put in their assault. Again the visibility caused curtailment of the RAF bombing. Defenders had been able to shelter in deep bunkers. The Fusiliers were started from nearby St Andre to which they had withdrawn during the bombing. Cleverly the Germans immediately treated St Andre with a heavy artillery barrage, assuming that the attackers would have to start from there. The attack of the Fusiliers was stalled almost before it began.

As the German barrage died down and Allied artillery support became available the Fusiliers reorganized and advanced on May. The continuing accuracy of all types of German fire made it impossible for more than one company of Canadians to obtain a lodgment in the village, only to find itself cut off from the battalion. The clearing of morning mist made the defender's direct fire more telling. By 11.00 hours stalemate was complete. The CO was recalled to Brigade Headquarters and fresh plans had to be elaborated to cope with this crisis on the extreme rear flank of Totalize.

Having now obtained use of the 1st Hussars tanks, Brig Young left some of them to attack Fontenay and brought the rest to St Andre. There they linked with British Assault RE's Crocodile flame-throwers. The artillery was briefed to provide five minutes of intensive barrage followed immediately by the laying of a smokescreen to the north of May (in the direction of St Andre). The historian Roy rounds off the story of May-sur-Orne, a thorn in the Canadian side for so long, with a graphic description:

> The terrifying sight of the jets of flaming fuel squirting towards them, combined with the quick advance by the infantry, had the desired effect on the enemy. Those who were not destroyed either surrendered or retreated southward as the Fusiliers entered and pushed through May-sur-Orne. Nevertheless, it was close to five in the afternoon before the battalion had completed the mopping up in the fire-blackened rubble of May-sur-Orne. With its solidly built field defences, its access to mine tunnels, and its well-sited and camouflaged defensive positions, the village and its garrison had frustrated and delayed the Canadians to the bitter end.[18]

On the other side of the main road, Brig Jim Cassells' walking infantry consisted of the Scottish 5th Camerons (Lt-Col D.L. Lang) and two battalions of Seaforths, the 2nd (Lt-Col G.L.W. Andrews) and the 5th (Lt-Col J. Walford). Their tasks and problems would be very similar to those of the Canadian Iron Brigade with a slight strategic difference. Whereas May and Fontenay represented only peripheral interference to follow-up troops, the 152 objectives were potentially vital obstructions to Phase 2 timing. Not only were there two armoured divisions moving up behind the Phase 1 troops, but there were in addition the supply and reinforcement echelons of four divisions, not to speak of convoys of wounded and prisoners needing to travel in the opposite direction. Once Rocquancourt had been cleared this left a fairly open 'Oregon Trail' on the right of the main road, including that arterial road itself. On the left flank the villages of Tilly and Secqueville, while they harboured anti-tank guns, could seriously delay, if not halt, daylight traffic from Cormelles to Saint-Aignan and Cramesnil.

The then Lt-Col Derek Lang, commanding 5th Camerons, modestly yields preference to 2nd Seaforths in his brigade's achievements during the night of 7/8 August, saying that the Seaforths had the toughest time. He still remembers features of the action:

> It was my first battle as CO and what a battle it was! The dust and general confusion because of the armour churning up the ground was intense. It was our first experience of Monty's Moonlight. My main memory is of Moaning Minnies (multiple mortar bombs fitted with sirens) which were frightening. It may have been a confusing night for us but much worse for the Germans.[19]

In fact the Camerons had quite a torrid time. They were required to advance towards Lorguichon, which 8 CRR was approaching from across the main road. The Camerons' route lay through high harvest-ready corn, apparently a partial source of cover for the attackers, but more significantly a prime hunting-ground for defending snipers. A throwaway line from an official historian records that this 'main objective' (one of two) was 'captured without great difficulty' by the Camerons. In fact, in the death trap of standing corn, the Highlanders only achieved their goal through good practice in traditional skills of gillies and poachers, ferreting out the individual snipers and machine-gunners from their lairs.

Brig Cassells had advised Lt-Col 'Geordie' Andrews that it was 2nd Seaforths' turn for the 'tough one'. The two of them had gone forward of the Canadian front line at Hubert-Folie and lodged in a hedge of the white house just outside the village. From there it was a wide open view to Tilly-la-Campagne, good for photography but fatal for walking infantry in daylight. The Canadians had already reached Tilly twice (in a total of five attacks) but had not been able to hold it. Their unburied dead could be clearly seen lying around a railway embankment, which was obviously an important feature in front of the village. Reading the lessons of previous unsuccessful attacks, Andrews opted for a 'silent attack' without prior barrage, under the cover of the noise of the armoured columns.

At 23.50, deep in the dust, smoke and thundering noise of the rearmost tanks, 'D' Company headed across that open ground towards the railway. 'A' Company followed, going left, and 'B' was directed right. The open ground was traversed in safety but as 'D' neared the embankment, Spandau fire commenced with that familiar and horrific ultra-fast ripping sound. German artillery accurately zeroed on the embankment. 'D' was heading for roughly the centre of the stretch of embankment which ran diagonally across their front, from nearest on the left to furthest away on the right . Beyond the embankment there was an orchard. As the railway line left the

Fields of Fire, near Saint-Aignan. (IWM, B8817)

embankment two roads coming into Tilly joined just where the village's houses commenced.

By 01.30 'D' Company was on its objective and 'B' reported that it had also arrived. In fact, in the dark, it had strayed on the right. On the left 'A' was meeting ferocious fire in the doubly dark orchard. 'C' Company was called up as reinforcement but casualties in the orchard were mounting. The CO was also having communication problems: one radio pack was smashed by a shell splinter, another had gone dead, runners were finding difficulty in locating sites in the darkness. Eventually Geordie Andrews managed to use the artillery net to contact brigade. Jim Cassells immediately requested a company from 5th Seaforths. Their 'D' under Capt Grant Murray was sent in and Andrews directed it to the right flank as the orchard area seemed impenetrable. For the time being Grant Murray's men disappeared into the unknown.

In the midst of raging battle Geordie Andrews came upon a personal microcosm of human cruelty and fear:

As the morning mist cleared, I went forward round the companies. . . . Several bodies were lying about and, as I passed that of a German, I saw him move as if to raise a weapon. Immediately recalling lurid tales of fanatical Nazis who shammed dead and then shot at you, I drew my pistol. He heard me cock it and at once began to moan for mercy, which left me acutely embarrassed. As I called some stretcher-bearers the affair struck me as a vignette of war – I had thought he was treacherous enough to shoot me, whilst he thought I was callous enough to finish him off. There was a moral in this somewhere.[20]

At 02.15 Capt Murray of 5th Seaforths was sent forward to the level crossing at the entrance to the village. Still in darkness and mist Murray took 'D' Company down the railway in a south-west direction to attack a point from which strong enemy resistance seemed to be stemming. This was a copse of trees about 800 yd from the village and near a second level crossing. The mist reduced visibilty to about 100 yd. Murray sent 17 Platoon under Sgt Barnes to attack the trees and himself followed on. In the ensuing battle Murray was killed.

Meanwhile it was apparent to the brigadier that only a major attack by 5th Seaforths could clear this vital village, which the underestimated 272 German Infantry Division was so doggedly defending. He consulted with Lt-Col Walford at 03.10, but the latter pointed out that there had been no recce of ground and no briefing of the battalion. An immediate mass attack in the dark and in ignorance could be a recipe for disaster. The brigadier agreed to await the colonel's own personal reconnaissance as soon as light permitted, with an attack to commence as soon as possible therafter. In the meantime he had requested Brig Scott for any tanks which might be available (no tanks were allocated to 152 Brigade at that point).

With support from 148 RAC and taking advantage of their Kangaroos, 7th Black Watch had carried out a quick clearance of the important area of the Garcelles-Secqville chateau and its woods so 148 were able to detach a squadron to drive the mile or so back towards Tilly, taking the defenders in the rear. Caught in a pincer between elements of 148 RAC, 2nd Seaforths and 5th Seaforths, which were backed by heavy artillery concentration, the defenders at last began to yield ground. The 148 tanks drove back and forward through the village, eventually encountering a German lieutenant. He proved to be the only surviving officer and asked for time to consider a total surrender. Given a stern warning by Lt-Col Walford, the young officer appeared at 10.50 hours leading some thirty surviving infantry. Tilly had been liberated at long last.[21]

Meanwhile, 5th Seaforth's 16 Platoon ('D') had at last flushed the final defenders out of the woods near Mont des Renes, which had claimed Grant Murray's life. Infantry moving into the area found the body of Grant Murray closely surrounded by dead of 17 Platoon and German bodies, evidence of a most bitter fight. Murray's under-strength 'D' Company had gone into action with only forty men and had lost himself and ten Other Ranks killed plus another ten wounded.

Bill Deeming, in 148 RAC, was most pleased, after the chaos of the night, to be riding back towards base, the rear deck plates of the Sherman now loaded with prisoners from Tilly. One of the significant factors of the entire Totalize Phase 1 battle was the discrepancy in rates of casualties between carrier-borne infantry and walking infantry, on both the Canadian and the British flanks. The Canadian official history records that their carrier infantry battalions suffered a total of 7 killed and 56 wounded, compared to

68 killed and 192 wounded of the walkers. 'The Rileys' (Hamiltons) lost 1 killed and 14 wounded in contrast to the Canadian Camerons' 30 killed and 96 wounded. While some of the disparity could be explained by the presence of the tanks, the value of the carriers was seen to be proven. It must be remembered, too, that the small numbers of Kangaroos available meant that many of the armoured column infantry travelled in the thinner-skinned White carriers, but these men still enjoyed greater immunity than the walkers. British casualty ratios were similar.

The many individual tragedies and the extremity of suffering are well illustrated by the experience of Wilf Mylan, of 33rd Armoured Brigade HQ, in his encounter with a wounded Canadian:

A Canadian, leg gashed, body shattered beyond belief, still breathing; wasps swarming on the bloody flesh of his leg, maggots already emerging; the medic saying, 'Best chance is bandage the wasps, maggots, all into the leg; provide some leeching'; the mass of wasps crunching into the raw meat under the khaki field dressing: in battle you learned about Nature's realities.[22]

Phase 1 Totalize objectives had been achieved on time or in good time. Phase 1 duties were not yet ended, for an early German counter-attack would fall on the tired, filthy, thirsty, bladder-swollen Phase 1 troops.

Chapter Six

Counterpunch at Saint-Aignan

'It was now afternoon, and they had led the army right through the villages . . .
when suddenly they saw the enemy coming over some hills in front of them,
numbers of cavalry and foot in battle formation. So they marched forward, and
the men in front came to a large wooded gully where the going was difficult.'
(Xenophon, 400 BC)

It was going to be another nice day. Stan Hicken and Rex Jackson looked out
from their driving compartment of Sherman 3 Baker, 'C', Northamptonshire
Yeomanry, through the morning mist which portended August heat. Behind
them was the stone village of Saint-Aignan-de-Cramesnil. In front the
orchards sloped gently to an innocent-looking thick hedge, out of which
sprouted tall trees. Beyond the trees, and through a gap straight ahead, they
could see the buildings of Robertmesnil farm. A reverent quietness belied the
fact that they were now sitting 3 miles beyond the enemy front line.

No. 2 Troop had been pushed forward through those trees. They had
reported crossing a gully, a mundane-sounding word reminiscent of a
rainwater drain along the edge of a roof or a gutter beside a road. Nothing
menacing! Stan stared across the fields. The mouth was free to chatter on
the wireless intercom channel while the eyes continued a disciplined watch.
Stan asked, 'Why don't we just go forward and take the other ridge? Give it
a few hours and those woods will be teeming with Jerry tanks and infantry.'
Cdr Ken Snowdon, up aloft in the turret hatch, replied, 'We're far enough
forward already. We're isolated enough as it is here.' But if Stan had been a
responsible general his words would have sent a shiver down the spine of a
certain Kurt 'Panzer' Meyer just a mile or two away.[1]

There was time for a makeshift breakfast prepared by Stan while the rest
of the crew broke off branches and camouflaged the front of the tank,
hoping to disguise its tall domed shape and let it merge into the apple trees.
The 1st Northamptonshire Yeomanry tanks stood in a rather crooked circle
among the trees, with the 1st Black Watch in slit trenches inside the circle or
in the stout farms and cottages of the village. 'A' Squadron looked south and
west towards the main Caen to Falaise road. 'C' Squadron faced south and
east out into empty enemy territory. 'B' Squadron guarded the rear where
German troops still lurked. The Black Watch had 'A' and 'B' companies
close up to the tank perimeter. On the right 'B' Squadron could see the flank
tanks of 144 RAC. On the left there was nobody to contact.

Tank crews sat and mulled over their unusual and sometimes frightening experiences of the night. Cpl Jim Stanley was one of the humorists of the squadron and had recently been issued with spectacles, which caused him to be the butt of some leg-pulling as a 'short-sighted commander'. Someone greeted him with the words, 'What? Still alive, Jimmy?' to which he snapped, 'It'll take a bloody good Jerry to finish me off!' Wally Tarrant was continously thinking about how quiet it all was: 'not at all what we had been led to expect'. Joe Crittenden was munching hard biscuit and bland processed cheese and wondering how long it would be before he could really stretch his legs properly. He had already suffered about ten hours of cramp. For a Firefly gunner there was less room in the turret than in a normal Sherman. Joe was a little concerned about the 17-pdr gun, which had only been fired once or twice. He knew there had been teething problems. Just before D-Day the Firefly gunners had been ordered to remove the extractors which pulled the spent shell cases out of the gun after firing. The extractors were then sent off by despatch rider to Cardiff for insertion of new spring plungers. This might, or might not, solve the problem of jammed shell cases which had happened on the ranges at Lulworth. A fine time for testing today! John Stenner, who had bloodied his nose in a crash on the Night March, saw everyone looking dishevelled and tired as they grabbed some breakfast, but he felt even more sorry for some Germans who appeared, bedraggled and absolutely horror-stricken from the shock of the Yeomanry attack. They wanted only to surrender.

The illusion of peace and tranquility persisted until about 10.30 hours when mortar bombs began to fall within the perimeter. The crackling wireless static cut out and a voice called, 'Medics forward. Big Sunray wounded.' There was consternation throughout the Yeomanry. Big Sunray was the colonel, Doug Forster, and the enemy's first blow had deprived the regiment of its revered commander. In the orchard where RHQ was located stretcher-bearers ran to the colonel's tank. Lt-Col Forster had been talking to 'B' squadron leader, the Hon. Peter Brassey, when a shell exploded and wounded them both, the colonel in the neck and Brassey on the hand. Signals officer John Crosby heard the colonel protesting vehemently about being evacuated, but the three stars of medical opinion out-voted the star and crown of military command.

Douglas Forster was typical of a certain breed of middle-ranking British officer whose praises might be sung more often. A regular Hussar, he had taken 'early retirement' just before the war. He was then called back as a major to train raw troops and then to lead them to the Normandy beaches. A quiet man of immense authority, he was the main reason why his territorial regiment had survived when others were broken up or diverted. He also brought assurance to the traumatic experience of the Night March. Now, in some pain, he would guide the half-track driver down a back route which would be more perilous in daytime than at night because the Germans remaining there were wide awake and determined to resist. 'Keep the sounds of firing on your left' (Tilly-la-Campagne), he urged the driver repeatedly as the corporal found his way down a poorly marked route.

At about 11.15 the first direct action took place. Beyond the gully Lt Bill Heaven ordered Jim Stanley to move his tank nearer to that of Sgt

Thompson. Breaking from cover, Stanley's tank was spotted by a German SP gun near Robertmesnil. The first SP shot brewed up Stanley's tank. It was an ordinary German gunner who caused Stanley's demise. Several other 'C' Squadron tanks noticed the flash from the SP. A fusillade of 75 mm and 17-pdr amour-piercing shot and high-explosive shells ripped into the hedgerow at Robertmesnil, repaying Stanley's debt in kind. The response had been instinctive, without formal word of command.

As noon drew near, Maj Wykeham, now commanding the Northants, was relieved to see tanks of the Polish armoured division approaching across the fields at the rear. The Poles had needed to steer through huge traffic jams across Caen and up the beaten track left by the Night March. Now they were due to pass through 1st Northamptonshire Yeomanry and 144 RAC and continue the attack. But, before that, their task would be eased by another great bombing raid of nearly 700 planes, this time from the US Army Air Force.

Tank commanders and platoon leaders knew about the raid. The first thing many tank crews and dug-in infantry privates knew was when the bombs started dropping right on top of them. The Northants adjutant, Capt Llewellyn 'heard a rushing noise like an express train. Suddenly the tank rocked, everything went completely black and we were smothered by a shower of earth and stones which continued to rain down on the tank for some seconds . . . I thought the end of the world had come.' Buffeted in their tanks, the troopers swore in a way that Shakespeare would have recognized, but the Black Watch bore the brunt. Two of 'B' Company's vital signallers were killed and their equipment smashed. The troops in the perimeter were not to know that far worse chaos was caused by the same raid in rear areas, causing further delays. The armoured pause while awaiting the bombers also resulted in the Northamptonshire Yeomanry having to undertake singlehanded a perilous defence. All the troopers knew was that real action had started, and that the theorists reckoned their Shermans would sacrifice from three to five tanks for every German tank knocked out; but that at that moment the score, with Stanley's tank still burning over there, stood at one all.

Thanks to the efficiency of tank wireless the most humble tank crew member could eavesdrop on battles near and not so near. The infantry were much more confined to their slit trench and narrow field of fire. They had endured an unaccustomed and eerie ride through the night. Now they were being bombed by their own side. Morale was difficult to maintain in such a situation. Sometimes a young soldier would lose his nerve and begin to act irrationally. Stan Whitehouse remembered this happening to a friend:

The ordeal of running the gauntlet . . . left us badly shaken and whilst most of us soon recovered, one or two were left in a pathetic state. Mushty, a young lad from Cornwall, began crying and sobbing to anyone prepared to listen . . . bemoaning his fate, all the while trembling uncontrollably. Our officer had sternly told us, 'There is no such thing as "bomb happiness" in the Black Watch'. 'Bugger it, Whitey, I'm shagged', [Mushty] said. He strolled about the front area in an upright posture . . . This became known as the 'deathwish walk', as opposed to the infantry crouch we had all instinctively adopted very early on.[2]

'Hullo, William 3 Charlie. Figures three nasties range twelve hundred alongside road. Look like Tigers. 3 Charlie, over.' The very slightly raised voice of 'A' Squadron's Sgt Gordon ushered in the time of fatal gambles among the orchards. Three Tigers! Only a few weeks earlier one lone Tiger had knocked out twenty tanks of another Yeomanry regiment. The Totalizator would surely set odds of 15 to 3 in this instance. The voice of Capt Tom Boardman, now well known from his Night March conversations, ordered Gordon to hold fire while a plan was quickly concocted.

Three of the 53-ton Tiger tanks, the most feared weapon in Normandy, were moving slowly parallel and near to the main road from Caen to Falaise. Their guns were traversed left to cover the far side of the road. Gordon's troop, commanded by Lt James, was therefore lurking in the orchards on the right of the Tigers. The German tank commanders appeared to feel that they were sheltered on their left by the trees beside the main road and by the road itself which was slightly raised at that point. None of the three Tigers appeared to be watching out to the right. Arriving close to Lt James, Capt Boardman ordered the three 75 mm Shermans, plus his own, to 'pepper' the turrets of the Tigers. The 75 mm shot would have little effect on the Tiger armour but would make the commanders close down and restrict themselves to periscope view. Gordon's Firefly would then shoot at the rearmost Tiger.

In 3 Charlie Firefly, Joe Ekins, the shoe clicker from Bedfordshire, lined up his sights and, as the Tigers prowled to within about 800 yd, Boardman gave the order to fire. At 12.40 hours Ekin's boot trod on the trigger button and the immense flash of the Firefly wrapped itself around the turret. Gordon and Ekins blinked deliberately and then opened their eyes to see the shot strike the enemy turret. Ekins fired again. The Tiger started to burn. Immediately the other two Tigers alerted began feverishly to traverse their 88 mm guns towards the Yeomanry. One Tiger fired and Gordon ordered his tank to reverse so that he could find other cover from which to resume firing. A third Tiger shot glanced on the turret hatch of the Firefly, doing no material damage but smashing the heavy steel plate against Gordon's head. Gordon staggered out of the tank and was wounded by a random mortar bomb.

Lt James ran to Gordon's tank, guided the driver into a new firing position under the apple trees and gave the fire order. 12.47 hours – one shot from Ekins and the Tiger's turret exploded. The 75 mm Shermans appeared to have done some kind of damage to the third Tiger, possibly smashing the commander's periscope, for the tank seemed to be circling as though looking for escape from the open field in which it found itself. 12.52 hours – and two more shots from Ekins. The third Tiger started to burn. In Ekins' own words 'this all happened in about 12 minutes. All I was thinking was "get them before they get us". I fired twice [at the third Tiger]. He started burning. We reversed into cover. We reloaded and sorted ourselves out and sat back waiting.'

Another tank reported about twenty enemy 'Nasties', probably Mark IVs, moving along a ridge about 1,200 yd away. The Mark IV was much smaller

Tpr Joe Ekins ('A', 1st
Northamptonshire
Yeomanry), Firefly crack
shot at Saint-Aignan.

than the Tiger but, with an upgraded gun, could still fight on more than
equal terms with a Sherman. Ekins was still waiting, as he says:

> We moved into a fire position and immediately saw a target at 1,200
> yards. I fired one shot and the tank brewed. . . . Suddenly there was a
> loud bang and sparks shot all around the turret. The order came from
> Lt James, 'We're hit. All out!' We scrambled out and ran back out of the
> orchard. A quick glance showed our tank burning. Bullets were flying
> around. Lt James was wounded when he went to report to the
> Squadron Leader. I never fired a gun again.

Having achieved an unparalleled success against the fearsome Tigers, Ekins
was not required to shoot in the next several actions. He then became a
wireless operator and, although serving on until the end of the war, never
fired another shot although, as a Sherman operator, he did load shells into
the gun for someone else to fire.

It was Tpr Wellbelove of 'C' Squadron who actually saw that the first of
the main body of German counter-attack tanks after the Tigers, advancing

in front of the rest, had been eliminated. Wellbelove's 2 Troop had crossed the as yet inconspicuous gully and obtained a good view of the Robertmesnil Ridge. Four tanks of the main formation came out into the open between two woods on the ridge. His commander, Cpl Giles, ordered Wellbelove to fire. Although the Sherman's Westinghouse traverse system was perhaps the fastest turret mechanism of any tank, the first Mark IV had passed out of sight. Wellbelove was a small, genial, popular lad who, as with many other tank crew, looked almost like a schoolboy in uniform. At that moment he became belligerent. Lining the sights, pumping the trigger, waiting the loader's slap on his leg, adjusting sights, firing, sighting, firing, he knocked out the other three tanks as they accelerated, trying to put the barrier of the woods between them and the Firefly gun.

The Germans had a priceless advantage. They knew the ground. 'Panzer' Meyer had served in the area long before the Normandy campaign. A very young officer in high command and ever at the front of battle, he now put his knowledge to good use. On air photographs of the time, the gully looks to be just another Normandy country track with thick hedges on either side.[3] The local inhabitants call it le Petit Ravin (the Little Ravine). However, the map contours do not do justice to the danger which this feature presents to an attacking force. A 'going map' issued for the attack marks the gully as a hazard,[4] but from a few yards away the gully looks like a simple Normandy hedgerow, an illusion which is not banished until a tank commander looks right down into it.

Running diagonally from the west and snaking towards Saint-Aignan in the east, the gully begins as a thick hedgrow and then becomes a wide track, eventually developing into the size of a small field. From its course to the point where the Robertmesnil track crosses it, and where 2 Troop had passed over, it is at times almost 30 ft below the level of the surrounding orchards and woods, thickly shrouded in trees, but with a kind of racetrack along which the largest tank could run freely.

The Northamptonshire Yeomanry tanks were already perilously placed forward of any support until the Poles were in position in full strength. It was not possible for the Yeomanry or the Black Watch to control the gully. Now the Mark IVs began to trundle along this ideal hideaway, able to come up at points on the banks and still be effectively screened by the thick trees. Total annihilation of the Yeomanry and the Black Watch infantry was not too much for Meyer to hope for, given also the general superiority of German weapons. Meyer's counter-attack objective was the woods at Garcelles-Secqueville, behind 144 RAC and occupied by 148 RAC with the Argylls and 7th Black Watch.[5]

If the Yeomanry and Black Watch could be either eliminated or forced to retreat this would expose the Canadian left flank. Only a day later a Canadian force of similar size on neighbouring terrain would be totally wiped out. The removal of the Saint-Aignan battle group would then leave the SS Panzer group on a forward high ridge, with good knowledge of the ground and adequate sylvan cover, and also fairly mobile SP 88 mm guns in support of the Mark IVs. They would be well sited to pick off the massed Polish tanks paraded on open ground, and then attack the even more exposed flanks of

144 and 148 RAC. It was quite a recipe for disaster. It would bite off the advance aiming to join up with the Americans and leave the threatened German troops within the embryo Falaise pocket with a clear escape route.

The stalking, hunting and killing contest of Saint-Aignan entered its peak hour. While there would be ruthless exchanges at a few yards range, Tpr Joe Crittenden fired the next shots at long range. Sgt Finney, his tank commander, discerned two Mark IVs moving through trees well over on the other side of the main Falaise road, about 1,800 yd away. 'Traverse right. Do you see them, Joe?' asked Finney. The two Mark IVs were about 50 yd apart. Again it was align sights, fire, 'the rear tank starting to burn, a slight traverse left, then fire . . . that too started to burn. The whole affair was over in two or three minutes'.

A Mark IV had arisen out of the gully. Nearby Shermans were much hampered by their turrets being high among the tree branches, thronged with myriad cider apples. The Mark IV gun telescope was at ground level. It calmly set about brewing up Shermans. Maj Gray Skelton saw his 'A' Squadron disintegrating into pyres of belching flame and black smoke. He called for an artillery 'stonk'. It came down right on the Northamptonshire Yeomanry tanks. Finney's tank 'rocked with the blast of exploding shells, and shrapnel rattled like hailstones on the turret'. Skelton had 'a heart to heart talk' on the wireless with the forward observer of the artillery. He then ordered Finney to go right while he himself went left in a pincer movement, assuming that the Mark IV would knock out one of them while the other repaid the compliment. Joe Crittenden was concentrating on his telescopic sight:

We had not gone very far when there was a loud clang and dust and flakes of paint appeared in front of my eyes. The commander yelled 'Bale out'. There were no flames in the turret so I hand traversed the turret to clear the driver's hatch, and then found myself on the ground still wearing my headset. When I looked around the rest of the crew had vanished completely. . . . I walked to the edge of the orchard where some infantry were dug in . . . finally I came to 2 Troop where Stan Bailey proffered a bottle of Scotch which cheered me somewhat.

Crittenden was more cheered later to learn that not only were his crew mates safe but Maj Skelton had knocked out the Mark IV. The give and take continued, punch and counterpunch. Bill Higham heard a loud bang and thought he had gone blind:

What had happened was that a bullet had skimmed the top of the tank, smashing my periscope and penetrating Cpl Bowden's tin helmet through one side and exiting out the back, just leaving a graze on his forehead. You may not believe it but I swear it is true. But his luck did not last very long.

Bowden's tank was called forward to help Maj Skelton in the search for the elusive, hull-down Mark IV. Bill Higham continues:

We moved off to try and spot the tank. Cpl Bowden directed me to where he thought it was and I fired a couple of shots to where we thought we could see it. Suddenly there was a tremendous bang and Cpl Bowden dropped down into the bottom of the tank. What happened was a shell hit the opened flap of the hatch and killed Cpl Bowden instantly. He was wedged under the main gun and the turret side. I couldn't rotate the turret, so we were a sitting duck. I took command and ordered the driver, George Smith, to reverse back. We got help and managed to get Cpl Bowden up and out of the tank. Later in the workshops we saw Sgt Ryan's tank which had been hit by a bazooka on the Night March . . . the shot had penetrated the projectile of an armour-piercing shell in the racks, leaving a neat round hole. If it had been a high explosive shell the whole tank would have blown up. So the crew had a bit of luck on their side, except for Sgt Ryan.

On the Northamptonshire Yeomanry left 'C' Squadron were experiencing similar patterns of hide-and-seek tactics. Another Mark IV rolled unseen along the now infamous gully, found a gap in the rear bank trees and came up behind the remaining tanks of 2 Troop. It was a matter of less than a minute to knock out those tanks before they knew what was happening. Wellbelove's tank blew up. Cpl Giles exited safely. Wellbelove also baled out, but in the confusion of battle he ran in the wrong direction. He disappeared in a blaze of enemy machine-gun fire. His body was found by a Polish padre the next day.

Rex Jackson watched the survivors of 2 Troop emerge from the tangled trees of the gully. Their troop leader, Lt Heaven, came to report to Lt R.S. McColl in the tank next to Rex's. The group of survivors seemed to be holding one another up and walking as though in a faraway dream. Rex and Stan Hicken were not too happy themselves. For some time they had been watching a ginger-headed man in a trench in front of their tank, where no Highlander should be. When the man failed to move they began to realize that it was not a man in a trench. It was a disembodied head standing on the ground on its own. For the rest of the day, amid all the turbulence of shot and shell, the head sat in the grass and stared at them.

There should now have been some relief for the hard-pressed Yeomanry for, at 13.35 hours, the Polish armoured division began to pass around their left flank, accelerating into a kind of cavalry charge formation towards the German positions. As another Polish formation passed on the right, Capt Boardman tried frantically to contact them on the wireless to warn them about the hidden German tanks. He failed. Many Yeomen like John Stenner watched in horror 'the Polish armour going along a ridge, being knocked off like a shooting gallery in a fair ground'. Lt Tony Faulkner, commanding the Yeomanry's left flank 1 Troop, also watched in something between admiration and horror as the Poles dared the open ground and paid the price. There was to be no relief for 1st Northamptonshire Yeomanry and 1st Black Watch as yet.

At this point Maj Skelton and Capt Boardman were still unaware of the full significance of the Tiger fight. For them it was simply a savage 'hunt and be hunted' task amid the trees. They did not know that if any half-troop of tanks in the Second World War could claim to be 'élite', and if any tank commander of the war could claim to be 'The Ace', then that force was still burning beside the Caen to Falaise road. The average Yeomanry tanker or Black Watch private was equally unaware of the fact that, whereas on the Night March and dawn attack they had coped with 'green' soldiers not yet inured to intensive bombardment, they had now passed into confrontation with what Hasting would describe as 'arguably the most formidable fighting force the Allies encountered in Normandy'.[6] Their Hitlerjugend opponents were one of the three German divisions which won most awards for bravery in the war, and the Hitlerjugend gained their awards in much less time than the other two divisions.[7]

To counter the gully run of the enemy, 'C' Sqn Ldr David Bevan now ordered Lt 'Bobby' McColl to dispose his 3 Troop nearer to the gully. It would have been suicidal to post tanks beyond the gully at this point as German infantry were infiltrating the copses, carrying with them the feared *Panzerfaust*, the throwaway, short-range, hand-held tank destroyer. McColl sent Cpl Ken Snowdon in 3 Baker to the lip of the gully where the track to Robertmesnil descended abruptly and from where they could see enough of the 'racetrack' to impede full use of the entire gully by enemy tanks. In that position an imperative need was for the tank to be able to reverse rapidly in the event of overpowering enemy fire. Meanwhile 'C' 1 Troop (Faulkner) and 4 Troop (Brown), farther left, were denying the wider part of the gully to the enemy but, like 3 Troop, were tactically unable to move against the narrower gully areas. Stalemate again! At that point the German forces had more elasticity of movement.

Poised on the lip of the gully in 3 Baker, Stan Hicken was worried because his clutch pedal was not working properly. It was apparent that the return spring had broken so that when depressed the pedal stayed down. Stan had been reduced to hooking his toe under the pedal and kicking it back up. Not a useful driving style when needing to reverse sharply! In addition he was beginning to suffer severe bruising of the shin every time the pedal shot back up into position. Always ingenious, he found a piece of telephone wire which had somehow got into the driver's compartment, tied one end to the pedal and the other end to his leg above his knee. Now he simply lifted his knee and the pedal came up at fairly normal speed. He thought wryly of the old story about a battle lost for lack of a bootlace. He soon had far more to worry about.

Capt Ken Todd, second navigator on the Night March, suddenly appeared guiding his tank in front of 3 Baker, waving Snowdon back and obviously concerned that 3 Baker was too exposed. Stan Hicken received his order to reverse and, as he operated his home-made clutch mechanism, there was the now familiar terrible crash, flash and odour of an 88 mm armour-piercing shot smashing into a Sherman, the close-range crash of the gun firing and the crash of the shot impacting, running into one appalling concussion. With flames obscuring the periscope, Stan thought his own tank had been hit but it was Todd's which had taken the enemy round. The crew of 3 Baker saw their friends Hoult and Hood wriggling out of the driver's cab, Martin and Capt Todd vaulting off the turret and, as the engine burst into flame, Eric Marchant, his clothes on fire, falling off the tank. There was a flurry as Todd's crew struggled to beat out the flames on Marchant's

L/Cpl Eric Marchant, HQ (F), 'C', 1st Northamptonshire Yeomanry, was badly burned when Lt Todd's tank 'brewed' at Saint-Aignan.

On partial recovery Marchant was discharged with terse official wording, 'ceasing to fulfil army physical requirements'.

denims and, at the same time, drag him to safety, if ducking under machine-gun fire counted as safety. Then the blazing engine ignited the turret ammunition in a 50-ft firework show which went on interminably it seemed after the crew had found safety with Black Watch people nearby.

'C' Squadron second in command, Capt Bill Fox, saw the firing and noticed movement on a distant ridge. He directed his gunner, Bruce Dickson, on to the spot. Through his telescopic sight Dickson could discern just 8 in of tank armour (verified next day) showing over the ridge as the tank reversed. He put a quick shot into that meagre target and knocked out what proved to be a self-propelled gun.

Stan Hicken now noticed movement along the gully and alerted his commander, who ordered the gunner to traverse, in time to shoot and brew up yet another hunted hunter. Rex Jackson was perplexed because the opposing tanks were so close that the one which 3 Baker had brewed might just possibly have been a wandering 'A' Squadron tank. Rex became even more perplexed because 3 Troop's 'Charlie' (the Firefly) had moved up to take part in the action. The huge blast from the 17-pdr's muzzle had seared through a large tree which came down, meriting a shout of 'Timber', right across 3 Baker's front.

On the extreme left, 1 Troop Cpl Charlie Rogers was also puzzled. His tank had comfortably nuzzled into a row of young pines. Without any warning the tops of the pines began to fall off. Farmer Charlie had never before witnessed such a phenomenon. His troop leader, Tony Faulkner, a few yards away, also noticed the pine disintegration but quickly realized that an enemy gun was shooting diagonally across the gully. Tank warfare in close country is extremely fluid. Cautious tank commanders will fire only a couple of shots from a specific hide before moving to seek another nesting place. Some German gun had moved into a hitherto unused lair to try to outflank Faulkner's troop.

Faulkner, realizing that he was dreadfully exposed, ordered his driver, Sutch, to reverse. Nothing happened except that two more shots zipped almost visibly across their bows (high velocity, 88 mm shots caused furrows of visible disturbance among leaves or across grass). Faulkner, irritated and fearful, yelled into his micophone, 'Driver, for God's sake reverse'. The response came from co-driver Pye, 'He can't. He's dead'. Faulkner gasped 'How can he be?', to which Pye replied, 'Head shot off, and I can't get him out of the seat. His feet are hooked under the pedals.' The tank was now stranded and immovable in the open at the widest part of the gully. Lt Faulkner gave the 'all out' order and waited to see that everyone but Sutch was safely out. Turning away to exit himself, he was astonished to see Pye standing in the middle of the gully, shooting his Sten gun at the vague area from which the German gun must be aiming. 'Run, you idiot!' he shouted, and set an example himself.

Faulkner, Pye and others mounted another tank. The lieutenant took over command, calculating that the enemy gun must be traversing or moving to shoot this next Sherman. 'Reverse, for your life,' he ordered driver Joe Preston. 'Never mind where. Just reverse like Hell!' Little Joe Preston, the speediest of football wingers, trod his pedals, crashed backwards unsighted, across the gully, through a hedge, across a road, knocking down a chateau boundary wall and coming to rest surrounded by a convenient barricade of fallen free stone. Tony Faulkner looked to his left and saw that Polish tanks had committed themselves to the open with such bravado that they were still being shot up, 'like a coconut shy at the fair'. Back in the gully, Sgt Sid Hulme had worked his Firefly into a position where he was able to knock out the gun which had killed Sutch.

Battles are untidy affairs and Phase 1 of Operation Totalize had now been subsumed in Phase 2. In an ordered war, the German Waldmuller battle group would have completed its counter-attack on Saint-Aignan, successfully or unsuccessfully, and the bell would have gone for the end of Round One. The Polish Armoured Division would then have inaugurated Phase 2 as an attempt to leap further forward from Saint-Aignan. In the event the Phase 2 action began while Phase 1 troops were still fending off the counter-attack. For the sake of clarity this book will treat the counter-attack as a separate Phase 1 event and return to the Polish efforts later on.

No. 4 Troop of 'C' Squadron was located centrally, driving forward along the lane which leads from the church past a large farmyard and into the fields beyond. In the lottery of tank movements, a German gunner now lined up his sights on the troop leader's tank. Lt Brown, an Australian, was badly wounded. L/Cpl Arthur Dwight took command. He had Tpr Monkman with him in the turret and L/Cpl Michael Hunt and Tpr Cliff Cuthbertson in the driver's compartment. Dwight called down to co-driver Cliff to come up into the turret and act as gun loader. All tank crew were interchangeable as regards the functions of the tank in action, although perhaps not all able to maintain the engine, repair the wireless or strip the big gun. Geordie Cliff performed the uncomfortable feat of squirming into the turret. As he left his seat a 75 mm shot smashed through the armour plating, destroyed the co-driver's vacant seat and wounding Monkman. Down to three men, Dwight had to reverse to obtain a reinforcement gunner. Michael Hunt had been stretching across the co-driver's seat, trying to work the machine-gun, when the seat exploded into splinters, wounding him too.

Incredible things continued to happen in battle. John Stenner heard the unmistakable clang of an armour-piercing shot hitting his tank and heard the commander, Sgt Johnson yell, 'Bale out'. John was getting used to bangs. Only a little while earlier 'friendly fire' had descended on their turret top, blown away their 'A' set aerial, leaving them deaf to normal messages and able to communicate only on the restricted 'B' set. By the time John had got his head out of the turret, Johnson was on his way back, saying, 'It's OK. No penetration. Get back in.' But the turret was not reacting smoothly. A call went out to the 'Tech. Adj.' who came up to have a look. He discovered that a freakish round had ploughed around the turret, shearing off its retaining bolts. Tech Adj Capt Frankham's advice was, 'Don't fire your gun. Your turret will fall off!'

By 14.00 hours Maj Waldmuller had managed to push his infantry up from reserve to back up his tanks. He had assembled Panzer Grenadiers from three weak battalions, still a formidable and experienced fighting force which moved forward resolutely across cornfields in the Robertmesnil area, and from there to the main road.[8] John Hopwood, CO of 1st Black Watch, viewed it all dispassionately:

> The shelling and mortaring increased in intensity and considerable fire was heard coming from 'A' Company's direction. It appeared that 'A' Company were being attacked by 200 infantry supported by tanks. This counter-attack continued for one and a half hours, the enemy infantry advancing to within 300 yards of 'A' Company's FDLs. The Northants Yeomanry, however, moved forward of our FDLs and did magnificent work against the Boche tanks. The Divisional Artillery brought down DF . . . the position had been stabilised and certainly heavy casualties had been inflicted on the Boche infantry.[9]

Waldmuller's infantry were a serious menace, especially if they could work their way through the hedges and copses and orchards around the gully. However, for the tank gunners, after the period of searching for minimal targets hard to identify, it was almost a relief to have a clear sight of infantry moving across cornfields. Viewed generally from the Northants Yeomanry positions the narrow part of the gully was a high green screen, but to both left and right open cornfields were visible at anything from 500 to 1,200 yd. The *élan* of the attacking infantry may have contributed to their fatal willingness to walk across open fields, or they may have felt that the harvest corn was high enough to shield them if they dropped into a crouch.

There were still about thirty Yeomanry Shermans fully operational, each with a cannon firing high explosive and with two machine-guns. The 1st Black Watch firepower was almost undiminished, while many of the 144 RAC tanks and the 7th Argylls had a flank view. This mass of fire now poured into the ranks of the advancing infantry. After a few moments of defiance the attackers relented and took to crawling forward, always forward. The artillery ranged in on to the cornfields and the tank tracer set fire to the dry corn. Some of Waldmuller's men were shot, some burned or suffocated, others continued to inch forward towards the shelter of the gully. Almost any other body of infantry might have called it a day and felt satisfied by their efforts. The Hitlerjugend survivors reached the far banks of the gully but found that area was no refuge. Some of them died there along the banks and others dug in back among the trees. Allied regimental diaries relate that 'the enemy continued to mount one attack after another until his losses made further attacks hopeless and he was compelled to withdraw'.[10]

Amid the high drama, fighting soldiers were often more preoccupied about niggling details. Peter Smith, moving here and there in the recovery vehicle to do rescue jobs and minor repairs, was irritated because he was not allowed to eat inside the vehicle, which was common custom, especially in the front line. His commander was an old desert hand who had become obsessed with the problem of flies crawling all over the food in sandy conditions. Even in the green pastures of Normandy he vetoed the 'consumption of rations' inside the vehicle.

With their turret useless Johnson and Stenner were driving through the orchards, loading the flat back of the Sherman with wounded and dead, tank and infantry, British and German. There was work in plenty for them. Jack Pentelow's crew were the most puzzled of all. Where had the war gone? When Lt Coakley was killed, a L/Cpl Clark was sent to command the tank with orders to guard the rear of the hedge at which the Night March had landed. Maj Wykeham himself had given the order. Now, hours afterwards, they still guarded an empty landscape while guns sounded in the near distance from almost every direction.

By about 15.00 hours, in spite of Waldmuller's best efforts, the situation had, in Lt-Col Hopwood's words, stabilized. The German infantry had gone to ground or retreated across the cornfields. Northamptonshire Yeomanry Tpr Buck swears that the last Panzer Grenadier to leave the cornfield deliberately turned, stood up and shook his fist at the distant tanks. Buck did not fire. The German mortar crews and artillery continued to make life uncomfortable in the fields and woods forward of Saint-Aignan. On the lip of the gully, 3 Baker was hit and seemed to be on fire, but to the relief of the crew it was only the camouflage of dry branches which burned. A fire extinguisher was adequate to that task.

The silence which followed the Waldmuller attack was almost as frightening as the attack itself. Most Yeomanry and 1st Black Watch soldiers had no means of knowing how many more German tanks and infantry

Officers of 'C', 1st Northamptonshire Yeomanry. Back row, left to right: Lt J. Haskard (killed in action), Lt W.G. Heaven, Lt E.S. Brown (both wounded at Saint-Aignan), Lt R.S. McColl (killed in action) and Lt A.W. Faulkner. Front row: Capt Bill Fox, MC, S.M. Turton (killed in action), Maj D.G. Bevan, MC, S.Q.M.S. Farnham, MBE, Capt M.S. Rathbone (Croix de Guerre).

might be just over the ridge. On the other hand there was time now to contemplate the carnage and fearful casualties which had been seen and sometimes touched. Rex and Stan still looked out of 3 Baker at the ginger-haired head, which gradually turned crimson as the sun eventually set.

It was a time when unemployed minds might turn to unhealthy panic. So Maj David Bevan decided to take a walk across the fields where, as yet, few people moved above ground. Idly swinging his ceremonial riding crop, as though on a summer stroll, he approached 3 Baker and pointed out to Cpl Snowdon that his 'A' set aerial had been snapped off. 'No wonder I couldn't raise you on the wireless.' To tank crews, the squadron leader's stroll spoke of great coolness and lack of fear. Bevan himself was to confess that, at the worst moments of the day, he sat on his tank turret, chain-smoking and wishing he could be as free from fear as his nearby second in command, the stern-looking but ever kindly Bill Fox, a rather older man. It would be years before Bill Fox in turn would confess to 'Hank' Bevan that, 'at that moment I was more scared than I have ever been in my life. I was shitting myself.' The stiff British upper lip was the order of the day. To an extent it was contagious.

Some people, no doubt, had even more reason than Bill Fox to be scared. There was Lt Wyn Griffith-Jones who had been hiding all night in a potato patch back along the route of the Night March. At dawn the mist had given him opportunity to explore and find help for a number of wounded men who were also in the potato field. There was a disabled Bren Gun carrier which the wounded driver thought might be driveable. Wyn's troop corporal, Ferrier, had turned up, so borrowing a machine-gun from an injured Black Watch private, he accompanied the lieutenant through the mists. Visibility was only about 10 yd but they found the disabled carrier. The carrier was difficult to control as to direction but the engine started up, so the lieutenant drove it rather crab-wise to wherever they might arrive. Fortunately they ran into a patrol of (5th) Black Watch who directed them to their headquarters.

Wyn requested an ambulance. A stressed but sympathetic sergeant-major asked him if he could find his way back to the potato field. When he replied that he could, the sergeant-major found a properly working White Scout carrier and a large Red Cross flag. The mists had now dissipated and the woods on the flank were still held by German infantry. These honoured the Red Cross flag and the carrier passed safely across the fields and back with no further harm to the wounded men from the potato field. On return to the Black Watch post the Northamptonshire Yeomanry lieutenant was saddened to find that his next task was to load on to the carrier the sympathetic sergeant-major, who had been mortally wounded in the meantime. Wyn Griffith-Jones himself had been hit in the throat by shrapnel which eventually emerged to the light of day some forty-eight years later in America! Cpl Ferrier was awarded the Military Medal for his part in this mission of mercy.

Referring to the trip under the Red Cross flag, and the observance by the watching Germans of international conventions, Lt Wyn Griffith-Jones stated, 'I am pleased to report (amongst so many gruesome events in war time) such honourable behaviour on the part of the enemy.' Unknowingly, 3 Troop, 'C', were, in a sense, reciprocating. After the cessation of the Waldmuller attack 3 Troop had a partial view along the gully where Dr Rabe and a group of German medical orderlies were searching the far banks of the gully, barely 50 yd away at one point, to check bodies lying among the trees and render aid where aid was possible. Maj Bevan, seeing movement in the trees, ordered retaliation, but Lt McColl and Cpl Snowdon were able to see clearly the Red Cross armbands and monitor the actions of the slow-moving medics. Bevan cancelled the retaliation order.

Anxious echelon people now began to find their way through the masses of reinforcing Polish armour and bring urgent supplies up to the front-line troops. None was more assiduous than the Northants Yeomanry's burly RSM, George Jelley, a 1914–18 veteran, who had so far been restrained only by a direct order from the divisional commander, Maj-Gen Rennie. The Yeomanry had fired off a tremendous amount of ammunition and would be needing more shells, machine-gun bullets and water especially. George Jelley had assembled what might be termed a relief column of carriers. Assisting him were reserve crews, like Percy Sumner, who would replace the day's casualties.

For Percy, bumping across rutted country in an uncomfortable half-tracked vehicle was nothing like an August Bank Holiday outing on a Sheffield tram.

Guarding the supply team were Honey tanks of the Recce Troop, commanded by Lt 'Acky' Atkinson, which had not been included in the Night March. Sgt Kenny Jack's elder brother had been captured with the original Highland Division in 1940 and Kenny was always up front in his Honey, seeking vengeance on the enemy. Lou Lakin, in his Honey, was not such an enthusiastic warrior as Kenny, but was anxious about pals who had been in action all night. He felt, like Mack Clague and Fred Musgrove, also commanding Honeys, that now their light tanks could be of some use in ensuring that the needed supplies got through to Saint-Aignan. There were still occasional 'do and die' enemy wandering in the open country ahead.

Also waiting impatiently at the base line, as insurance against a collapse of the forward spearheads, the 'firm base' 153 Brigade was able to begin moving forward to guard the flank gap behind 154 Brigade (1st Black Watch *et al.*). The 153 (Murray) consisted of 1st Gordons (Cumming-Bruce), 5th Black Watch (Bradford) and 5/7th Gordons (Renny). The Sequeville woods were still smouldering from the massive RAF raid during the night, but 1st Gordons could now occupy the area, taking ninety prisoners in the process. There was no safe hiding-place that day and 5th Black Watch had been hit by daylight bombers 2 miles behind the new front line. Their CO, adjutant and HQ medical orderlies had all been thrown out of their vehicles by close bomb blasts but had survived. They now completed the clearance of the village of Sequeville (not to be confused with Garcelles-Sequeville) while 5/7th Gordons pushed towards Conteville on the wide left flank of Saint-Aignan.[11]

Meanwhile 152 Brigade (Cassells) had been working as 'walking infantry' behind 154 Brigade (Oliver). The often unsung machine-gun battalion of the division, 1/7th Middlesex had, during the total action, loosed off 250 bombs from each of their mortars and fired 44 belts from each of their machine-guns. The Crocodiles (flame-throwers) of the Royal Engineers had also formed part of the 'firm base' until they should be wanted for dealing with difficult resistance in narrow village streets.

As the light began to fade on Tuesday 8 August 1944, it was clear that the spearheads of Phase 1 of Operation Totalize had not been dislodged by a ferocious counter-attack, and that the perilous flanks and spaces behind the spearheads were being successfully filled. Phase 2 was another matter and did not directly concern the forces of the left flank of Phase 1. The immediate objective of the counter-attack, the woods around Garcelles-Secqueville had not been achieved. 154 Brigade still sat firmly between the attacking SS Panzers and those woods. 1st Northamptonshire Yeomanry and 144 RAC could now withdraw to refuel, undertake maintenance and minor repairs. The Highland troops were well dug in around Saint-Aignan and Cramesnil. The Poles were present in massed numbers to support the 'Jocks', although that had not been their principal purpose.

There was still room for a little humour amid the devastation. Ray Ager, exhausted after a night and day in the driving compartment of Capt Tom Boardman's Sherman, was unexpectedly amused when he saw some enemy infantrymen coming in to surrender to nearby Polish tanks. The prisoners-to-be were clapping and cheering. They proved to be Poles unwillingly conscripted into the Nazi armies and now surrendering to the Free Poles, who were not reluctant to recruit such trained soldiers into their own ranks.

Statistics of enemy vehicles knocked out are notoriously fallible. In this case 1st Northamptonshire Yeomanry had the opportunity of returning to the same battle positions the following day when, the battle having moved forward, officers were able to tour the 8 August battlefield and identify knocked-out enemy tanks. Based on that survey, the Yeomanry claimed to have destroyed twenty tanks or SP guns, including five Tigers, four Panthers, six Mark IVs and five SPs. The regiment itself lost four tanks on the Night March and sixteen at Saint-Aignan, a total of twenty. Some of the German tanks knocked out could have been 'shared' with other units but all had been hit by Northants fire. A 20–20 score was creditable in view of two factors: the general expectation of losing three to five Shermans for every enemy destroyed, and the fact that by 10 August the Yeomanry had been brought up to full tank strength again from the apparently endless 'conveyor belt' system which brought new Shermans from the factories of the USA. German tanks were virtually irreplaceable. For the Yeomanry twenty tanks lost meant merely a day's delay in resuming full operations, whereas tanks lost for the Germans meant further pressure on their very efficient workshops to try to cannibalize and cobble together replacements, in lesser numbers, from what wreckage might be salvaged during a retreat. It also, indirectly, meant more use and loss of valuable infantry and more drafting into infantry duties of skilled engineers and other support arms.

As the daylight died, so did any German hope of causing total chaos in the Allied ranks by pinching off the exposed left flank. It will be seen later that the counter-attack achieved another purpose which delayed the Allied advance. However, from 03.00 hours until 12.00 hours on that day the 1st Northamptonshire Yeomanry and 1st Black Watch armoured camp at Saint-Aignan had 2–3 km of open flank. At dawn the Poles were still making their way through and around the city of Caen, coming from Bayeux. A successful German right hook past the area of Saint-Aignan church and a dispersal of the Yeomanry and Black Watch in disorder would have left a powerful German force on high ground, with distant vision over open fields of fire, a knowledge of the terrain and the ability to do to the tightly massed Polish columns of march what a lesser force of 88s had done to the tanks of Goodwood. The Northants tanks had maintained their one advantage, that of being sited in woods and orchards and able to hunt while they were hunted. The tall profile of the Sherman was a disadvantage in the orchards but the tank's mobility and refined mechanical reliability compensated to an extent. One of the 'crack shots' of the Saint-Aignan battle, Tpr Bruce Dickson, reflects:

> Didn't the . . . Armoured . . . send a Squadron over a hillock line abreast and were they not all destroyed by two anti-tank guns? I think we scored by having a hunting tradition which permeated down the

ranks. The qualities that were abundant amongst commanders were individuality based on guidelines, initiative and common sense. I don't think Rowan Atkinson could have drawn material from the NY for 'Black Adder'. It is one thing to observe rising dust and enemy vehicles ten miles or so away but a completely different problem coping with cover offered by buildings and hedgerows.

The 1st Northamptonshire Yeomanry refuelling and reinforcement base was to be at the ruined village of Hubert-Folie, near the Night March start line, less distance for RSM George Jelley and his echelon to travel but still a weary journey back in the dark for exhausted crews. The tank crew strength of the Yeomanry at the commencement of the Night March was 292 total personnel. Of these 12 had been killed and 51 wounded. A general might consider that a minimal 'butcher's bill' for what had been achieved. However, a serious aspect was the loss of 13 officers and about the same number of NCO tank commanders. Maj David Bevan was quite firm in his opinion that NCOs with several years of training were not necessarily less efficient tank commanders than very young officers with accelerated training. The bane of the tank CO's life was the constant need for replacement of commanders who found it more convenient to command a tank when riding with the fragile human head projected high aloft out of the turret.

Joe Crittenden, who had counted fourteen hours before he was able to relieve the cramp in his legs, was now counting forty hours since he had slept. Rex Jackson had watched through binoculars several British infantrymen being marched as prisoners along a distant ridge. He had then seen the German medics at work among the fallen bodies. One German Red Cross man was so unconcerned, or maybe stupefied, that he dropped his trousers and relieved himself in full view of the British tank crew, which refrained from reacting out of respect for the international emblem of mercy.

Now, back at Hubert-Folie, while others of the crew prepared a meal and carried out essential maintenance, Rex climbed on to the flat back of the Sherman where the crew's bedding rolls were wrapped up in a tarpaulin. He began to unroll the tarpaulin and then fell asleep amid the bedding rolls. A few rude shouts from the crew roused him sufficiently to throw down the bedding before again curling up on the warm engine covers and, without bothering about the meal, catching what sleep might be possible before the 02.30 hours reveille.

A day of preparation had merged into a night of horrors. That night had fused into a day of ferocious retaliation. Now the day had diminished again into a midnight of petty squabbles and continuing skirmish, not sufficient to waken the crews on, beside or underneath their tanks.

Chapter Seven

A Points Victory

'On the next day they set out and the enemy fought back at them. They made the
road-block in front of the vanguard ineffectual by trying to get on to higher
ground than those who were manning it. . . . The enemy . . . were very good.
Their arrows went right through our shields and breastplates.'
(Xenophon, 400 BC)

In Operation Totalize Simonds had gone for a knockout. He aimed to drive
through to Falaise in two days. He eventually reached Falaise in nine days,
arriving on 17 August (it should be remembered that D-Day of 7 August had
its H-Hour only minutes before midnight so that effectively Totalize started
on 8 August). The 'Falaise Gap' or 'Falaise Pocket', both rather misnomers,
was eventually closed at Chambois on 21 August, after thirteen days. Totalize
lasted only to 11 August, and was followed on 14 August by 'Tractable'.

The knockout was not achieved. Some self-appointed referees have scored
Totalize as a draw. Continuing the boxing terminology, a 'Victory on Points'
might be more appropriate. From H-Hour 7/8 August until 11 August, Totalize
achieved an advance of 9 miles. This was a considerable inroad into enemy
territory compared to Goodwood gains and contrasted to Goodwood losses. It
also bears some comparison with the more celebrated 'Cobra' break-out of the
Americans, against a much weaker German defensive system. So the word
'victory' does apply, even though the progress of Phase 2 was disappointing
when related to the perhaps exaggerated and unwise expectations of higher
command. It has been commented that Montgomery himself criticized Crerar's
expectations that the Germans would run away after an efficient bombardment.
Yet the whole concept of Totalize (or at least the expectations of it) appear to
have been posited by Montgomery and others on the same vain hope that a
dose of night confusion would see the Germans rabbit-tailing it at dawn.

The overt purpose of this book is to focus on Phase 1 as the victory which
the victors forgot because of disappointment at the sequel. Isolating Phase 1,
it may not be unreasonable to claim that, marks out of a hundred, Phase 1
was perhaps a 95 per cent success in distance and timing achievement. Even
if the writer settles for, say, 80 per cent achievement this would surely set
Phase 1 of Totalize very high in the league of battle results. It is therefore
necessary to look at what went wrong subsequently.

In the early morning of 8 August most of Phase 1 battle groups were on
or nearing their targets. There was at that point no question of total failure
but simply frustration at delay along the extreme right flank and at Tilly. By
normal battle standards, casualties had been light. It looked as though the

enemy were 'there to be taken'. The Canadian 4th Armoured Division was assembling near Fleury and the Polish 1st Armoured Division was heading into Cormelles where 1st Northamptonshire Yeomanry and 144/148 RAC had assembled the day before. Simonds had planned another leap forward from the armed camps of Saint-Aignan, Cramesnil, Gaumesnil and Caillouet. Anything was possible. Totalize is a gambler's word. There was a large element of gambling in the expectations raised by Totalize, as with Goodwood. Simonds was doing his best to equate expectations with reality in a situation where the gamblers had forgotten to hedge their bets.

Back at Cormelles, Fleury and Ifs conditions were, if anything, worse than for the well-marshalled Night March. The armoured columns had devastated assembly areas and roads. Advance lanes, already badly cratered before the Night March, were further complicated by the inevitable detritus of the confused battle. Wyn Griffith-Jones, revisiting his potato field, noticed the six knocked-out armoured vehicles clustered together 'at handshaking distance'. This obstacle course was also being used in reverse by the returning traffic of wounded and prisoners, as well as vehicles being towed for repairs. The Germans had sent a considerable barrage of heavy shells down on the assembly areas. Capt Robert Anderson, temporarily with the 1st Black Watch echelon, had climbed a high water tower to see the sights. He came down quicker than he went up when it received close enemy artillery attention.

Dragoon Birt described the exhilarating but frightening situation which greeted the early daylight:

> Even stranger were the experiences of the dangerous hours at dawn when the mist rolled over Caen plain, making it impossible for those who were lost and those whose tanks were lying at crazy angles among the bomb craters to tell where they were or where was friend and where was enemy . . . the country was full of scattered parties of Germans who had not been rounded up. As they were quite without news of the result of the fighting, stranded crews dismounted their machine-guns and stood their ground, waiting for the mist to lift and release them from the nerve-racking doubts about their positions.[1]

For Phase 2 the Canadian armour, under Maj-Gen Kitching, had formed an advanced guard called 'Halpenny Force'. This consisted of 22 CAR (the Grenadier Guards of Canada) and a motor regiment, the Lake Superior. The force was commanded by Grenadier Lt-Col Halpenny. It was ordered to move up from the assembly area at 08.45. By noon it had moved very little distance because of problems of traffic and terrain, as well as the disturbance caused by continued resistance in Fontenay and May and also across the main road at Tilly.[2] Up to this moment there might not have been any irretrievable damage done. But a new element was about to make its impact.

The Night March had been successfully supported by RAF bombing. The plan was that Phase 2 should commence with a similar air bombardment by the US Army Air Force. The bombs would begin to fall at 12.26 and continue until 12.55 when the Phase 2 tanks would roll forward. The air-raid

A Highland medic, John Watt, 1st Black Watch, prepares his kit for the Night March. In action medics were universally attentive to the wounded of other units and, where possible, to those of the enemy.
(IWM, B8804)

targets were on a line about a mile forward of the Phase 1 troops at locations where it was assumed the enemy would be either digging in, in desperation, or massing for a counter-attack. The margin of safety between bomb targets and ground troops was much larger than for the night raid.

A force of 678 heavy bombers was assembled for an attack on four targets. One target at Gouvix was difficult to identify and a sole Flying Fortress bombed that site. Altogether 492 bombers identified targets and dropped bombs. Three of the targets received the majority of those bombs. However, subsequent debate has centred on two tragic aspects of the raid. The first aberration was when two of the air groups dropped their bombs on Allied positions. A second debate of wider strategy relates to the timing of the raid. German critics have pointed out that a lacuna of several hours existed between the arrival of the first Phase 1 troops on their objectives and the launch of Phase 2. This interval enabled the enemy to organize rapid but effective counter-measures. Phase 2 was firmly locked into the timing of the American raid. Had it been possible to vary or cancel the air raid, it is argued that ground troops could have surged forward, as Lt-Col Gordon and Maj Radley-Walters proposed (and as driver Stan Hicken and other troopers wondered about), catching the disorganized defenders before they could produce any buffer moves. This can be argued later in the book.

It might seem that a few 'friendly' bombs should not have disrupted such a massive mission as Phase 2. In a number of instances the misplaced friendliness caused serious casualties and the total impact on Phase 2 may well have been decisive in swaying the balance between a difficult task and an improbable achievement. The US Air Force's own historian judged it to be 'gross errors on the part of two twelve-plane groups'.[3] This may have been a little unjust in one case, for the best evidence seems to be that a lead bomber was hit by anti-aircraft fire while still over Caen, causing it, possibly without human intervention, to shed its bomb load. As was the system, the remaining bombers of the group followed suit and dropped their bombs. In the other incident it was considered to be a miscalculation by the leading bombardier, which again was imitated by some, if not all, of his group. The impact on individual and particular units was dramatic. Charlie Robertson of 7th Black Watch was back in the assembly area on echelon duty, fully 4 miles short of the bombers' objectives, when bombs began to fall 100 yd or so away, 'plastering a Canadian Medium Battery'. Ian Hammerton vividly describes the horror of friendly fire:

> We looked upwards, and they were so low we could read the identifying numbers and even see the crews in the planes as they passed over us. Their bomb doors were open and to our horror we could clearly see the bombs falling from their racks . . . as the scream of the missiles reached us we could not believe our ears or eyes. The crump of the bombs as they exploded in the field beside us stimulated us into instinctive action . . . we sprawled on the ground breathing in dust under the tank.[4]

The sight was not horrific to everybody. A German officer tells the story about German troops jumping out of their slit trenches and cheering because they thought the Luftwaffe had at last mounted a raid. When the soldiers realized that the Allies were bombing themselves their cheers changed to laughter.[5] Some Allied ground troops were beginning to refer to the 8th and 9th US Air Forces as the 8th and 9th Luftwaffe, because of friendly fire incidents.[6] A survey of casualties removes any tendency to find the occurrences amusing. The Canadian official historian quotes an authoritative survey which took place three days later:

> The casualties caused by this bombing, including the Poles', were estimated as about 65 killed and 250 wounded. Four medium or heavy guns, some 55 vehicles and a considerable amount of ammunition were also lost. The Canadian unit hardest hit was probably the North Shore (New Brunswick) Regiment . . . it lost about 100 officers and men and one company was wholly ineffective for the operations.[7]

In fact the North Shore Regiment, which went ashore on D-Day, lost more men to the 8 August bombing than they did in the assault on the beaches on 6 June. Maj-Gen Keller, commander of the Canadian 3rd Infantry Division, was badly wounded and had to be evacuated. The CO, adjutant and medical team of 5th Black Watch were all thrown out of their vehicles but survived.

In 148 RAC their RSM, Keegan, was killed. Veteran RSM Jelley of 1st Northamptonshire Yeomanry, who had seen the ravages of the First World War, saw men disappear in the bomb blasts and remarked, 'No trace of 'em. Not even a hand to shake goodbye to, like you found in the old trenches'.[8]

There is probably little that is more demoralizing to troops than to be the recipients of fire from their own side. In the congested conditions of the assembly areas it was inevitable that casualties and damage would be serious. Even more serious was the delay caused to the Polish division which was already struggling to arrive at its start line on time. Such haste was not conducive to cool appraisal of situations. And in the meantime, having seen the first USAAF marker plane flying across their lines and having taken advantage of the lull in the Allied advance, the Germans had contrived to patch together a dangerous counter-attack group and insert it into the area forward of the Allied positions which would not be bombed. The general outcome of the air raid was more damaging to the Allies than to the enemy, in more ways than one.

The Polish Armoured Division had arrived in Normandy with great enthusiasm and impatience to join the battle, now two months after D-Day. They had many grudge debts to pay off against the enemy which had opened the First World War by launching the first real Blitzkrieg against their homeland. Some of them had actually been fighting on and off since 1939, before any of the other Allied troops were actively engaged. Their general was the high commander with longest current war experience. Now they were almost in sight of the enemy and, as one of the Poles, Zbigniew Mieckzkowski, of the 2nd Armoured Regiment said, 'We were just waiting to get at them'.

The Polish commander was Maj-Gen Stanislas Maczek. He had fought in the First World War and had also seen action against the Bolsheviks in 1919–20. A regular Polish officer, he was given command of one of the Poland's first two armoured formations in October 1938. This was the 10th Cavalry Brigade which was equipped with 7-ton Vickers tanks at a time when most of the Polish cavalry still used horses. The war began on 1 September 1939 and on that day Maczek went into action with his brigade. It fought with such tenacity that its members were named the 'Black Devils' by the Germans. One of those who fought in Normandy recalled those early war days:

> [in 1939] well disciplined and patriotic this Polish Army inflicted on the Germans, twice their number and superior in equipment, losses similar in casualties but greater in tanks and equipment than they sustained later when defeating the Anglo-French forces in 1940.
>
> Amongst the Polish Cavalry Brigades the 10th had already become mechanised before the war. Under the command of Colonel Stanislas Maczek, from its first encounters south of Cracow and up until the defence of Lwow, she delayed in battles the advance of the enemy Armoured Corps, often fighting against the 2nd German Panzer Division. A few years later luck gave the 10th Cavalry Brigade the well deserved revenge by surprising the same Division at night in Normandy, dispersing its headquarters and spreading general confusion.[9]

The Poles arrive. Montgomery with Maj-Gen S. Maczek inspecting. (IWM, B8762)

Once the German invasion had overrun Poland many Polish soldiers were made prisoners by the Russians advancing from the east. Then, when the Germans in turn invaded Russia those prisoners of war were released to join the free Polish forces. Others, in the chaos of 1939, found their ways through the byways of Europe, Asia and Africa, first to France (before the Dunkirk debacle) and then to Britain. So to describe the 1st Polish Armoured Division as 'green' is only partially accurate as regards the formation and totally inaccurate in describing its general and many lesser ranks.

As a result of their many journeyings the Poles earned another soubriquet from the Germans, this time as 'the Sikorsi Tourists', from the name of their supreme commander of free Polish forces. Sikorsi gave to Maczek the task of forming the 1st Polish Armoured Division around the 10th Armoured Cavalry Brigade for the 'Second Front' in Europe. For the two months since D-Day the division had continued training in Britain but their complaint was that no information on tactics had been passed through from Normandy. It was clear that the conditions encountered in Normandy would require special consideration but the Poles found it difficult to obtain guidance. To make matters worse, Maczek's chief of staff was sent to Normandy on a fact-finding mission and was killed there. So one of the Polish soldiers subsequently stated that the first four days in action during Totalize were in reality a further training period for the division, a stint which might have been undertaken prior to arriving in France.[10]

Even if their training proved rather inadequate, there was an aura about the Poles which cause certain trepidation in the enemy ranks. The British XXII Dragoons provided flail support for the Poles and one Dragoon, Ian Hammerton witnessed something of that unique reaction. He had come across a wounded German soldier and called a Polish doctor:

> He agreed to send two burly stretcher-bearers to carry our prisoner to the side of the track and promised to pick him up later. When the two Poles bent over the youngster to lift him onto the stretcher, he caught sight of their arm flashes, 'Poland. Nein,' he cried, 'Nein, Nein!' I often wondered what became of him.[11]

One problem which had not been adequately addressed was that of language. The attitude of higher command seems to have been at the least lackadaisical. Another Dragoon remarked on this:

> Our task was made exceptionally difficult because none of us spoke Polish and very few Poles spoke English. Radio communication was out of the question, and in the time available for discussion it was not easy to explain to Polish commanders that our machines were not merely so many extra gun tanks, but were special devices to be employed if they ran into minefields.[12]

This might produce its comic moments but a comic moment at a serious juncture may not be the best strategy. Angus Stewart was GSO3 at 51 HD headquarters at the time:

> Their Liaison Officer with us kept us in fits of laughter. He had married a girl in Perth but she couldn't have understood much of what he said. He rushed in very excited one day and said, 'Is informations of much Germans tank. Is not good! Is two hundred fifty Tigers in wood.' Later he came back and said ' Is good, only forty to fifty tank.' At first he had only heard '. . . to fifty' in a report of ' forty to fifty'. In fact they were only seven, and those not Tigers.[13]

As Maj-Gen Maczek made his final plans most Poles were aware of Montgomery's challenge to the division. Using his familiar 'hinge' imagery 'Monty' had demonstrated how the Americans were opening a door through the German lines on the far right, while the hinge of the door rested upon the Caen area. Now the Poles were to be sent in to smash the hinge. In more practical terms that meant an immediate attempt to break through to the area of Cauvicourt and Saint-Sylvain about 2 miles south of the front British positions at Saint-Aignan. The first wave would be provided by the 10th Armoured Cavalry Brigade with the XXII Dragoons bringing up their flails, followed by one anti-tank battery and one anti-aircraft battery plus a company of Engineers. In close support would be the Polish 8th Rifle Battalion. The 10th Mounted Rifle Regiment, with an anti-tank battery, would seal off the left flank which had been perilously open since 1st

Polish armour moving up to battle. Shermans left, Cromwells right. (IWM, B8835)

Northamptonshire Yeomanry had completed their Night March almost ten hours previously.

Maczek's own 1939 command, the brigade, was now commanded by Col T. Majewski. The Recce Regiment, 10th Mounted Rifles lost its commander, Lt-Col J. Maciejowski, and Maj J. Wasilewski took over. One of the armoured regiments, the 24th Lancers, also lost its commander, Lt-Col J.W. Kranski, who died of wounds, with Maj R. Dowdor replacing him. The other armoured units were 1st Armoured Regiment (Stefanowicz), 2nd Armoured Regiment (Koszutski) and 10th Dragoons (Zgorzelski).[14] These units had formed up behind Saint-Aignan. They had been delayed by traffic through and beyond Caen. They were still in place early enough to have to wait until the planned bombardment by US planes had saturated the defences against which they were to advance. In the event, the supposedly static German defences had not been obliterated and German formations were between the bombing line and the Allied Forward Defended Localities. It may be that language inhibited total exchange of information just then.

There appears to be some discrepancy about the actual time of the Polish advance, with various accounts citing 13.00, 13.35 and 13.55. The history compiled by officers of the division in 1945 states the time as 13.35 hours. Together the two leading Polish regiments moved forward. 24th Lancers had a complement of 52 Shermans (43 × 75 mm, and 9 × 17-pdr) and 11 Honey light tanks, and personnel of 45 officers and 620 Other Ranks. That regiment was to move between 1st Northamptonshire Yeomanry and 144 RAC, striking south towards Cauvicourt on the right. 2nd Polish Armoured Regiment, with a similar full-strength complement, was to loop around the left of the Yeomanry and 1st Black Watch, passing Robertmesnil in the general direction of Estrees and Saint-Sylvain. There were a number of fatal factors which presaged doom. Firstly, the leading regiments did not seem to be fully aware that numbers of 88 mm anti-tank guns and tanks still dominated the distant ridge; or that Panzer Grenadiers had infiltrated into woods and hedgerows, although without ousting the Highlanders and their tank support; or that two Escort Companies (HQ defence units) were being rushed up in the gap between Robertmesnil and Saint-Sylvain. Secondly, there appeared to be an idea that the mobile and reliable Sherman at full speed could drive into the enemy lines and enable the tough Polish fighters to exact the vengeance they so much desired against their 1939 oppressors.

The Yeomanry tank crews had suddenly become veterans in tank warfare and fully realized the Sherman's inability to cross open fields unscathed. They were also very aware of the enemy dangers lurking in the undergrowth and behind clever camouflage in hedgerows. Guns capable of shattering a Sherman turret at 2,000 yd were now waiting within 200 yd just beyond the gully. The German counter-attack, which had collided with the defences of hidden British tanks, now reverted itself into defensive positions where its equipment was superlative.

On the far left, Lt Tony Faulkner, who had recently been brewed up and was now commanding another tank behind a ruined wall, watched in horror. A squadron of Shermans came rumbling along behind the chateau. Tony thought it was the Northants 'B' Squadron coming up to reinforce 'C'. Then he saw the distinctive Polish cap badges, much bigger and easier to distinguish than the Yeomanry's little silver horse. He wanted to shout a warning. The tanks were theoretically in open order but only a touch of the gun traverse apart one from another. The gunners in two German Mark IVs must have been utterly flabbergasted to see the sight, but lost no time in firing shot after shot. While Tony Faulkner watched speechless, from Sherman after Sherman there blossomed the unmistakable flowering of flash, smoke and dust, marking the impact of armour-piercing shot. Then the puff of flame and smoke out of turret or engine. The scramble of men, some immune, others on fire, out of the blazing vehicle. The devastating roar of turrets being blown off and ammunition sending fireworks high into the air.

Many of the Polish tanks tried to fire their guns but without any clear sighting of opponents. More tanks brewed. Others began to circle and dash for shelter. Machine-gun fire plucked at survivors. Someone remarked that it was like watching a field full of haystacks set on fire by an arsonist. A freak of battlefield positioning meant that although the German defenders within 200–500 yd of the 1st Northamptonshire Yeomanry had the Poles in full view, the thick belt of trees along the gully blocked the Yeomanry's view of any German gun. Shots were fired towards the German position and once or twice a tiny glimpse of armour was seen but there was nothing that the English Yeomen or accompanying Highlanders could do to save the Polish squadron during the fatal five minutes or so when it was totally exposed. The defenders had demonstrated that by that time of the day there was no daylight route around the east of Robertmesnil on 8 August.

On the right, Capt Tom Boardman had tried to call the Poles, whom he saw heading for similar trouble. These were the 24th Lancers. Their enthusiasm was such that it is unlikely that they would have been totally deterred from at least an initial charge against the enemy.[15] Another history describes their fate:

> From hedges along the road teams of SS men armed with *Panzerfaust* and *Panzerschreck* waited patiently, while behind them the anti-tank guns opened up at maximum range and destroyed the tanks of the first wave. Polish tanks began to burn . . . machine guns opened up on the tank crews racing for cover . . . petrol from the burning tanks had ignited the corn.[16]

Again, as with timing, there are discrepancies in the descriptions of the battle, as is common in the heat of complicated action. One account speaks of guns firing at maximum range. Driver Stan Hicken, looking for a spare escape hatch for 3 Baker the next day, counted sixteen Polish tanks 'in an average field of about five acres. There were two SP guns facing them'. The SPs were also knocked out and still lodged in the hedge at the end of the field.

Polish troops continued to probe forward, but the original concept of a cavalry charge over 2 miles had changed to a cautious inching through thick undulating country. Maczek records the division's losses as more than 40 tanks that day. Over the three days of Polish effort in Totalize the total losses rose to 66 tanks plus 12 other guns. Personnel casualties were 656 killed, missing and wounded.[17]

Detailed returns of the 2nd Armoured Regiment on the left show that their available 43 Shermans (75 mm) had been reduced to 23, their 9 Firefly tanks to 4, and their 11 Stuarts (Honeys) to 9, a total of 27 lost, although some of these may have been normal breakdowns as the regiment recorded 20 tanks lost. Their lieutenant, Roman Sikora, was the first man killed in action. He and 10 other ranks of the regiment died; 3 officers and 32 other ranks were wounded and 1 officer and 5 other ranks were missing at the end of the day. Similar records of 24th Lancers reveal 30 tanks destroyed or under repair on the evening of 8 August. For those Poles who had not previously seen action this could truly be called a baptism of fire. The baptism of fire had inevitably become a cremation by fire for those who rode what the Germans, so apt with nicknames, called the 'Tommy Cookers'.

The 4th Canadian Armoured Division under Maj-Gen Kitching was due to start its Phase 2 advance on the right of the main Caen to Falaise road at the same time as the Poles on the left. Units of the 4th did move at the planned time of 13.55 hours. However, there seemed still to be some confusion, both of traffic towards the rear, and of mission. Some German accounts speak as though the Canadian armour was suffering to the same extent as the Poles. The official history records a hold up caused by German resistance at Gaumesnil. That village was eventually occupied by one of the Phase 1 units, the Royal Regiment of Canada, at 15.30 hours. Maj Radley-Walters' 'A' Squadron, which had completed the Night March with only three tanks lost, had been sitting on the Gaumesnil position for several hours

Polish tanks on parade. This aptly illustrates the difference between the 75 mm Sherman and the Firefly. At Saint-Aignan the ratio would have been only one Firefly for every three 75s in a troop of four tanks. (Tank Museum, photo 2725/E4)

before it was officially occupied by infantry. And 'Rad's' squadron, the nearest to the main road, was not wiped out in the eventual epic battle with the Wittmann troop of Tigers. At times a suspicion of exaggeration enters into the records of the day on both sides of the battle lines.

A reasonable reading of events could be that the Canadian Phase 2 armour on the right continued to penetrate the enemy positions, but without any of the dangerous Polish *élan* and perhaps with a little too much of the opposite vein of caution. What Simonds had demanded was a rapid advance, presumably paced somewhere between the first Polish tearaway tactics and the 4th Canadian 'feel your way', the latter course very understandable in the circumstances around 14.00 hours. By that time, the gap seen by Mel Gordon and Radley-Walters, and feared by 'Panzer' Meyer, had disappeared. The 4th Armoured had unfortunately inherited inappropriate expectations. Towards 18.00 hours the Argyll & Sutherland Highlanders of Canada with the South Alberta Regiment had entered Cintheaux. Some of the Argylls pushed on until they encountered the massive quarry beyond Haut Mesnil. On the extreme right, the Calgary Highlanders and Le Regiment de Maisonneuve with the 1st Hussars captured the key town of Bretteville-sur-Laize, although they were delayed because the available artillery was still supporting another attack. The entire Canadian Phase 2 push had been carried on against a considerable screen of 88 mm guns from the Luftwaffe, which acted with some independence within the military dispositions.[18]

At any other moment since D-Day, on the British and Canadian sector of Normandy, the 8 August advance up to nightfall would have been heralded as a significant advance by troops, the more experienced of whom had come to consider 500 yd a well-won victory. In the light of the requirements imposed on Totalize the advance was less than planned. It provoked the kind of disappointment which might be suffered by a gambler at the Totalizater who had put all his money on a horse which was unlikely to win a very hazardous long-distance race.

Again in the context of the requirements imposed on Totalize, what happened next was even more detrimental to expectations. Simonds required the forward Phase 2 units to continue pressing forward during the night. They failed to respond. No real reason has been advanced for this. The Phase 2 forces were markedly superior in numbers to the defenders who were tired, short of supplies and attempting almost ridiculous feats of military improvisation. The 4th Armoured Division had worked its way into a spearhead position along the main road which Simonds wanted extended during the night, while the Poles would gradually move to a site from which they could attack Cauvicourt at first light. The 344 Independent Searchlight Battery, RA, which had provided Monty Moonlight for the Night March, now moved 3 miles forward to set up a further display for the benefit of the attacking and reconnoitering forward troops. These orders and preparations did not produce a significant move forward except for one endeavour which ended in tragedy and possibly brought to an end all hopes for a knockout conclusion to Totalize.

Brig E.L. Booth, commanding the 4th Armoured Brigade, ordered the British Columbia Regiment (28 CAR) with the Algonquin infantry to advance to Point 195 by first light. The British Columbia commander, Lt-Col D.G. Worthington, took charge of what came to be known as Worthington Force. Their advance involved a left hook, around Bretteville-le-Rabet village, and then a right incline across the main road, not the simplest of operations for a new unit. In the open but confused country, with sporadic opposition and indistinct light, Worthington Force lost its way, passing to the left of Estrees village instead of to the right. The force eventually consolidated on high ground almost 4 miles from its objective, having confused the D131 with the main Falaise road. At 06.50 the group reported it was on its objective. By about 08.30 enemy tanks had located and attacked Worthington Force. Soon the Canadians were encircled and attempts to locate them and provide support were unsuccessful. To all intents and purposes the force had ceased to exist, in spite of heroic individual efforts by the hopelessly isolated soldiers. At the end of the day (9 August) a few men managed to find their way through the German encirclement, but Worthington himself was killed. The British Columbia Regiment lost 47 tanks. The tank regiment and the two companies of the Algonquins which had accompanied them lost a total of about 240 officers and men, including about 80 who were taken prisoner. Stacey rounds off the tragic story with the apt comment:

Such losses would have been deeply regrettable even had they been the price of success. Unfortunately they were suffered in the course of a tactical reverse which did much to prevent us from seizing a strategical opportunity of the first magnitude . . . the episode, with its tragic mixture of gallantry and ineptitude, had been appallingly costly.[19]

The momentum of Totalize had been lost. A considerable amount of territory had been gained and serious blows dealt to the enemy's strength. The battle was poised, as the Germans were aware, so that the next hammer blow would inevitably smash through to Falaise or wherever else a trap could be closed on the German 7th Army. That was not as much as Simonds' plan had envisaged or deserved. It was certainly not what Montgomery wanted in the time-scale. It is always easy to criticize with hindsight and the facility of a computer keyboard which does not shoot back. An eminent historian has commented, particularly with Worthington Force in mind, that, 'it was an awful warning of the dangers inherent in cornering first-class German formations, however battle-worn and whatever the odds stacked against them.[20]

Greater strategic opportunities may have been missed, but for the footslogger and the tankie on the ground it had been a tough fight, leading more than once to the elimination of an entire unit on one side or other. One of the British Dragoons surveyed the scene:

We lay in a rough orchard beneath whose meagre skin of soil was a deep layer of limestone that made the digging of shelters a task only for the strongest . . . the trees were torn by shellfire, and among them was spilled the wreckage of battle – the scorched frame of a Spitfire, two abandoned German self-propelled guns, a litter of shell cases, and the graves of two or three German soldiers hurriedly buried beneath mounds of limestone, from which under the sun there drifted the sickly stench of corruption . . . the mosquitoes and horse-flies were merciless, robbers of our rest.[21]

There were long pauses between outbursts of strife. In those fairly quiet moments the men nearest to earth found the insect life more annoying than the man-made wrath:

Flies and mosquitoes became more than just a nuisance. While up front I was bitten so badly about the face that I had to stop shaving after slicing the tops off the half-healed bites. The Sergeant-Major saw my stubble and reported me to the company commander, who gave me three days 'spud bashing' when the Argylls passed through us and we were placed in reserve.[22]

Peter Simonds, the brother of Guy Simonds the Canadian commander, was himself up front and recorded the human tragedy:

. . . the corpses of German anti-tank gunners scattered in grotesque positions round their gun. It had been put out of action by the crew, now dead, of the last of nine Polish Sherman tanks, which was burning merrily 65 metres away. . . . Not far away, Peter Simonds, whose duties with the Royal Canadian signals led him to supervise the laying of telephone lines along a new slice of captured road, noticed a German who appeared to be hanging over the metal fence of a field. It was only half a man. Simonds spotted the other half of the trunk lying in the middle of the road. . . . He approached . . . and read on the lapel of the tunic the number of the 89th German Infantry Division.[23]

Meanwhile, for some of those of Phase 1 still in jeopardy behind the enemy lines, things were working out rather better than they might have hoped. L/Cpl Dursley had been taken prisoner when he was a driver in Lt Wyn Griffiths-Jones' troop, which had been the first to suffer losses during the Northamptonshire Yeomanry's Night March. He was expecting to spend the rest of the war behind barbed wire somewhere in Germany. Held for the time being in one of the strongly fortified villages, he was called before a rather nervous German commander who stated that they were about to surrender the village. Would Dursley certify to the incoming troops that he had been treated well by his captors? Dursley felt that the Germans had observed the Geneva Convention except for the inevitable initial rush to search him for souvenirs such as his watch, pen and pistol. He assured the German officer that he had no complaints.

Dursley's capture was, in itself, a most courteous event. He was crawling along a ditch in the potato field, trying to distance himself from his burning tank. He came face to face with a German tank man also crawling along the same ditch in the opposite direction, also trying to escape from a possible explosion of his tank. The German spoke good English. He suggested that, as the Germans were in the majority, and well armed, in the potato field, Dursley should become his prisoner. Now that the tables were again turned, the German commander found a large white sheet and a pole to which to attach it. He then asked Dursley if he would march out with him at the head of the village garrison, who were already lined up smartly in the village square.[24] Do the gods of war forget? Later, in Holland, Dursley's tank was knocked out. He was again taken prisoner, for the rest of the war!

About the time that Dursley was leaping out of a blazing Sherman tank, John Torrans was jumping out of a blazing Lancaster bomber. He landed in a field near a canal in thick fog. After wandering for a while he took the risk of seeking refuge in a French farm and was happy to receive a warm welcome. He had 'landed' on the Resistance. So, too, had his navigator, Flt Lt Hill. Their pilot had also survived, but badly wounded and needing hospital treatment. This could only be obtained as a prisoner of war. Torrans and Hill were kitted out as farm labourers of a slovenliness not becoming RAF air crew. Hill had broken an ankle during the jump but the French had loaned him a bicycle and after cycling about 4 miles near Le Havre he was then carried to a cave where Torrans was hiding. A local Resistance man, Emile Schild, brought a Dr Evin to treat their injuries, John Torrans having a bullet lodged in his thigh although able to walk.

They were given hospitality and refuge on the farm of M. B. Beauvais near Oudalle for three weeks until British troops arrived in the area. Their return to duty was by motor cycle to an artillery unit, by Auster aircraft to the Normandy beaches and by tank landing craft back to Britain, arriving back about four weeks after H-Hour of Totalize.[25]

Escapers! Shot down during Totalize, Flt Lt Alan Hill (right) and flight engineer John Torrans disguised as French farm labourers while being sheltered by the French Resistance.

It was very much a case of swings and roundabouts. Tom Boardman, who had navigated the Northamptonshire Yeomanry through the Night March and then fought Tigers, was promoted to major, given command of 'B' Squadron, wounded in the leg and repatriated to Britain, all within about twenty-four hours. Brig Harry Scott had sent a letter of congratulations to his three colonels of 33rd Armoured Brigade for their part in Phase 1. The CO of 148 RAC, Lt-Col R.G. Cracroft, MC, read his letter and almost immediately was killed by a shell. The men of 148 had hardly recovered from the shock of losing their colonel when they learned that the regiment was to be broken up and dispersed as reinforcements to other units. Some reward for their work in the cauldron of Tilly-la-Campagne!

TOP SECRET.

APPENDIX A.
I.S.9/WEA/2/357/2055.

The following information was obtained from BRITISH personnel who
have been repatriated.

If further circulation of this information is made, it is important
that its source should not be divulged.

EVADER'S NAME, etc.:- 123999 F/Lt. Alan Faulkner HILL,
582 Sqn., Bomber Command, R.A.F.

DATE OF INTERVIEW:- 4 Sep 44.

DATE.	NAME AND ADDRESS.	REMARKS.
(1) 8 Aug - 1 Sep 44.	M. B. BEAUVAIS, ELEVEUR, A OUDALLE (N.W. EUROPE, 1:250,000, Sheet 4, L 62), SEINE INF.	Food and shelter throughout.
(2) Aug 44.	M. Emile SCHILD, (address unknown, but often at above farm).	Leader, local Resistance Group. Contacted LONDON by French Intell. (Und.).
(3) Aug 44.	Docteur EVIN, ST. ROMAIN DE COLBOSC (L 62), SEINE INF.	Bandaged burns and sprains.

D. Johnson S/O

I.S.9. Lieut. Colonel.

Top Secret! Part of Alan Hill's Evader's Report cites French helpers.

After Totalize had stuttered to a temporary halt, it was decided to launch
another well-planned offensive called Tractable. This would, to use the word of
the day, 'bash on' finally to Falaise and close the Falaise pocket. In this operation
the Poles showed their true mettle against some of the most fanatical defence of
the entire war by the diminishing numbers of survivors of the Hitlerjugend.
Although Falaise was captured at last, this did not seal the trap on the retreating
Germans as the bolt of the trap had shifted east to Chambois where the
northern Allies would meet the Americans. Polish units were cut off in the last
phase of the Falaise battle and also in finally closing the Chambois trap. They
had the misfortune to seal the gap and become the target of every German
attempt to break out. When the gap had been closed the Poles found that:

once the destruction was achieved the Polish units were not able to cross
over to hill 262 South, as the road was completely blocked with the
wreckage; heavy smoke exuding from the still burning fires hid everything
from view. The crisis reached its height on the 20th. The Germans fully

realising that their last road of retreat had been blocked, directed their attacks in a concentrated fury born of desperation on each and every unit of the (Polish) Division. . . . They managed to penetrate . . . cutting off the road to Polish Supply Companies carrying essentials to the fighting troops and threatening Polish positions from a hitherto secure direction. Hills thickly covered by trees and bushes were very difficult to patrol and German tanks approached the very edge of Polish positions. An excellent illustration of this was the wrecks of Panthers and Shermans standing facing each other, gun to gun, destroyed by nearly point blank fire. . . . Supplies by air drop, arranged from England, proved a failure. Attempts to evacuate the wounded ended in failure. The soldiers were using the last of their ammunition . . . exhausted by lack of sleep . . . the suffering of the wounded, among whom the mortality rate was mounting quickly, became more harrowing. . . . Prisoners began to outnumber the defenders. The soldiers were at the end of their endurance.[26]

By 21 August the German efforts began to weaken and masses of prisoners surrendered. Most of the Poles felt that they had exacted some kind of vengeance for 1939, the defeat of an army against the defeat of an army. An added source of gratification for the Poles was that a German SS officer whom they had captured in 1939 (and who was released when the Germans proved victorious) was now captured for the second and final time at the Falaise or Chambois gap.

On 9 August the 51st Highland Division battalions, which had been forming the firm base for Totalize, moved forward and to the left and, by taking the villages of Conteville and Poussy-la-Campagne, finally closed off any danger from the fields sloping down from Saint-Aignan. The Highland Division and the 33rd Armoured Brigade were then removed from the control of Lt-Gen Simonds' corps and reverted to British 3 Corps, which was also under command of the Canadian army. The 51st and 33rd Armoured grouping, which would persist until the River Rhine, was directed towards the River Seine via St Pierre-sur-Dives, Lisieux and Bourg-Achard.

This advance, which was slowed down more than once to await flank troops moving less quickly, was a supporting 'side show' which, given other concepts in the high command, could have been raced ahead to make a double lock on what is still frequently known as the 'Falaise Pocket'.

148 RAC had assisted in the capture of Poussy-la-Campagne. The crews were then called together and told of their posting to other units, 140 of them to 144 RAC and 80 to 1st Northamptonshire Yeomanry. Tank crews from the East Riding Yeomanry arrived and took over the 148 RAC Shermans and Honeys en bloc. By 27 August the brief life of the 148 RAC had come to an end, the fate of the most junior numbers in the army lists. The 59th Infantry Division was disbanded on the same premise that, efficient or not, the junior numbers must be cannibalized to provide reinforcements for senior formations.

The commander of the 4th Canadian Armoured Division, which had experienced such a torrid time in Phase 2, Maj-Gen Kitching, was relieved of his command, albeit reluctantly, by Simonds. The corps commander had also intended to relieve Maj-Gen Foulkes, but was not supported in this by Crerar.[27] Simonds had learned two lessons which he put to good use later on. He was able to build up the tiny force of quickly adapted Kangaroos into battalion strength, now using the Canadian Ram tanks (Sherman derivatives) with turrets removed, as the 'Holy Rollers' had to be returned to their owners. He also repeated a version of the Night March later in the war near Calcar in Germany. For a time Simonds commanded the 1st Canadian Army while Crerar was on sick leave.

After the war Simonds served as senior instructor at the Imperial Defence College. He then commanded the Canadian National Defence College. Eventually he was appointed Canada's Chief of the General Staff, but not, surprisingly, until after that position had been occupied by the man whom he had tried to depose in Normandy, Foulkes. Lt-Gen G.G. Simonds, CB, CBE, DSO, was CIGS during the Korean War in which Canadian troops were again in action.[28]

Lt-Col Doug Forster returned to command the 1st Northamptonshire Yeomanry after recovering from wounds, only to be seriously injured again on the banks of the River Rhine. There the Yeomanry were driving amphibious Buffaloes to ferry 51st Highland Division across that wide obstacle. One of their first duties after landing was to bring back the body of the much-lamented Maj-Gen Rennie, the 51st commander who had been in charge of the left flank of Totalize Phase 1. Capt Tom Boardman became an MP, a government minister and a life peer as Lt-Col the Rt Hon. the Lord Boardman, MC, TD, DL.

Of other Phase 1 commanders, the British Camerons' CO became Gen Sir Derek Lang, KCB, DSO, MC, DL, including in his career the command of 51st Highland Division. John Hopwood, 'Geordie' Andrews and 'Rad' Radley-Walters all became brigadiers (or brigadier-general). Among the other ranks, crack shot Joe Ekins went back to shoes and became a factory manager. Aiming for a less offensive type of conflict he became a Judo expert and was chairman of the Championship Committee organizing Judo national and international events at the Crystal Palace. Rex Jackson won the Military Medal in Holland and Stan Hicken became well known among veteran car enthusiasts as a Shelsley Walsh hill climber.

The fate of the Poles was not always so kind. Many of them realized that they would no longer be welcome in their homeland under a Communist regime. Many of them settled in Britain and a number of them congregate from time to time at the Polish Institute in London, with its museum and war archives. There Zbigniew Mieczkowski and others are always happy to share their recollections of 1944 with any visitor. Another hero of Falaise, recce lieutenant Jerzy Niewinowski, who had become a 'Sikorski Tourist' from Lwow University, married one of the Polish women soldiers liberated by the Polish Armoured Division from Oberlangen Camp in 1945. They elected to return to Poland. As a result of his service in democratic countries, 'George' Niewinowski was subjected to many years of interrogation by secret police and suffered resultant psychiatric disorders, dying in 1980 after completing the memoirs quoted briefly above.

In some ways the most tragic yet consummate life history was that of Lt-Gen Maczek himself. Unable to return to Communist Poland, with the Polish army in Europe disbanded, no pension and no civilian skills, he drifted back to Scotland. He was partly supported by friends but also worked as a part-time barman in Edinburgh in order to show some kind of independence. He lived in poverty and relative anonymity until the age of a hundred. Came the Gdansk shipyard strikes. Came democracy in Poland. Came Lech Walewska to Scotland. The patriotic shipyard worker, now President, promoted the heroic 'Sikorski Tourist' to the rank of full general with an appropriate pension from democratic Poland in 1992.[29]

Chapter Eight

The Opponent's Corner

'Soldiers, our position is undoubtedly difficult. . . . All the same, what we have to do is to surmount our difficulties like brave men, not to give in, but to try, if we can, to win honour and safety by victory. And, if that is beyond us, then at least to die with honour.' (Xenophon, 400 BC)

The tough young commander of the tough young Hitlerjugend Division, Standartenführer (Colonel) Kurt 'Panzer' Meyer, was having one of the worst days of his career:

> I got out of my car and my knees were trembling, the sweat pouring down my face . . . before me, making their way down the Caen-Falaise road in a disorderly rabble, were the panic-stricken troops of 89 Infantry Division . . . . I lit a cigar, stood in the middle of the road, and in a loud voice asked them if they were going to leave me alone to cope with the enemy.[1]

Ever since Meyer uttered those dramatic words to Milton Shulman in an interview during August 1945 his graphic portrayal has tended to colour all other views of the action between Phases 1 and 2 of Operation Totalize. Whether intended or not, the words tend to show the SS Panzer commander as heroic, if not cool, and the infantry of the 89th ordinary division as a broken horde of cowards. It does not entirely pervert the truth, but it is somewhat less than fair to many men of the 89th.

The Canadian official historian admits that 'the forces available to the enemy to deal with "Totalize" were, on the face of it, very inadequate'. Nevertheless, as has already been quoted from Keegan, it was most unsafe to underestimate a cornered German formation, however heavily outnumbered. The 89th Infantry Division was stretched across the entire front chosen for the Canadian columns. The 272nd Infantry Division on the right would face the British. Although there were elements of the 12th SS Panzer Division Hitlerjugend available in reserve, a battle group had been detached to counter a move on the German left flank by another Allied force. The British 59th Division had crossed the River Orne at Grimbosq. Battle group Wunsche (a composite force commanded by Maj Max Wunsche) of 12th SS Panzer Division was sent to repel this threat.

The great strength of the German line was in anti-tank guns and mortars. Estimates made by various authorities indicate that there were about 100 anti-tank guns (or guns that could be used in that role) of either 75 mm or 88 mm on the Totalize sector. Battery 3 of Werferregiment 83 had its mortars trained on Saint-Aignan. The II Panzer Regiment commanded by Sturmbannführer Prinz was a few kilometres down the main road near Bretteville-le-Rabet, with thirty-nine Mark IV tanks. The I Panzer Regiment of Sturmbannführer Jurgensen had thirty-eight Mark V Panthers available. Also on hand were between eight and ten Tigers of the 101st Heavy battalion commanded by Michael Wittmann, already famous in Germany as the ace tank commander of the war. Tank workshops in the woods near Falaise were ready to exercise the vital German skill of repairing the irreparable, according to Georg Isecke who, at the time, was adjutant of the 12th SS Panzer Regiment.[2] Given the configuration of slopes and woods and villages favouring the defender this was still an imposing force, considerably stronger than that which had inflicted such casualties in the early moments of Goodwood, and better disposed to deal with any frontal attack.

Immediately after the war the term 'SS' attracted such notoriety, because of Nazi concentration camps and the Holocaust, that some writers seemed wary of praising the military skills of the Waffen (Weaponed, or battle) SS. It was frequently pointed out that the ordinary German army, the Wehrmacht, tended to behave impeccably, in accordance with international conventions on warfare, whereas there was a grave shadow hanging over some of the actions of the Waffen SS. By the 1990s it seemed that the pendulum had swung to the other extreme and writers were almost idolizing the Waffen SS, distinguishing the fighting SS divisions from the concentration camp guards in almost the same way that earlier the Wehrmacht was distinguished from the entire SS structure. There is no doubt that some SS divisions (though not all) were élite fighting machines. It is also true that some fighting SS divisions have been accused of atrocities. Certainly the worm's eye view of the ordinary tank man, like the writer, in August 1944 was that the Wehrmacht would obey the rules of war but the SS might not. The word 'SS' probably came next after 'Tiger' and 'Panther' in the hierarchy of fear. Even the 'Moaning Minnies' could assume a familiar feminine guise which made them somehow more endurable and less odious than the 'SS'. Such was the common ranker's 1944 attitude.

It is not the purpose of this book to rehabilitate the SS Panzer Divisions, wholly or partially, but simply to try to present as factually accurate a version as possible of the Totalize events. As an SS formation provided at least half of the defensive action it is therefore reasonable to look briefly at what 'SS' really signified.

The formation can be traced back to the mid-1920s when political violence was rife on the streets of Germany. Goering, one of Hitler's earliest supporters, organized a bodyguard consisting of an officer and ten men in each district. These groups would provide protection for Hitler wherever he travelled in Germany. Goering had been a pilot in the First World War and he borrowed a term which was used in the air force for the support group of the ace pilot, the 'Schutz Staffel'.[3]

Himmler developed the SS as an élite guard which in 1933, as Hitler assumed power, had risen to 50,000 in number. It was invested with the mystique of the old Teutonic Orders of Knighthood with appropriate pageantry. Its very distinct sign, the flattened double S, was an adaptation of ancient runic writing. With Hitler's accession to power a company of the SS took over the task of guarding the Reich Chancellery and became the Leibstandarte Adolf Hitler (LAH). It was always quite separate from the normal German army structure. The Wehrmacht tended to recruit from urban areas while the SS trawled rural areas, thus developing an expertise in fieldcraft. Although Himmler used SS units to guard the new concentration camps, with the onset of war complete front-line fighting units of SS were formed. The LAH eventually became 1st SS Panzer Division (LAH), which, with the 2nd, Das Reich, became recognized during the war as two of the three 'most élite' fighting divisions. These two divisions were originally recruited from men of what was known as the 'true Aryan type', that is, blond, tall, healthy, with no dental cavities, and so on – quite the antithesis of their master, Himmler. Later SS Divisions (numbered into the twenties) were recruited from non-German nations. While a few were successful from a military point of view, others were a total failure. For instance the 23rd SS Division was intended to consist of Bosnian Muslims and was forming from January to October 1944. It was then disbanded, because of a bad disciplinary record, without ever being issued with a regimental badge.

The name 'Hitler Youth' was familiar before the war as a kind of Nazi Boy Scouts organization, which was often seen parading in great masses and carrying agricultural implements, sports equipment or swastika flags. It was not until the war was in progress, however, that the idea emerged of forming an SS Panzer Division from the cream of Germany's emerging youth. Hitler himself issued the order on 24 June 1943, creating such a unit with effect from 1 June, just a year and a few days before D-Day. Viewing the record of the Hitlerjugend in Normandy it is difficult to digest the idea that only a year before its exploits near the Normandy beaches it was forming in the Antwerp area. Conceived as a Panzer Grenadier unit it was changed in October 1943 (about the time that British Totalize units were receiving their first Sherman tanks) to 12th SS Panzer Division Hitlerjugend. A cadre of experienced officers from LAH would train and command an intake of youths born in 1926. In Normandy about 65 per cent of Hitlerjugend were aged eighteen, but none were younger, although this has sometimes been the subject of mistaken comment related to the allegedly extreme youthfulness of boys impressed into the German front line. (89th Infantry also had its quota of youths, as did many British reinforcements arriving in Normandy.)[4]

The old cinema pictures of vast battalions of Nazi storm-troopers goose-stepping past Hitler on his saluting base perhaps gives a false impression of the preparation of Hitlerjugend. The youths joining the unit in 1943 were indeed subjected to a high degree of Nazi indoctrination but the traditional type of 'square-bashing' was prohibited. All members of the civilian Hitler Youth received cadet-type weapon training before being drafted into military service. The Hitlerjugend regime developed this initial skill training into a very high level of weaponry and fieldcraft. There were none of the massed Nazi rally style of functions. The Hitlerjugend was almost prudishly puritan. Boozing, smoking, visiting brothels and even serious 'girlfriending' were officially denied, while major emphasis was put on sport and fitness. The contrast with other German units, or many British regiments, is rounded off by what Reynolds notes, 'that the only soldiers in Normandy not to have short hair were those of the Hitlerjugend' (and some tank crews in the 1st Northamptonshire Yeomanry!).

The word 'fanatical' is often used of formations like the Hitlerjugend when describing their style of warfare in impossible situations. The word may have connotations of berserk fury with little rationality. The entire mode of training of Hitlerjugend denied this aspect of 'fanaticism' and emphasized instead technical skills, strict self-discipline and a cool ability to employ tactics like allowing an enemy to pass by and then attacking from the rear. Hitlerjugend was first commanded by Fritz Witt, an original member of the 1930s Chancellery Guard. He was killed in Normandy, and by the time of Totalize Kurt Meyer had taken charge. He was the son of a sergeant-major of the First World War. Since 1939 he had fought in Poland, France, Greece and Russia and had been decorated several times. He became the youngest German general at only thirty-four years of age.

The much-maligned 89th Infantry Division was an even more recent formation than Hitlerjugend, having been set up near Bergen, Norway, in February 1944. It was composed of Grenadier Regiments 1055 and 1056, each with an establishment of three battalions; the 89th Fusilier Battalion; 189th Artillery Regiment, together with engineer, signals and anti-tank units. According to its own Lt-Col Gevert Haslob, 64 per cent of the division were aged nineteen or younger. The division had no tanks or self-propelled guns. It was qualified only for defence missions and not for attack.[5] One historian describes the division as 'in a poor state. It lacked armoured support and was without heavy anti-tank guns. Its artillery was entirely horse drawn and it had no mobile reserve'.[6]

The anachronistic infrastructure of the 89th led to a jibe from the SS as they were relieved by the new division: 'What do you want here with your horses?' The 89th Division soldiers themselves seemed to be sensitive about the primitive nature of some of their equipment and nicknamed the unit the 'Wheelbarrow Division'. The more official name of the unit was the 'Horseshoe' division, from its badge. The 'horse' connection was also said to relate to the names of its two regimental commanders, Col Rossman and Col Roesler, 'Ross' in German being a steed or a horse. The division, which had been training in Norway, was commanded by Lt-Gen Konrad Heinrichs.

As the Allied columns lined up for Totalize the 89th Division was responsible for the sector from the Rivers Orne and Laize to the main Caen to Falaise road, the road itself coming within the 89th's sector. On the east of the road the 89th linked up with 272nd Infantry Division, a weaker unit numerically than the newly arrived 89th. The 272nd held the line from the main road past Bourguebus and through the Secqueville woods area and the 89th Division had 271st Division on its left beyond the rivers. The 1055 regiment was on the right covering Rocquancourt, and 1056 on the left in front of May and Fontenay. Its 88 mm (Pak-flak) artillery force was spread between the villages of Caillouet and Gaumesnil. The 189 Fusilier Battalion was near Bretteville-sur-Laize in reserve and the Divisional Headquarters had been located in an old mine nearby.

Lt (later Lt-Col) Gevert Haslob, 89 Infanterie Division, postwar organizer of reconciliation groups.

In contrast to 'Panzer' Meyer's horror-stricken image of 89th infantry running away in panic, the 89th records seem to reveal a clear awareness of the tactical situation and coolness in a situation of extreme jeopardy. The division had been alerted by the Leibstandarte Adolf Hitler, in a terse message as it pulled out, 'Feindl. Grossangriff von Caen her unmittelbar bevorstehend!' ('a major enemy attack from Caen immediately imminent'). The division was still moving in on the night of 6/7 August but, by 00.15 on 8 August, 1055 Regiment was reporting an accurate bombing raid by enemy aircraft reaching deep into the regimental area. A few minutes later 1056 Regiment made a similar report.[7] Minutes later still, Allied artillery shells were falling around the Divisional Headquarters itself.

The first appreciation of the weight of attack was a brief message, 'Im rechten DivAbschnitt Panzereinbrueche' ('an armoured breakthrough in the right section of the Division'). As early as 08.00 hours the army commander himself, Gen Eberbach, appeared at Divisional Headquarters to discuss the situation. Between 09.00 and 10.00 deep penetration along the main road was reported and the division was referring to villages as 'islands' ('Inseln') in hitherto divisional territory. The heaviest weight of enemy inroads was recognized as lying on the German right, and the lesser penetration on the left (that is towards the rivers). At about the same time an Allied prisoner had vouchsafed the information that the Polish Armoured Division was involved (although it was not to enter action for another three hours), cooperating with 'Canadian infantry'.

A major concern of 89th Division was an artillery bombardment, stated to have commenced at 11.00 hours (German time) and lasting for one-and-a-half hours. This, combined with the (US) air bombardment, caused considerable problems in the delivery of ammunition and other supplies from the echelons behind the lines. It was considered that the psychological effect of the bombing could quickly be overcome but the temporary physical impact was disturbing. Reference was made to detonations, near misses, air blast, the resulting grit and dust interfering with sight and movement.

By 14.00 hours, as the second phase attack rolled in, the situation was near disaster. The divisional commander himself went out to his right wing to give personal leadership to units under terminal strain. The divisional adjutant was sent to organize the allocation of the reserve of Fusiliers to meet the waves of Canadians pushing through to the very doorstep, or mine entrance, of Divisional Headquarters. The counter-attack of Hitlerjugend, and the irregular pattern of Allied penetration, enabled the 89th as a battered but still operational unit to move back to a new defence line, and eventually to fight other battles until standing on German soil. The divisional commander, appearing once too often in the front line, was killed in action, and Col Rossman would write to a battalion commander, Maj von Kalm, who lost his right arm in Totalize, 'What is remaining from the Regiment since that time? Burned out to a cinder . . .' [8] The 6th Company lost ninety-four dead in the battle and 5th Company was wiped out.

Over on the other side of the main road 272nd Infantry Division had shared the experience of the 89th during the night and morning. It had suffered the earliest penetration right through to objectives and was not fresh and at full strength as was the 89th. It offered furious resistance at Tilly-la-Campagne and claimed to have repulsed attacks towards Conteville and Poussy, although Highland Division records suggest that these attacks took place at a later time. It has to be said that the defence of Tilly, while causing many problems for following echelons, did not prevent the main Polish armoured strength from reaching the Cramesnil/Saint-Aignan start line on time. The remaining units of 272 retreated as they were able, either side of Saint-Aignan, and formed a new line well back the next day.

Reference has already been made to Kurt 'Panzer' Meyer's quick reaction to the emergency and his recognition that if 'I did not deploy my division correctly, the Allies would be through to Falaise, and the German armies in the West would be completely trapped'. Since Milton Shulman interviewed Meyer in August 1945 the Meyer version of events has dominated the study of the Totalize 'interim', the gap between the successful Phase 1 and the slower follow-through.[9] There is no doubt that prompt action was taken in a situation of utter confusion. Saint-Aignan was reported recaptured when it was not. Cintheaux was reported recaptured before it had been captured. An attack on Conteville was beaten off before there were any attackers near it.

The German reaction was disciplined and skilled. Max Wunsche and his battle group had been detached to meet a left-flank danger at Grimbosq. That group was brought back and soon dealt the mortal blow to the misguided Worthington Force near Estrees. Hans Waldmuller was to launch another battle group, which would attack through the area of le Petit Ravin, while divisional escort groups swung wider in support on the right flank and, by luck or good judgement, just opposite the Polish left flank. An 88 mm unit formed a further line of defence near Bretteville-le-Rabet, about 4 km back from Cintheaux. While these were small groups compared to the Allied numbers, they were still powerful forces when defending on favourable ground. There was also support from the divisional artillery and a considerable number of the very effective mortars of various calibre.

If there was a flaw in the German dispositions it must have been the failure to integrate fully a tiny but potentially deadly Tiger force with other counter-attacking Panthers and Mark IVs, supported by Panzer Grenadiers. What must be counted as the most formidable troop of Tigers in the German army was on the spot and could have wreaked havoc among the massed formations of new Canadian and Polish armour. On 9 August, five knocked-out Tigers were identified down the eastern side of the main road, all in quite exposed positions and apart from the main mass of counter-attacking troops. Had they been used in a more elusive and better-supported role the delay to the Allies could have been far worse.

The available Tigers (only perhaps seven being really battle-ready and one or two still being rushed out of workshops) were commanded by the now legendary Michael Wittmann. On 8 August neither Rad Walters nor Tom Boardman had ever heard of him. In the German army and to the German nation he was already a much-decorated hero. Following the air traditions of the First World War he was termed an 'ace'. As with legends, his demise has been coloured by various accounts, but the simple fact is that, whereas five Tigers might be expected to account for twenty-five enemy tanks (or in the massed Totalize columns maybe fifty!), the five Tigers identified on 9 August had cost the Allies no more than the same number of the more vulnerable Shermans. In fact at this moment, the author has only been able to identify with certainty two Northants and possibly two 27 CAR tanks which may have been knocked out by Tiger shots. This could, of course, be incorrect at this remove in time. Patrick Agte, Wittmann's biographer, from the German side identifies the knocked-out Tigers as those of Wittmann, Dollinger, Iriohn, Kisters and, at some distance, Hoeflinger.

Wittman was born into a farming community just before the First World War broke out and so was thirty years of age in Normandy. He did military service in an infantry regiment from 1934 to 1936 (national service) and rose to Gefreiter. In 1937 he began again, volunteering and gaining admission to the élite 'Leibstandarte', then developing from a 'palace' guard into a full-strength fighting unit. By the outbreak of war he held sergeant's rank in armoured cars. He fought in the Blitzkrieg of 1940 but it was not until the German invasion of

Greece in 1941 that he was given command of a tracked vehicle, as distinct from the wheeled cars. There followed service in Russia where he distinguished himself by handling a self-propelled gun like a tank, the SP not having the advantage of a traversing turret, and knocking out numbers of Russian tanks.

In 1942 his actions resulted in posting to officer training and a commission on 21 December 1942. It was only in 1943 that he first commanded an actual heavy tank, a Tiger of the LAH's heavy armour company. He took part in several astonishing tank battles, both in Russia and in Normandy, and at the time of Totalize was calculated to have been responsible for knocking out, in Russia and Normandy, 138 tanks and 132 other armoured vehicles and guns. Surprisingly, he was known as a very modest, quiet and likeable man, who never boasted of his prowess. He had also gathered around him a group of kindred spirits, although a number of his extraordinary exploits, such as the elimination of an entire British squadron at Villers Bocage, were achieved when 'hunting' in a single Tiger tank.[10]

The events of 8 August 1944 have been clouded in some mystery and debate, but appear to have been fairly simple. Early on that day SS Capt Franz Heurich had taken a group of Tigers down the main road without orders. Hearing this, Wittmann was concerned because it was Heurich's first day in action. Wittmann quickly called for his Volkswagen and, with his good friend, Capt Dr Rabe, drove to Cintheaux where the Tigers were well hidden for fear of air attack by Typhoons and other ground support aircraft. German sources suggest, with some surprise, that RAF ground support was not called on, possibly because of the raid by USAAF heavy bombers which had been planned.

Wittmann met and conferred with Maj Waldmuller, who was finishing his briefing for the counter-attack, and 'Panzer' Meyer. Meyer had already studied the serried ranks of Allied tanks visible in the distance (the follow-up forces of Totalize). The instinctive reaction of the three experienced tank commanders was to hit before being hit, and the Garcelles wood and chateau were indicated as an appropriate target from which a German group could then dominate a wide panorama of open slopes packed tight with Allied armour in almost as perilous a situation as the vehicles at Villers Bocage. The decision may have been a desperate throw of the dice in the knowledge of the scarcity of their own resources. As Keegan has commented, '[the tank] companies were now so weak that half-repaired tanks had to be driven out of the battalion workshops only a mile behind the lines. Ominously too, some of the Tigers had to drop out of the action for want of fuel, which was not coming up the line of supply.'[11]

Wittmann himself had to take a Tiger (no. 007) other than his usual mount. Although Meyer had left liaison officers in Saint-Aignan and other villages it is debatable whether the three commanders at Cintheaux were fully aware of what awaited Wittmann's troop, or whether the bait of the massed hundreds of static tanks was too much temptation, blurring their logic. What, in fact, awaited was 27 CAR, on Wittmann's left, 144 RAC ahead, and 1st Northamptonshire Yeomanry on the right, all fairly well hidden. These three regiments counted at that moment with about thirty-four Firefly tanks in total, all likely to be within range of Wittmann's route

Michael Wittmann, Germany's tank 'ace', killed in action, 8 August 1944. His grave was not discovered until 1983 and he is now buried in the German cemetery at La Cambe, grave 47.III.120. (Photo © Bundesarchiv)

and each capable of knocking out a Tiger within the scope of the day's probable action.

It seems likely that Maj Radley-Walters' 'A' Squadron had the first shot at Wittmann, who was on the far (eastern) side of the main road from the Canadians. This caused all four Tigers within range to traverse left and look for the enemy gun flashes. This move meant that the SS tank commanders' backs were turned to the 1st Northamptonshire Yeomanry's 'A' Squadron deep in the orchards and well within 17-pdr range. As it happened, only one of the Yeomanry Firefly tanks was required for the action, so exposed were the Tigers. Radio operator Bahlo, on SS Lt Dollinger's tank, reported that the shot which destroyed his tank came in through the right side wall, which would have been from the direction of Joe Ekins' Firefly. More than one witness saw Wittmann's turret blown askew by another shot. There could have been little hope of the commander surviving such an impact but almost immediately the tank's ammunition started to explode and the tilted turret was blown clear of the tank.

The violence of the removal of Wittmann's turret has led to some thought that the damage might have been done by a Typhoon rocket, although neither Germans nor Allies seem to have been aware of ground support aircraft operating until somewhat later in the day. It has also been suggested that, before it was destroyed, Wittmann's troop had been the chief agent in the destruction of numbers of Polish tanks. The recollections of a number of soldiers who were there at the precise moment, including the author, are to the effect that the Polish tanks were still behind the British forward Shermans until some while after the demise of Wittmann.[12] Dr Rabe saw the incident from a distance but could not approach the destroyed tanks because of the outbreak of intensive firing from all arms and also because of the fires in the destroyed tanks themselves. Panzer Adj Isecke later sent Dr Rabe again to try to confirm Wittmann's death but the task became increasingly impracticable as the Allied host pushed forward. The loss of Wittmann was a great blow to his comrades.[13]

Wittmann's last charge was a most forlorn hope. Had his troop not been dealt with by the forces immediately in sight there were numbers of other Firefly and anti-tank guns at hand. Tactically, had he caused more harm to 27 CAR, 1st Northamptonshire Yeomanry and 144 RAC, this would not have been of great importance, for they were already on their objectives, waiting for the new mass of armour to pass through. To an extent the second phase of Totalize had already been set back by the need to await the scheduled air bombardment (and Meyer had passed Wittmann through the area of that bombardment before it commenced). When the new armour did at last move forward the worst destruction was wrought by German guns and infantry which had waited in good defensive positions. Even Waldmuller's main push, which had moved minimally too late and fractionally too far away to support Wittmann, was a net loss of irreplaceable tanks and material.

Perhaps because officers of the Northants Yeomanry were themselves so surprised to have inflicted one-for-one losses on the German armour, the opportunity was taken next day to visit and identify the various German tanks knocked out on 8 August. Peter Smith remembers:

> As soon as it was safe to do so, the Squadron Commander ('A',1NY), Major Gray Skelton asked me to take him and . . . other commanders (on my half-track) to see the result of the 'A' Squadron shooting. I have vivid memories of seeing a group of three destroyed Tigers, of which the turret of one was lying upside down alongside the hull. Charred parts of the crew were present mainly in the hull but also evident in the turret . . . one of the tank commanders made a sketch of the Tiger's insignia on his map case for further identification. . . . I also remember being amazed at seeing a neat, fist sized hole, commensurate with a 17 pounder strike, punched through the front plate of one of the Tigers – armour which I now know to be about four inches thick.[14]

At least four other Allied field officers from that action (Maj Radley-Walters, Bevan, Boardman and Brassey) visited the site during the following three years when destroyed German tanks were still *in situ* and when human beings could walk the fields in leisure and with impunity. The main tactical and topographical details are therefore quite clear. Veterans of the Northants Yeomanry, no doubt like those of other regiments, have also had a number of opportunities to explore the battlefield in the company of French residents, who were evacuated for the actual battle but were able to return to their homes before some of the German bodies had been buried. The remains observed by Peter Smith in Wittmann's' tank were buried 'temporarily' nearby, not to be discovered and identified again until 1983.[15]

Those who opposed the Waldmuller counter-attack, and other similar actions, were often amazed by German discipline and loyalty at a time when some German military men had already attempted to assassinate Hitler and when there appeared to be no hope of military success. Wittmann and Waldmuller, with perhaps fewer than 50 tanks, were in effect attacking probably more than 900 enemy tanks of all kinds and more than 30,000 men. In subsequent times histories have tended to imply that the Allies were generally better motivated because they were fighting to eradicate the evil system of Nazism and that, in some way, the German soldiers must have been far less motivated, as well as being aware of impending defeat.

Mortar squad commander Karl-Heinz Decker, a civilian Hitler Youth leader and volunteer for the Hitlerjugend division, sneaking by night from one hideaway to another during Totalize, relates that his main concerns were about air activity, the lack of it from the Luftwaffe and the Allied domination of the skies. For him the Allied planes meant terror, and he was angry with the Luftwaffe, not understanding the problems of German airmen. Nevertheless for Karl-Heinz the real blow to his morale was later in the war when he read that the three Great Powers had decided that his homeland of East Prussia would cease to exist. Whatever happened in the war, he would now have no homeland to go back to.[17]

A factor in the good morale of German troops was undoubtedly the way in which their generals were highly visible to the front-line soldiers. A present-day British general refers to the meeting of Eberbach and Meyer on 8 August: 'thus we have the equivalent of Dempsey or Hodges less than 5 kms from the nearest enemy troops on a front which has already collapsed. No wonder the German soldiers had respect for such officers!'[18] In fact when Eberbach called at 89th Infantry Divison HQ that morning he was less than 2 km in a direct line from where Maj Radley-Walters was perched in the turret of his Sherman, well within Firefly range.

The Polish officers who compiled a history of their division stated another factor in the German's iron will to resist. 'The German High Command fully realised that every kilometre ceded around Caen, would mean a retreat of hundreds of kilometres in case the "prising open of the hinge" proved successful. In the light of this fact, it is easy to understand why the German defence was so consistently stubborn.'[19] There was also the general expectation that a German defender could expect to make an Allied attacker pay up to a five-to-one ratio of casualties for every advance.

German troops generally had great confidence in the quality of their equipment, although often concerned about shortages. It is significant that Sherman crews gave the nickname 'Ronson' to their own tanks, and the Germans added 'Tommy Cooker', but there were no similar derogatory names for German armoured vehicles. One Yeoman, Fred Gibbs, spoke of his 75 mm shots bouncing off German armour plating like tennis balls,[20] while, almost unbelievably, an officer at Villers Bocage, Bernard Rose, reported his 6-pdr shots bouncing off Wittmann's tank at a range of eight – repeat 'eight' – yards.[21] Both Reynolds and Hastings, to mention only two, have made striking comparisons of German superiority in material, tactics and training, including other arms such as 'the 1,200 rounds-a-minute rate of fire of the German MG 42s [machine-guns] . . . compared . . . with the American or British equivalent of 500 at best'.[22]

There is some evidence that the equipment situation in the German army was not 100 per cent perfect. One report from German prisoners described the vaunted *Panzerfaust* as 'inaccurate and, according to eye witnesses, [it] did not always penetrate'.[23] A different complaint was that on roads 'there were no emergency barriers or road repairs because engineers were fighting as infantry'.[24] Hitler suffered a temper tantrum about the time of Totalize because of *Panzerfaust* shortages:

'Who issues these weapons?' asked Hitler angrily. Keitel shrugged his shoulders. 'That was the quartermaster general, Wagner'. 'Aha!' Hitler said triumphantly. 'The swine! He did well to shoot himself. . . . In the open countryside of the Ukraine we have bazookas in abundance. And in the hedgerows of Normandy we have none!'[25]

Already at Totalize the German army's shortages resulted from three main causes: inefficiency of the national supply system, RAF destruction of factories and communications, and continuing front-line attrition. Karl-Heinz Decker was worried about shortage of mortar bombs. Lt Ian Hammerton, like many other Allied soldiers, was astonished to find out how hungry a German prisoner was:

I shall never forget the look on his face when we gave him a mug (of tea) and a huge slice of white bread with butter and jam. In his haversack we had found only a small hard chunk of black bread. . . . He was fifteen years old and came from Dresden. He had not heard from his family for months.[26]

A major cause for complaint, ranging from Karl-Heinz Decker to Hitler himself, related to the shortage of Luftwaffe aeroplanes in the sky.

'At every conference the Führer goes on for hours on end about the Luftwaffe', lamented Koller in his diary on August 8th, 'he strongly reproaches the Luftwaffe. The reasons are our lack of aircraft, technological shortcomings, and noncompletion of the replacement squadrons in the Reich.'[27]

Goering's response to the problem had been to go to bed. The Luftwaffe also had another problem, with the magnificent 88 mm dual purpose gun. It had originally been designed as an anti-aircraft gun to be manned by the

Karl-Heinz Decker,
commander of a mortar crew,
25th Panzer Grenadier
Regiment.

Luftwaffe. In Normandy these guns were still under the control of a Luftwaffe general, Pickert. The 5th Panzer Army commander, Dietrich, was in a state of constant strife with Pickert over the location and use of the guns. He remembered, 'I constantly ordered these guns to stay forward and act in an anti-tank role against Allied armour. My orders were just as often countermanded by Pickert, who moved them back . . .'[28]

The Luftwaffe itself was much hampered by Allied air force strikes against airfields and communications. Although 800 German fighters were moved to the west to counter the invasion, they were never an effective force commensurate with their numbers. The head of the Luftwaffe 'Fighter Command', Galland, reported:

Most of the carefully prepared and provisioned airfields had been bombed out and units had to land at hastily chosen landing grounds. The poor signals network broke down. . . . Many units came down in the wrong places. The alternative airfields were too few, poorly camouflaged and badly supplied.[29]

The same historian who interviewed Galland records that 'in addition, many underground cables were cut by French saboteurs. An investigation by OKL revealed also that some of the faults which developed after D-Day had been "built into" the land-line network by the French technicians who had laid it for the Luftwaffe.'[30] The Luftwaffe pilots themselves, whose personal bravery was never in doubt, had therefore almost as much cause to complain as the benighted infantrymen and mortar crews who scuttled furtively from cover to cover at night and almost totally disappeared during the day, because of the incessant menace of Allied air forces.

It was Dietrich also who graphically pointed out the negative aspect of Hitler's personalized conduct of the war. When von Kluge followed Hitler's intuitions, ignored the Totalize breach and continued attacking the Americans, Dietrich commented, 'There was only one person to blame for this stupid, impossible operation. That madman Adolf Hitler. It was a Führer's order. What else could we do?'[31] Hitler had made some good intuitive decisions before the war and in the early days. This fact, added to his own innate, not inconsiderable self-confidence, convinced him that he was more competent in grand strategy than most of his generals. In addition, the High Command seemed incapable of conveying to him the reality of situations. Had his best divisions been at full strength in early August 1944 he might have held the Caen-Falaise sector and still counter-attacked effectively against Patton's extended forces at Mortain. But most of those divisions were down to half strength or less, and the requisite air support was almost totally lacking. He was, in a sense, playing at war games, although a properly conceived war game incorporates casualties.

As much of the Totalize story revolves around an SS Division, and the SS organization was associated with atrocities, it is relevant to mention this aspect as it affected the Normandy campaign. The stories or rumours about atrocities can have a dual impact on military morale. Atrocities committed against one's own side can make soldiers fight harder and more ruthlessly against a foe they despise. It can also cause the more fearful rankers to fight more cautiously than if they are facing an enemy which, like the ordinary Wehrmacht unit, is reputed to follow the rules of war on such items as treatment of enemy prisoners and the use of the white flag.

There were rumours and probably incidents of atrocities on both sides in Normandy. The author himself, when commanding a tank, was advised by a Black Watch sergeant of the misuse of a white flag, waved to induce the attacking infantry to stand up as good targets for enemy guns. In the main the author's experience was that the enemy behaved impeccably when surrendering. On the enemy side, Karl-Heinz Decker was angered when he was told stories about Canadian atrocities by eye-witness comrades, though he had no way at the time of checking those stories.

Accidents happen in the heat of battle. Lt-Col Andrews remembered almost shooting a badly wounded German who made a suspicious movement in the turmoil of Tilly-la-Campagne. The 89th Division Col Haslob quotes a sad incident seen by Lt Willy Scheuermann on 8 August:

. . . his medical first aid corporal when he tried to help a wounded messenger of the 6. Comp was killed. He remembered 'I still see him when he jumped out of his foxhall (*sic*) waving a white cloth and shouted often against an enemy tank which was standing right in front of him "Red Cross! Red Cross!" But the machine-guns didn't hear him and it didn't take long when his shouting grow dumb' . . . His name was Anton (Toni) Mayer born 30 June 1906. He was not a so-called 'strammer soldat' – smart soldier, but a brave soldier always ready to help and make sacrifices to his next person.[32]

The death of Toni Mayer could well be misunderstood by an angry comrade. From 3 Baker, 'C', 1st Northants co-driver Rex Jackson tells a somewhat happier story:

We had watched several Germans wearing Red Cross arm bands going through the gully, presumably looking for their wounded. We were very surprised by their apparent lack of concern at our presence as, unless they were blind, it seemed impossible for them not to have seen us . . . either that or they had great faith that we would respect the Red Cross, which we did. One of them was relaxed enough to drop his trousers and relieve himself by a tree. But, with second thoughts, perhaps he had seen us!

Driving alongside Rex, Stan Hicken had been very impressed after a previous Yeomanry battle nearer Villers Bocage. He had gone to look for the body of his pal Rawlins, with whom he had planned to open a garage after the war. Amid the shambles of an early Bocage battle the Germans had buried the Yeomanry dead with neat crosses over the graves and the deceased soldiers' identity disks attached to the crosses. Wyn Griffith-Jones points to his perilous journey back to the potato field to collect the wounded when, in a state of maximum confusion and ferocious hatefulness, the German machine-gun teams had sedulously observed the ritual of the Red Cross flag. There was also the case of L/Cpl Dursley and the almost medieval chivalry with which he was treated as a prisoner and then later was requested to lead his captors (of 272 Division) in their own surrender.

The Canadians did not easily forgive the shooting of a number of their men when taken prisoner in the earlier battles of the Bocage. An American diary records that 'Clarence Huebner, whose 1st Division had suffered badly in storming Omaha, said on June 25 to General Hodges – "with his mouth curling into a smile" as Hodges noted approvingly in his diary – that his men refused to take prisoners. "Could have taken four yesterday easily, but preferred to kill them" said Huebner'.[33] Armies train and incite men to violence and it is surprising that there were no more confirmed reports of atrocities between soldiers in Normandy than are on record. One of the most horrific instances of hatred and vengeance must have been when the long-suffering Poles closed the 'Falaise Gap' and German troops did their utmost to reopen the escape route. Yet the record compiled by Polish officers, while acknowledging the ferocity of the fighting, has very little indication of atrocities being committed.[34]

These remarks give the writer an opportunity to mount one of his hobby horses on the idea that violent men make the best soldiers. Films like *The Dirty Dozen* have developed plots whereby criminals were deliberately recruited to undertake military operations which, it is assumed, normal soldiers would 'funk'. Those who served in the front line often observed that the most valiant deeds were performed by the most considerate and least aggressive of men. A good example of this is the German Wittmann, whose life has now been meticulously researched by a number of authors. Each one has had to portray him as a most sensitive and unassuming man, the antithesis of the 'Dirty Dozen' image. In many instances the drunken braggart proved to be of the lineage of Pistol, the character created by that perceptive military commentator, Shakespeare. Having received a bruising beating as punishment for desertion, Pistol would 'get me patches to these scars and swear I got them in the Gallia wars'.

As already mentioned, Konrad Heinrichs, commanding the ill-fated 89th Infantry Division, was killed exactly a month after Totalize Phase 1. Kurt Meyer, apparently unaware of his promotion to general, was taken prisoner and when interviewed by Milton Shulman (then a Canadian Intelligence major) professed continuing loyalty to Hitler but became a prime source of information and comment on Totalize. Staff Off Hubert Meyer produced a massively researched history of Hitlerjugend. That division ended the Normandy campaign at weak battalion total fighting strength but was reformed to fight again. Panzer Adj Georg Isecke was wounded and captured two weeks after the Saint-Aignan battle. Gevert Haslob was wounded on the Rhine, but was discharged by an Allied 'Discharge Collection Centre'. He then became a moving force in a number of initiatives to promote reconciliation between enemies.

Mortar bomb NCO Karl-Heinz Decker has possibly the most unusual story. His nightly move from hideout to hideout ended when he was taken prisoner. With a pocket knife he amputated the shredded leg of a comrade. Taken to Wales he worked as a prisoner on a farm, work which he knew well. When repatriation time came he had no homeland to go to, being an East Prussian. He elected to stay as a farm worker in Wales and eventually married a Welsh-speaking girl. Injuring himself in a farm accident, he saw an advertisement inviting war veterans to apply for jobs with the (British) Post Office. He applied. To his great surprise he was accepted and ended his career as a British civil servant in North Wales! This says something about the logic of wars.[35]

The last word from the opponent's corner shall come from a young soldier of the often maligned SS. He suggested:

The tactic of unbroken artillery barrages lasting for hours was a gruesome mental and physical torture. For me, when politicians today toy with the idea of sending young men off to war, they should be made to take part in an exact reconstruction of the action at Tilly-la-Campagne and experience personally what it means to be a soldier.[36]

Chapter Nine

The Champion Dethroned

'It is therefore necessary that the generals we have now should take much greater
care than those we had before, and that those in the ranks should be much better
disciplined and more ready to obey their officers now than they were before.'
(Xenophon, 400 BC)

The British invented the tank. The British first employed it in battle. The British won the first battles using tanks. In 1916–17 Britain was, as one might say, the Tank Champion of the world. How then did the British tank equipment and strategy of 1939–44 become such a shambles? How was the champion so easily deposed? Why did so many British (and French and Canadian and Polish) tank crews die unnecessarily and their infantry go unsupported into the valleys of death?

It might have been otherwise. Phase 1 of Totalize demonstrated that, properly handled, Allied tanks could compete with the inventors of the Blitzkrieg. On the Eastern Front the less technologically developed Russians quickly produced a tank equal to or better than the Tiger, while the largest advanced manufacturing nation in the world had to rely on continuous assembly-line replacement of a basically inadequate product. And it was well beyond the midway point of the war before the inventors of the tank perfected a model which, in a specific role, could compete with the best (the up-gunned Cromwell). Yet a military genius called Percy Hobart with his 79th Armoured Division was able to produce variants of tanks which could swim, spout flame, explode mines under the earth's surface, bridge trenches and streams, and whatever other strange task might be demanded.

On the other side of the battle line, in 1918 the only tanks which the Germans had were derivatives of the British or clumsy adaptations. Until 1933 Germany was restricted in its ability to manufacture tanks and exercise armoured formations. British thinkers had continued to develop theories of tank warfare, although French and German theorists were also at work. When the crunch came and the Phoney War ended in 1940, great hosts of efficient German armour swept through the Allied armies. Britain's only significant response was one relatively small group of tanks of dubious quality which, at Arras, held back the flood of Blitzkrieg armour for a few hours.

As the war continued, the roll of armoured catastrophes grew with names like Knightsbridge in the Western Desert, Villers Bocage, Operation Goodwood and Worthington Force. This prompts the question as to whether there was a failure to learn from history, and whether that failure was perpetuated beyond 1945? Quotations from Xenophon can show that many aspects of battle endure from generation to generation. History has much to teach. The history of the tank is relatively brief.

The tank was first used in battle at Flers on the Somme on 15 September 1916. Its promoters had argued for an initial well-prepared attack in massed formation. Only forty-nine tanks were delivered at the Front in time for Flers and only thirty-two reached the start line. Only nine survived breakdown or crashes to make a major impression on the battle and enable the capture of Flers. The German recipients of this surprise recorded:

> The arrival of the tanks on the scene had the most shattering effect on the men. They felt quite powerless against these monsters which crawled along the top of the trench, enfilading it with continuous machine-gun fire, and closely followed by small parties of infantry who threw hand grenades at the survivors.[1]

The limited success and the terrorizing of the German front-line defenders obscured the first great lesson for subsequent study: much of the impact of surprise had been wasted by too hurried an introduction of the weapons and because inadequate numbers were employed.

Exponents of tank warfare celebrate the battle of Cambrai on 20 November 1917. This was the first time when substantial numbers of tanks were employed after reasonably adequate preparation. The details of Cambrai bear a striking similarity in some ways to Phase 1 of Totalize, except that this was a daylight attack. In both battles a force of something in excess of 350 tanks was employed. Both battles omitted the customary preliminary artillery bombardment. Both advances in their initial stages gained several miles across open rolling country with occasional woods and fortified villages. Both forces, on attaining their first objectives, halted for several hours before Phase 2 could be launched, thus giving the defenders time to regroup. Both forces included the 51st Scottish Highland Division and the Fort Garry Horse (in 1917 their Lt Strachan won the VC). At that point the similarity ceases. The 1917 counter-attack by the Germans pushed the British back in most places to the start line and in some places beyond it. In 1944 the advance continued, gaining what, by the previous standards of the campaign, were substantial areas of enemy territory.

Ominously, even before the Cambrai attack, a German major-general commanding one of the defending units, Freiherr von Watter, had already been training his artillery gunners to fire at large moving targets. The general's brother had been one of those to suffer the surprise at Flers. Here too at Cambrai there were lessons for the future. In places the infantry did not advance closely with the tanks. The delay between the first and second phases lost the impetus of the attack and resulted in a devastating enemy retaliation.[2] Was this latter lesson taken to heart?

At Cambrai some tanks had been designated as supply tanks, while others carried bridges, cables or even, in nine cases, a wireless. In 1917 the Mark IX tank was designed 'to meet a requirement for carrying infantry and stores over broken ground in an enclosed armoured vehicle'. Yet twenty-seven years later Simonds was having to improvise such a vehicle.[3]

Reference has been made to the 1944 generals' awareness of the significance of the date 8 August, which marked the battle of Amiens in 1918. The Canadians, and also Australians, were foremost in this attack, which again employed a force in excess of 350 heavy tanks, plus nearly a hundred of the newer whippet tanks. Taking advantage of thick mist, an hour before sunrise, the troops surged forward, overrunning the defence and penetrating well to the rear. So much for Phase 1, and then the attack 'flickered out'. Part of the reason for the difficulty of continued advance was that the ground troops were then crossing the old battlefields of 1916 through ancient barbed-wire forests and across collapsed trenches. However, Liddell Hart pointed out another reason which might have been noted in 1944:

> The original front of the attack had not been wide, and it is significant that almost all successful advances in the World War seem to have been governed by a law of ratio, the depth of the penetration being roughly half of the frontage of the attack . . . being strictly frontal, the more it pushed back the enemy the more it consolidated their resistance.[4]

Although improvements and innovations in the construction of tanks were made under the extreme pressure of war up until 1918, the next twenty years saw Britain lose the opportunity to retain pre-eminence in tank design and construction. Any apathy in that respect should have been dispelled by the Blitzkrieg example of 1940. Britain developed its own heavier tanks but none of them had the enduring value of, say, the German Mark IV or the overwhelming power of the Tiger or the Soviet T34. The excellent Firefly was so late in its adaptation that gunners had no time to practise properly before D-Day, and people like Joe Crittenden and Joe Ekins were still very concerned about this new weapon, knowing about its teething problems and wondering whether the ejection mechanism would jam in action. Some of the ideas which found their way into tank design were amazing. One example was an external jettisonable petrol tank to extend the range of the Churchill tank. This begs the question as to what would happen if the petrol tank was hit, bearing in mind the inflammability of the relatively well-protected petrol tank of the Sherman.[5]

There were, however, rays of hope in the general gloom of Allied tank design. For a time the Valentine and Matilda tanks did good service. One Yeomanry tank officer is not as critical as others:

> I have little patience with any who compare our tank crews unfavourably with the Panzers, when the latter always had the 88-on-wheels to make a screen behind which they could withdraw. . . . Just look how Valentines retrieved Kasserine against Mark IVs and Tigers by sheer good training and guts (steep losses) and with the help from our 25 pounders in the front line firing over open sights! Don't anyone tell me our air arm compensated for ground weaponry inequality. In Tunisia until the final six weeks air supremacy belonged to the Me and Stuka.[6]

The Mark V Panther thought by some Allied tank men to be more dangerous than the less mobile Tiger. This Panther did not survive. (IWM, B8947)

As late as July 1944, on D + 27, Eisenhower made a formal complaint to his War Department after a meeting at which 'from Monty and Brooke E (Eisenhower) learn that our anti-tank equipment and our 75 mm in Shermans are not capable of taking on Panthers and Tigers'.[7] What kind of information had Eisenhower been receiving until then? From late 1941 he had been at the brain centre of the US army in Washington, meeting with war production managers and others to set up the vast American war effort.[8] The German 88 mm gun was available for inspection in America soon after Eisenhower's arrival in Washington.

Some critics have pointed out the possible folly of Britain's armaments programme which organized tank design and gun design as two different functions in two different establishments. Whereas the 17-pdr gun was being produced in mid-1941, it did not find its way into an appropriate tank (the Sherman Firefly with its less than adequate armour) until it was too late to do more than supply one Firefly per troop for D-Day + tanks. One of the critics, himself an expert in the field, wrote the scathing judgement, 'It is not unfair to say that little of the labour and materials expended on the 25,000 British-built tanks helped to win the war'.[9]

It is little wonder, therefore, that British tank units suffered catastrophes in Normandy. A well-known example is the incursion of Michael Wittmann into Villers Bocage in a single Tiger tank, when he knocked out some twenty British armoured vehicles in a short run along a hedge. This was, in truth, a freakish incident and not truly typical. It required an 'ace' commander and an excellent gunner in a dominant tank to come unexpectedly on an enemy which was resting in unsuitable formation and apparently uninformed as to the vulnerability of its location. Yet that very juxtaposition of circumstances revealed something about the tactics, or lack of tactics, practised by the participants.

In more formal set-piece battles it is unclear as to whether those responsible for operations had an accurate sense of what tanks could do. The Night March of Totalize was a risky undertaking but everything possible had been done to anticipate problems and provide answers. The experience of 2nd Northamptonshire Yeomanry during the major Epsom battle suggested a none-too-clever improvisation. In the area of Brettevillette the two squadrons of 2nd Northamptonshire Yeomanry then ashore were resting after replenishment at 22.30 hours on the night of 29 June 1944.

> Suddenly there was a call for Troop Leaders to proceed urgently to Squadron HQ. It was obvious that, loosely speaking, there was a panic on . . . there appeared to be a sudden attack developing in the Beval Farm area . . . it was thought at HQ that the situation could be secured by our two Squadrons being sent out immediately to help the Scots. (2NY were equipped with Cromwell medium tanks without night sights.) Our orders were to 'sweep the area'. It was pitch black so there was nothing else we could do but advance in column. . . . As we advanced firing increased – the logical conclusion was that the opposition was a large enemy force who had bypassed the 15th Scottish and were using our road as their centre line. Our first tank was hit. We started to pass crews walking back and it became obvious that the forward tanks had been hit. . . . A second request to withdraw was refused – so began the destruction of 'A' Squadron. We had run head on into an SS Panzer Division attack in strength.[10]

The corporal writing his experiences did not know on that fatal night that his squadron had been directed straight at the 12th SS Panzer Division Hitlerjugend, who were virtually at their full strength of over 20,000 men and full complement of tanks. 'A' Squadron, 2nd Northamptonshire Yeomanry had been sent off, with minimal briefing and no reconnaissance, along a narrow road with high banks on each side, to 'sweep the area'. They had no infantry in support and had not yet made contact with any infantry ahead. In fact ahead were enemy tanks much more powerful than the Cromwells. There was no room for the squadron to deploy. When it ran into fire which could not be properly returned, its request to be allowed to find another route was rejected. When the German guns began to take their toll, with the Cromwells still ineffectual, a second request to be withdrawn was rejected. As the Cromwells moved in the total darkness the enemy were shooting at the flames from the tanks' exhausts. Only seven of 'A' Squadron's tanks returned, having achieved nothing and never having been in a position to achieve anything. While it is understandable that someone in higher authority wished to get some support up to the Scottish infantry (who were also unknown to the 2nd Northamptonshire Yeomanry), it is perhaps permissible to wonder how it was ever thought that the movement as ordered could be carried out.

The 2nd Northamptonshire Yeomanry, back with its own division, 11th Armoured Division, was also one of the regiments involved in the 'Death Ride of the Armoured Divisions' during Operation Goodwood. The battle has been written about and the ground walked over so often that only a brief reference needs to be made to it here, but the brevity does not in any way detract from the horror of the full facts. A month after D-Day the Allies had entered the pivotal city of Caen. Immediately beyond Caen lay a river and then the slopes of the Bourguebus Ridge. Caen itself was a place of almost impassable ruins. There was no easy way in which a major force, such as three armoured divisions, could pass through the ruins of Caen, cross the river and then attack the slopes. At the same time there seems to have been a trend of thought that, after the tiny fields of the Bocage, the Bourguebus area was good open tank country. The plan was therefore for the armoured divisions to do a circuit of Caen, crossing the river north of the city, passing down the east side and then turning left up the open slopes. Much of the time the columns would be clearly visible to the enemy. A mad charge might overwhelm the enemy before they could take too great a toll of the tanks.

At reunions of veterans after fifty years it is not unusual to hear tank crew members still wondering at the mentality which sent parades of tanks up those open slopes under the noses of the most fearsome gun ever used in a major war. It does appear on the surface that tank regiments were sacrificed without benefit of surprise, cover or infantry support in this way. Taking the wider view, Montgomery was under tremendous pressure to make an urgent attack. His own long-term strategy also required this. In fact the Goodwood concept might have achieved one or all of three possibilities:

1. It might have made a wide breach in the German defences which would have permitted a fast drive towards the Seine and Paris;
2. It might have cost the enemy more proportionally in irreplaceable losses of men and equipment than it would cost the well-supplied Allies;
3. It would cause the Germans to continue congregating around the hub of Caen while the Americans were preparing to launch their Operation Cobra breakout on the Allied right.

Another consideration in Montgomery's mind was that he was lacking in infantry while there was an endless supply of tanks, both in Normandy and from the depots stretching from England back to Detroit. Total tank losses sounded catastrophic but they represented mainly replaceable material. Human losses were much lower than in an infantry attack. A general cannot avoid casualties and the soldier knows that his trade makes him a potential casualty. Montgomery, like other Second World War Allied generals, is credited with having seen the waste of human life in the 1914–18 trenches and having decided to avoid that sort of 'butcher's bill' as far as possible.

Studying Simonds' approach to Totalize Phase 1 and the British approach to Goodwood, and having made all possible allowance for particular local problems, one is still left with a sneaking suspicion that Goodwood need not have been such a 'Death Ride'. For instance, there is that matter of carriers for the infantry. Not only would they protect the infantry as individuals. They would also provide the tanks with immediate infantry support within the armoured column, as in Totalize. The British general, O'Connor, wanted carriers, but his idea was rejected. Simonds decided he would have carriers and made the necessary arrangements. Both were corps commanders. It may well be that Simonds was more concerned because he was working with some 'green' troops, whereas nobody would dare to treat, say, the British Guards Armoured Division as 'green' troops, which they were. The very *élan* of the British armour may have meant that Simonds was more free to innovate and protect than his British counterparts.

The statistics for the Goodwood operation are revealing. Of the tanks taking part 36 per cent were knocked out and 5.14 per cent of the personnel became casualties. The casualty rate among infantry officers was 12.33 per cent compared with 9.69 per cent of tank officers. Infantry other ranks lost 8.85 per cent compared to 4.31 per cent of tank crews. The 2nd Northamptonshire Yeomanry started on 17 July with 72 fit armoured vehicles, on 18 July that had fallen to 46 and on 19 July to 35 ready for action. However, across the three armoured divisions replacement of tanks was rapid. Starting on 17 July with 1,369 fit tanks they were left with 880 at the end of 18 July. On 19 July this had risen to 1,000, and on the next day to 1,060. Some of the losses would have been accident or mechanical breakdown.[11]

Perhaps an ordinary tankie can best portray the flavour of Goodwood:

As we advanced up the ridge, what a sight met our eyes – the whole area strewn with the smoke-blackened carcasses of the 29th Brigade's Sherman Tanks which had 'brewed up' and burnt out, some with their turrets blown off, other still 'brewing' with gouts of orange flame shooting skywards from turret hatches as the ammunition exploded, dead bodies hanging from escape hatches at grotesque angles; dismounted crews were glimpsed trying to rescue wounded comrades from the wrecked vehicles while others were attempting to mend broken tracks amid the swirling black smoke from burning fuel and the flashes of mortar bombs raining down.

No sooner had we emerged from the (railway) arch than we came under heavy fire – these were ANGRY MEN and they were firing AT US. They had the advantage of concealment . . . the next thing I knew was a frightening thud as a shower of sparks enveloped my feet. An AP shell had ploughed through the armour-plate, shattering the idler wheel, and missed the co-driver's and my feet by inches – we both were burned by the heat generated as the shot sheared through the metal. Another thud quickly followed, bringing the tank slewing to a stop minus one track. A cry of 'Bale out!' sent us all running like 'bats out of Hell' for the cover of the railway embankment, with MG bullets zipping around us kicking up the dust.[12]

From one general's point of view what was happening to that tank was entirely logical in that location:

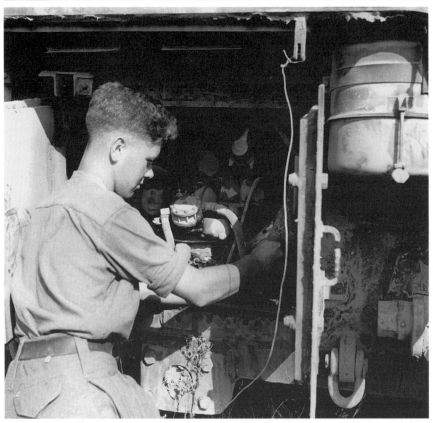

Driver Jock Scobbie, 'C', 1st Northamptonshire Yeomanry, maintains the huge engine. The size of the engine was a major determinant in the design of the Sherman's dangerously tall profile. (IWM, B8797)

The open terrain, with wide horizons extending to more than two kilometers, assured the Germans of superiority in the duel between our Shermans and Cromwells on the one hand and their Tigers and Panthers 'ainsi que l'incomparable canon de 88 mm' on the other.[13]

It was little short of a miracle, as another Yeomanry officer, A.E. Saunders, remarked that although 'our Cromwells, very comfortable tanks were under weight, under gunned and under armoured yet' 2nd Northamptonshire Yeomanry 'somehow managed to clear the ridge around Hubert Folie' of the well-protected defenders.[14]

Don Gillate did not have the protection of even a Cromwell tank. He was mounted in an infantry scout platoon carrier of 8th Battalion, the Rifle Brigade. His platoon had been encouraged at first by the preliminary bombing:

All the bombers in the world came over and dropped their cargo . . . we wondered whether there would be anything left for us to do . . . we came to the line of the railway . . . looking over the embankment we saw a solid wodge of dug in tanks and anti-tank guns . . . they picked off our tanks which went up like boxes of matches set on fire . . . the worst was the sort of noise an AP shot makes . . . a terrifying noise . . . if you can imagine putting your ear right up against a solid metal bath, and somebody the other side of the bath hitting it with a sledge-hammer. . . . You hear the shots and wonder which is the one with your number on it.[15]

Maczek made another comment which harks back to Liddell Hart's First World War formula about the relation of width of front to depth of penetration of the attack:

The tactical mission of exploiting the breach and rapidly gaining Points 195 and 205 caused two armoured divisions to make a rigid frontal attack on a very limited front. This is precisely the only form of action which an armoured division cannot undertake because its armour is too feeble.[16]

Although Maczek's comment was specific to Operation Totalize, it could be applied with even more relevance to Goodwood. In the latter battle the armour had to make its way through an extremely narrow corridor before it could hope to spread out on to a front below Bourguebus Ridge. Even that eventual front was still narrow for three armoured divisions, being only slightly wider than the Totalize front.

A further observation might be made about the concept of 'typical tank country' as applied to open rolling slopes. By contrast, tight, closed small farming country seems to have been regarded as non-tank country. Yet more than once tanks operated with success in the Bocage if coordinated well with the infantry. An example is the liberation of Noyers-Bocage, in which the 1st Northamptonshire Yeomanry figured. For this advance, which was also to some extent a feint before Goodwood, the tank squadrons each worked with an infantry battalion of 59th Division. The formations had not previously worked together in this way. The advance would be through typical Bocage fields intersected by very narrow lanes. The lanes were bounded by hedges which could be higher than the head of a man standing on the tank turret – a personal experience of the author, eyes about 16 ft above ground level and still not able to see over the top of the hedge. The hedges were, in turn, set on steep banks which might be up to 3 or 4 ft high in cases. Not 'typical tank country'.

On 16 July Shermans of 1st Northamptonshire Yeomanry did their Beecher's Brook leap over the first hedge banks, crashing through into fields which were so small that they would hardly have provided room for a decent tennis court, much less a football pitch. There was usually operational room for only one tank in each field and generally a tank could not see what was happening in the fields on either side. Typically a troop of four tanks would be advancing through three fields with the Firefly behind in reserve. The troop leader would coordinate the advance by sensible use of wireless and map. The successful penetration of a hedge by the tank would be followed by a 'brassing up' of the next hedge and then an infantry dash to that hedge, covered by tank guns. While theoretically this setting gave an advantage to the defenders, the tightness of ranges deprived defending Panthers of their great superiority at ranges of 500 yd or more.

Flame-throwing Crocodiles and rocket-firing Typhoons (against approaching Tigers) also took part. The 1st Northamptonshire Yeomanry knocked out three anti-tank guns, drove off a Panther formation and took nearly 500 prisoners for the loss of 3 of their own tanks, 1 on a mine. On one day 'A' Squadron took 310 prisoners, including 5 officers, which was a record at that stage of the Normandy campaign. But not in 'typical tank country'.

The temporary collaboration between 59th Division infantry and 1st Northamptonshire Yeomanry, together with the success of Simonds' Night March formations, inevitably raises the subject of 'battle groups', common in the German army and coming into favour in the American army in 1944. The first day of Goodwood was fought with, at times, no infantry and, otherwise, insufficient numbers of infantry. The tank spearheads of Goodwood did not have, as did the tank spearheads of Totalize, an entire infantry battalion, just 100 yd back and able to speed up to the front in armoured carriers, to say nothing of the various auxiliary vehicles also at that remove.

While it has been customary to write off First World War tactics as typical of generals described as 'donkeys', one or two recent writers have pointed out that tactics did indeed evolve in that war, especially in relation to the newly introduced element of armour. One writer points out that as early as the battle for High Wood on the Somme in 1916 a battle group was formed in which, as an integral part of the infantry attack, there were a cavalry brigade, field engineers with bridges, two armoured cars, a machine-gun squadron and a field artillery battery.[17]

The same writer says that 'Cambrai did help to crystalize the need for a concerted programme of tank training with other arms, even though this also meant spelling out the tank's limitations very early', referring to the fact that it was noisy (wireless sets installed could not be heard), blind, tore up signallers' wire, was in danger in built-up areas and woods, ran into difficulties with large craters and in mud and was already vulnerable to enemy armour-piercing shot and to mines. So the tank needed protection from all these dangers.

This early identification of the need for combined training highlights the criticism of a more recent British general:

> The majority of Allied infantrymen had never trained closely with armour and had no idea how to communicate with the tanks they could often see only a stone's throw away. For instance, it was not until they arrived in England in late February 1944 that the men of the 30th US Infantry Division 'for the first time . . . practised in earnest working with tanks'. . . . The tank telephone – housed in a simple box on the back of a tank so that someone outside could talk to those inside – was not in service in June 1944.[18]

The above statement is a reminder of Capt 'Bing' Crosby loaning the infantry a tank 'B' set before Totalize. It was also the author's experience, commanding a tank in September and October 1944, that the method of the, by then, good friends of the Highland Division for communication with a tank was a bang on the steel plates with an entrenching tool and then a shouting match which might have suggested a competition for hearty lungs at the Highland Games. Where British and Canadian tank units worked regularly with the same infantry units a good understanding quickly arose, leading, for example, to the 51st Highland Division commander, Rennie, insisting on retaining the link with 33rd Armoured Brigade after Totalize. But all such arrangements tended to be on an *ad hoc* basis with no move towards actual reorganization on the part of higher authority.

The dilemma in which some tanks units were placed in their relationship with infantrymen – as contrasted to the later 51st Highland Division and 33rd Armoured Brigade collaboration – is well illustrated by the experience of that abused regiment, 148 RAC, after its arrival in Normandy. Although ostensibly part of an established armoured brigade, it suffered a 'pillar to post' instability. From D + 8 landing to D + 58 it came under command of, or worked with, 33rd Armoured Brigade, 49th Division, 7th Armoured Division, 56th Brigade, 2nd Gloucesters, 2nd South Wales Borders, the 1/6th Queen's, 53rd (Welsh) Division, Army Reserve, 51st Highland Division, 32nd Guards Brigade, 51st Highland Division, 9th Brigade, 6th Airborne Division, 49th Division and back to 51st Highland Division, before, as an integral part of its own 33rd Armoured Brigade, taking part in Totalize with 7th Black Watch. Not an ideal way to promote close tank and infantry collaboration!

Lt-Gen Guy Simonds is given the credit for a number of innovations in his Totalize plan, such as the use of Kangaroos, the Night March and so on. To this should be added his deliberate and effective use of battle groups at a time when the regimental system still held sway. Not every writer has been happy with the British army's attitude towards tank and infantry cooperation or the attitudes within the structure of armoured troops:

> The long-standing problems of cooperation were at the heart of the situations now found in Normandy . . . it also stemmed from the old and seemingly never-ending jealousies inspired during the interwar period when the Royal Tank Corps was considered nothing more than a support arm of the infantry. . . . When the Royal Armoured Corps (RAC) was created after the outbreak of the Second World War, it was staffed with many ex-cavalry officers who had no great desire to serve in this new force. . . . In practice each cavalry regiment remained distinct and exclusive. The officers of the Royal Tank Regiment were deemed outsiders unworthy of admission to this exclusive club. . . . The Germans had no such problems when they created the panzer division, which was built around the concept of a combined arms team.[19]

The same historian quotes Brig Hargest about an action of 7th Armoured Division on 11 June:

> They could not locate the enemy opposition which was well hidden and so could not get on. Although they had an infantry brigade under

command . . . there was no supporting infantry company within three miles of the front . . . our tanks are badly led and fought. Only our superior numbers and our magnificent artillery support keeps them in the field at all. . . . My opinion is that a great deal of their failure is due to the retention of the absurd Regimental system. Because there is no work for cavalry the Cavalry Regiments were given tanks.

Brig Hargest's opinion is undoubtedly unjust to other tanks units, which were well led and well fought, but his basic points merit consideration. How, in Normandy beachhead conditions, could tanks be expected to operate when there was no infantry within 3 miles? As to the regimental system, which gave a tremendous boost to the morale of its members, under the pressures of war it did begin to adapt. In many cases lower ranks moved to a new regiment and became accepted as individuals or as small reinforcement units. Stan Whitehouse's Ox and Bucks platoon moved into the Black Watch, continued there as a platoon, but integrated well and found the Black Watch officers and senior NCOs efficient and accepting of the transfusion of Sassenach blood. Bill Deeming and others eventually became happy in the transfer of their loyalty from 148 RAC to 144 RAC or 1st Northamptonshire Yeomanry. Larger formations moved outside the territorial confines of peacetime. The very Scottish 1st Highland Light Infantry served in the Welsh Division. Tom Renouf, MM, quotes the Tyneside Scottish who moved to the Black Watch. The Devons, Dorsets and Hampshires were a long way from home in the Northumberland Division. And, of course, a county Yeomanry regiment with tanks could be reinforced by young trained conscripts from any and every other county in the country.

There is room for criticism too in the area of minor tactics. Consider, for example, the Mark IV tank at Saint-Aignan which shot, hull down, its gun at ground level, against Sherman tanks with their turrets high in the apple trees – how appropriate for such a moment were the months of normal tank training on Salisbury Plain or Thetford Heath when the old orchards and small farms of Herefordshire would have been better terrain? How much consideration went into the idea of using the Firefly secret weapon as a single unit in a troop of four tanks, rather than as a united troop? The contrast is the German practice of forming an entire troop of Tigers.

One writer already quoted points out the weakness of the squadron net wireless system, whereby squadrons operated on the 'A' set while RHQ worked on the separate 'B' set frequency (although this sytem was not universal – 2nd Northamptonshire Yeomanry used it but 1st Northants used a total regimental net):

[It] had the disadvantage that the only information reaching the colonel on regimental net was the squadron rear link captain's impression of what was happening. If the squadron commander was too preoccupied to pass to his captain snippets of 'picture' from time to time over the short range 'B' set, the captain's information, denied the chance to listen in to squadron net by the requirement to stay tuned to the regimental one, could be quite limited.[20]

Simonds' own ADC, Stearns, underlined this communication problem on a wider scale, saying, 'I am certain in my own mind that General Simonds felt that the lack of communication, liaison, wireless, from formation to formation, leading units to leading units, etc., had more to do than anything else with the failure of the armour to get on as planned.[21]

Before leaving the specific point of tank and infantry cooperation it might be germane to ask if subsequent battle commanders have been more ready to read the lessons of previous failures? Hastings remarks that 'Lieutenant Andrew Wilson, who fought as a British tank officer in north-west Europe and worked on occasion with American infantry, visited Vietnam a quarter of a century later as a correspondent and noted the same carelessness on the battlefield that he had observed in 1944–45'.[22]

Perhaps it is now far enough away from the event to dare to ask questions about the Falklands War. At the time there was much public interest in, and admiration for the British infantry attack at Goose Green. Yet why was the British army still using tactics which were already outmoded by July 1916 at High Wood on the Somme? This was a direct, frontal attack across open ground against automatic fire. Tactically it was inappropriate and strategically it was unnecessary, for Goose Green was not anywhere near as important, if left behind the army's line of advance, as Tilly or Fontenay were during Totalize.

There does seem to have been an element of arrogance in the British attitude to the Falklands combat, in that the self-styled élite units felt that they could easily win that little scrap without having to set up a proper war formation. They did, of course, win. The cross-country 'yomping' may have made for picturesque television action, but was it all necessary? In one book on the war the word 'Armour' only occurs (on the British side) as the surname of a Marine corporal. The Argentines had arrived firing from Amtracs (armoured carriers).[23] Presumably the planners of the British response held that the logistics of carrying, landing and maintaining British armour so far away, added to the influential foot soldiers' confidence in their own abilities, meant that at least some British soldiers paid the price of lack of heavier support, if only a troop or two of armour, at crisis moments.

By the time of the Gulf War the British Armoured Brigades were using the battle group although, from a regimental point of view, still adhering to the traditional structure. The Staffordshires (infantry) were a part of the 7th Armoured Brigade, which inherited the 'Desert Rats' tradition. For the important break-out overnight on 25 February 1991 a battle group was formed of the Scots Dragoon Guards and 'A' Company of the Staffords. Points of interest in that battle were, first, the brilliant use of night sights (which would have been most useful during Totalize); secondly, political imperatives had deprived all tank regiments of the ability to fight a full war establishment, and therefore the chosen regiments had to be brought up to strength by temporary drafts from other regiments; and thirdly, bearing in mind the technological problems of night navigation during Totalize, Brig Cordingley in the Gulf had to halt his night operation for fifteen minutes because the space satellites, upon which his GPS navigation system depended, had temporarily moved out of range.[24]

Harking back to Totalize, and having dealt with tank and infantry cooperation, it is necessary to refer again to ground-air cooperation in view of the friendly fire suffered during Totalize. Day bombing, as on 8 August, was repeated during later phases of Totalize and Tractable. One airman, Ralph Briars, refers to the simple faith which tank crews put in their yellow smoke bombs. Standing instructions for crews were that, if attacked by friendly aeroplanes, you release yellow smoke as identification. Briars comments, 'unless done in very large quantities, it would be hardly noticeable or effective to high flying aircraft, especially if mixed with smoke or mist'.[24] It had also been pointed out that on one day air groups were using yellow target markers which would easily be confused with tanks' yellow smoke.[25] Another airman, Roy Grey of 582 Pathfinder Squadron, emphasized the importance of artillery guidance for air navigators. He says that the Totalize raid was successful because of 'our marking and the Artillery star marking which was seen to land every 10 seconds on the aiming point. There was considerable smoke at ground level and we were continually adjusting during the assault.'[26]

During the interim between Phase 1 and Phase 2 of Totalize the traffic problem was such that the echelon bringing up the necessary coloured shells did not reach the artillery until minutes before the US Air Force marker bombers were due. The gunners were still unpacking the shells as they fired. They had needed to move their guns forward to shoot beyond the new front lines. However, the great breakdown in momentum, which surprised Panzer Meyer and which was caused by the Phase 2 armour awaiting the bombers, was more of a diplomatic problem. Simonds could have moved the armour earlier by simply cancelling the bombers. His own biographer found a good reason for his failure to do that:

Meyer did not understand that an important imperative of Simonds' retention of the bombing was that, from the 21st Army Group downwards, the army had been at pains to acquire air support, but was still having trouble with procedures. The 83rd Group insisted on vetting all army requirements, and they took so long to do it that, in the words of Brig Churchill Mann, Crerar's chief of staff, 'The situation as it stands at present makes it quite impossible to expect that there can be any heavy or effective air attacks within a matter of several hours. . . . Cancelling arrangements made after such a laborious procedure would have been a political error and would have mortgaged future air support.'[27]

The cancellation problem was exacerbated by the current bad feeling between British and Americans, with the Canadians, as it were, in the middle. Some of the American commanders and politicians were exasperated by what they perceived as the slow progress of the British and Canadians around Caen, and angered by Montgomery's attitudes and even outright verbal criticism of American actions. For Simonds to have cancelled, at the shortest notice, a raid by a fleet of American bombers which was already in the air would have provoked an outcry, and might have been countermanded by higher authority than Simonds, even if such a cancellation had been feasible in the system of the day.

The reference to bad feeling at 'the top' suggests that there should also be some brief review of what one might call 'command–troops cooperation'. It is well and good for sergeant-majors or adjutants to call troops to attention on the parade ground and expect a uniform click of heels. It is a totally different matter when soldiers are being killed, others wounded and others burying their pals, at a time when it seems that what has been called the 'War between the Generals' is absorbing more attention than the generals' concern for the battle. Much has been written about Montgomery's popularity with the troops and his concern for their morale. Perhaps it is enough to say that the popularity was not necessarily universal or without reservation. The general, clever as he was, often presented a supercilious or arrogant face to the world. It is a very minor thing, but he wore two badges in his hat, which may have endeared him to the people who wore the same badge but it was an infringement of discipline from a man who expected total obedience from others. He often appeared in 'scruff order'. There is a photograph of the Supreme Commander welcoming the Poles as they arrived in Normandy for their own 'Death Ride of the Tanks'. The Poles have paraded immaculately. Montgomery has appeared in dress that for some soldiers would reasonably have merited seven days behind the guard mounting or round the parade ground in FSMO before reveille.

Again, perhaps these are quibbles but they are also the gnat stings of a group of prima donnas in uniform, whose main concern was not always the battle. One writer refers to Montgomery's 'fetish of requiring his superiors to visit him rather than the other way around'. He also criticized Eisenhower both implicitly and explicitly and 'lectured Eisenhower on how a Supreme Commander should remain above the battle'.[28] One who took part thought that Montgomery was dreaming of repeating El Alamein on the rolling plains of the Goodwood battle, but found that the rolling plains were not the desert.[29]

One of the author's advisers has warned him, 'Don't confine any complaints to Brit and Canuck brass, because boobs between SHAEF and a number of Allied lower commands were, in my opinion, flagrantly more significant. Our WW2 British crowd were, on the whole, so very much better than their forebears in the Great War that I tend to be uncritical'.[29] Point taken. There was arrogance and incompetence on all sides. Patton, however brilliant in action, was totally undisciplined, to the point, at times, of irresponsibility. Eisenhower seemed to have had problems with his various roles. Von Kluge was a vacillating toady, but not so bad as Keitel nor as vicious as Schoerner.[30] What cannot be refuted is that, overall, Montgomery's strategy in Normandy 'had worked, although it had taken longer and cost more than he had anticipated. . . . The quality of his divisions, and their commanders was very varied, and he knew it. . . . He was sensitive to the morale of his soldiers. He knew there were limits, beyond which he could not push them'.[31]

A last word might therefore be said about the vexed subject of 'The British', or 'The Canadian Soldier'. It is generally accepted that the German army was, at its best, composed of well-trained, brave, sometimes fanatical, and technically skilled soldiers. Brig G.L.W. Andrews, a battalion CO in Totalize, made an honest appraisal of the relative attitudes:

The German soldier remained on the whole our superior in fighting skill and determination. It may not be a valid comparison, but the contrast between two photographs in Max Hastings' book 'Overlord' impressed me. One . . . 'classic portrait of a British infantryman in Normandy' shows a slouching, unshaven soldier with his helmet on the back of his head a cigarette drooping from his mouth. The other, of a German prisoner, is of an erect figure gaunt with fatigue but with a proud and hawk-like air even in defeat.[32]

Others are, perhaps, a little more sympathetic. One survivor of Goodwood, not a Desert Rat, thought that criticism of the 7th Armoured Division in Normandy as being 'tired' was unfair. 'They had a lot to be tired about. . . . It is a great mistake to think that the more experienced you are, the more skilled you become. Continual combat takes such a toll of your morale that eventually you are going backwards.'[33] Many of the troops encountered situations which they found most depressing and not a suitable preparation for combat:

A former officer recalls that prior to the operation (Totalize) his regiment had been stationed for several days near Soliers. In the area were some fifty knocked-out British tanks. For troops yet uncommitted to battle, he felt that this sight not only had a depressing effect on their morale but was to make them overly cautious when they first went into battle.[34]

In some cases it was inadequate training which was to blame for individual lack of skills. One tank crew reinforcement recalls:

we did not have time even for a rudimentary introduction to the Sherman. Our commander had not led a tank into combat, the gunner, as far as I knew, had never fired a 75 mm, I had never fired a Browning MG or driven a Sherman (as co-driver), and John (the driver) was in a similar situation himself. Only Norman was fully efficient at his job. However, things soon fell into place and we very soon became a proud part of the Troop and Squadron.[35]

Perhaps a balanced, as well as authoritative comment would be the following:

Again and again in Normandy, British units fought superbly, with great bravery, only to lack the last ounce of drive or follow-through necessary to carry an objective or withstand a counter-attack. The inexperience of American, British and Canadian formations must be measured against the performance of the 12th SS Panzer. This, too, was a 'green' division which had never fought in battle before 7 June.[36]

The need to qualify that general opinion, which has much to support it, by citing exceptions to the rule is a reason for writing this book. In Phase 1 of

Totalize British and Canadian troops did carry their objectives and withstand the counter-attack in the victory, which the victors have so often forgotten.

To put it another way, what would have been the result if, in the Goodwood battle, the British tank crews had been sitting up on the ridge armed with 88 mm guns, and the German soldiers had been forced to drive through a narrow, long corridor in inferior tanks with inadequate guns under the open sights of the 88s?

Chapter Ten

The Verdict

*'I should like you to think next what a great achievement you thought it was in
the past to gain all that you have now conquered, and now hold. I am perfectly
sure that you would have prayed for the achievement of all that has been
accomplished, rather than for many times the amount of money.'*
(Xenophone, 400 BC)

In Operation Totalize men planned brilliantly, men achieved gallantly, men
died with little glory and men suffered a lifetime's physical disability or
psychological bedevilment in breaking through one of the strongest
defensive positions of any war, manned by some of the most skilled and
valiant soldiers. This book therefore seeks to provide a balance to the
general assortment of information available on the Normandy campaign.

Firstly, there have been fewer studies, and even fewer pages of
commentary in the realm of military history concerning Phase 1 of Totalize
compared to, say, Phase 2, Operation Goodwood or the simultaneous
American Cobra. Each of those in certain respects lacks the level of military
innovation and success to be found in Phase 1 of Totalize.

Secondly, where Totalize is given space, a number of errors and
misunderstandings have crept in and need to be corrected. For instance, one
respected author quotes an eye-witness as saying of Totalize Phase 1, 'It was
such an easy one . . . after getting all keened up to fight hard, there was very
little resistance and the objective was taken in one of the easiest actions of the
war.'[1] This may have been true of individual tank crews, some of whom did
sleep in tanks in the centre of Night March columns, but as a reflection of the
entire picture of Phase 1 it is a gross misstatement. It is most unfair to men
like 'Rad' Radley-Walters, or Tom Boardman, and especially Des Coakley
and others who lie in the cemeteries of Banneville-Campagne and Cintheaux.

Thirdly, it raises questions about military studies which so often tend to
emphasize Allied, and particularly British, defeats and shortcomings and ignore
some of the more positive actions on the Allied side. There does also seem in
some works a tendency to rectify former disdain of and horror about the
reputation of SS Panzer Divisions by moving the pendulum to a position where
German troops could do no wrong militarily and German material must
inevitably surpass Allied products, much truth though there be in such assertions.

Simonds' biographer complains that:

Since the German army became an ally in the cold war, British and
American historians, by tending to agree [with some German

criticisms], have downgraded their own side. Moreover German criticism is blessed with hindsight and cannot, by the nature of the evidence, compare like with like. The Germans did not enjoy offensive successes themselves in the later stages of the war. Nevertheless the spoiling defence by thin and exhausted battle groups that faced the Canadians and Poles in Totalize and Tractable excite our admiration and make us question the competence of the attackers. Yet, whilst the Twelfth SS Panzer Division was as green at the start of the campaign as the Third Canadian, they had veteran officers and NCOs to lead them, and that helped them to avoid making many tactical errors.[2]

As to errors, the present writer is all too aware of human fallibility, having been caught, in times past, quoting Browning machine-guns as firing .303 bullets (instead of .300) and Custer riding with the 17th Cavalry (7th). Some errors result from misunderstanding of the situation at the time and others have arisen from inaccurate criticism. One Polish survivor, J.W. Suchitz, is still annoyed by enemy criticism that the Poles were late for Phase 2 of Totalize because they were eating their breakfasts instead of moving forward. As can now be seen, the Poles were held back to avoid the American air assault. A minor, but more relevant military error committed by a number of authorities shows the infantry units as comprising or commanding the Night March columns. The infantry colonels did not take over from the armoured regiment commanders until the debussing points.

A picturesque description of the Wittmann attack has fifty-two 1-ton Tigers roaring along in open wedge formation – probably a misreading of the fact that the Tiger weighed 52 ton. The Germans themselves reported Cintheaux recaptured before the Canadians had captured it. Wittmann is variously reported as having been in action earlier than his death fight, or duelling at length with overwhelming odds. It seems clear now that he advanced only once on 8 August, and that he did not perish, as in one famous illustration, fighting single-handed in his Tiger, surrounded by five Firefly tanks at a range of 20–50 yd.[3] A well-known note in the Canadian corps HQ log records the Poles reporting twenty Tigers near Saint-Aignan in the afternoon of 8 August (probably Mark IVs). The 33rd Armoured Brigade has been variously described (when actually mentioned!) in Totalize accounts as the 33rd Armoured 'Division' and the 33rd 'Tank' Brigade ('tank' brigades and 'armoured' brigades being somewhat different creatures).

Perhaps the gravest error of military criticism has been, with few exceptions, to allow Phase 1 of Totalize to be totally overshadowed by later events. This raises yet more questions. It has already been suggested on other pages that the tragedy of the later phases of the advance on Falaise was not so much the actual time taken to cover so many miles of ferociously defended, strategically vital road, but the expectations against which that timing has ever since been measured. Take away the expectations of Montgomery and Crerar, consider only the achievements of Simonds, and the march to Falaise would be accorded a much more positive and glorious position in military history, even with the aberrations of Worthington Force and the first mad charge of the Poles. Casualties and delays are endemic in military strife.

During the Normandy campaign itself there was much dissent among Allied commanders as a result of misunderstandings, more than once arising from Montgomery's inflated proclamations or his failure to correct the false impressions of others. His own head of operations and planning was quite clear that Montgomery's battle objectives were less ambitious than was generally understood. On the subject of the apparently disastrous Goodwood venture he states: 'Montgomery . . . set up a force of three armoured and four infantry divisions . . . not to break out . . . but to hold the German armour by a very limited but concentrated attack to the Bourguebus ridge. He succeeded in his purpose.'[4]

If others had misunderstood, it seemed that Montgomery was saying, 'That doesn't matter to me. If they are not intelligent enough to understand my strategy without explanation, let them carry on in ignorance.' At the same time he, or people linked with him, did make rather ambitious statements. The need to reach airfields in Normandy was a constant preoccupation of air commanders, which 'Montgomery had called vital for improved tactical support for his troops. . . . Montgomery had confidently predicted that the territory would be quickly in Allied hands, but it was still out of reach'.[5] He also failed to contradict erroneous statements:

> At a press conference (8th August) at Montgomery's headquarters, de Guingand and the Canadian army commander, Crerar, stated that the war would be over in three weeks. Butcher told Eisenhower of that wild boast, so detached from any reality; Eisenhower regretted it, but there was little he could do.[6]

Montgomery himself did not deign to deny the 'wild boast' emanating from his own headquarters and uttered by the two men most likely to know his mind on the continuing Totalize situation. It is most likely that Montgomery was misunderstood by lesser mortals. It is not unlikely that he allowed himself to be misunderstood. While he had learned many lessons from the tragedies of the First World War it seems that he had not chosen to avoid the earlier generals' habit of indicating unreasonable objectives to difficult military endeavours.

All that has been said above is simply to highlight the atmosphere of misunderstanding and distrust which prevailed among Allied leaders (military and civil) during August 1944. While Hastings did not necessarily accept that Montgomery was in any way stampeded into less than judicious decisions by this prevailing atmosphere,[7] it is a factor that must be taken into account. Although there is no direct evidence to support the proposition, it is likely that Simmonds was cleft into a mental dichotomy, between professionally planning an operation as ordered to meet outrageous expectations (Ifs to Falaise in two days) and intellectually recognizing that the facts portended a less ambitious outcome. There is certainly evidence that two of the foremost leaders of Goodwood, O'Connor and Roberts,

A Gordon Highlander escorts German prisoners during Totalize, their faces revealing all aspects of surrender – relief, stupor, arrogance, resignation. (IWM, B8818)

approached their tasks with a will to succeed but a recognition that all was not well with the premises of the proposition.[8]

Perhaps it is difficult for senior generals to instruct corps commanders like Simmonds to 'make a further attack up the Falaise Road, planning optimum outcome for available input'. As with all commanders, Simmonds would accept responsibility for any shortcomings in his planning. He might be 'blamed' on four points:

1. Totalize took place on a very narrow front, to which both Maczek and Kitching objected. But Simmonds used the entire width of country which was available to his corps, and also judged that his new formations would be less at risk if confined within close boundaries. Worthington Force went astray when asked to undertake a more complicated manoeuvre.

2. There were immense traffic jams which might have been foreseen. But there does not appear to be evidence of any undue operational delay on a large scale. Also there appear to have been failures at a lower command level to cope with such problems.

3. He did not allow fully for the delays caused by enemy resistance in Tilly, May and Fontenay. However, had he done so, his entire plan, to conform to the ordained time targets, would have been impossible to schedule.

4. He allowed the pause before the American bombing, giving the enemy time to regroup. But it has already been seen that there were

reasons for not changing or cancelling the American raid at the last moment. In any case the armoured force available should have been able to receive the German response (as at Saint-Aignan) and then break through again.

One of the unsolved mysteries of Totalize is the failure of the Germans, such skilled defenders, to put down an adequate line of anti-tank mines in the open spaces between fortified villages along the ridges. Very few tanks in the seven columns were knocked out by mines. A thin continuous belt of mines between May-sur-Orne and La Hogue could have caused much delay to the Night March while flails dealt with the mines and explored the possibility of a deeper belt. Perhaps the defenders were relying on direct daylight shoots as in Goodwood. Or perhaps there was a dearth of engineers available to lay the mines. The use of engineers as stop-gap fighting infantry did mean that a number of specialist engineer tasks were left either unfulfilled or badly delayed.

A number of commentators, contemporary and more recent, have considered that the Totalize forces might have reached Falaise sooner than they did and thus could have closed a pocket at Falaise instead of later at Chambois. Maczek was not of that opinion. He had doubts before the operation and in retrospect saw it as impossible:

> My personal opinion – the armoured divisions (Polish and Canadian) were not able to break the German lines on days 8 to 10 August because that was beyond their possibilities. 4 kilometers of first defences were penetrated by the Night March but at Soignolles and Quesnay woods there were 'truffees d'abris' and pill boxes at 8 to 10 kilometers beyond the first line.[9]

Panzer commander Kurt Meyer was in no doubt as to the danger which the Night March penetration represented, in the course of his now famous 'soliloquy' near Cintheaux:

> I was afraid because I realized that if I failed now, and if I did not deploy my division correctly, the Allies would be through to Falaise, and the German armies in the West would be completely trapped. I knew how weak my division was and the task which confronted me gave me at that time some of the worst moments I had ever had in my life.[10]

Another German who was there, Panzer adjutant Georg Isecke, after half a century of study and reflection, still considers that the way was open for a complete break-out:

> [as] to your night assault with successful occupation of the area around Cramesnil, we had to fear the further offensive in the morning, together with all [your] divisions . . . Yes, it was our opinion that the decision of the Div. Kdr. [Meyer], with 5 hours time, was right for the counter-

thrusts. In consequence, it enabled us to defend the north front of the beginning [of the] Falaise pocket, for some days more.[11]

A number of factors conspired to assist the defenders in their hazardous task against overwhelming forces. Maj-Gen M.F. Reynolds, CB, points out that, in his opinion, the vital gully between Saint-Aignan and Robertmesnil, le Petit Ravin, had been 'overlooked by those planning the operation because it is clearly marked on the map as a tank obstacle and yet the Polish 24th Lancers were directed straight into it! . . . the "going map" still exists and . . . it can been seen in the Polish Institute and Sikorski Museum near the Albert Hall in London.'[12]

Another factor may have been the precipitate nature of such an innovative assault. Simmonds himself clearly recommended more training time in his original plan and argued for it subsequently. Ideally he wanted a week. He was given what looked like four days but in reality some units did not have any opportunity at all to practise.[13] The entire Polish Armoured Division had to be rushed up from the beaches with no time for the complicated business of translated front-line briefing. Simmonds' request was vetoed at the highest level. In fact, some exercise of restraint or patience at that level could have resulted in a faster break-out only a day or two later.

A number of advantages would have accrued:

1. Obviously better staff organization and adequate training of specialized units in their specific tasks, e.g. negotiation of sunken roads and embankments in the dark (fairly brief tank training took place at night on quite level ground at Gazelle, north of Caen).
2. More time for ground–air coordination, possibly avoiding some of daylight 'friendly fire' and also ensuring more use of low-flying ground attacks during the day of 8 August.
3. Adaptation of more Kangaroo-style carriers and developing their use.
4. Improvement of navigation and other technical aids – both the artificial moonlight and the radio direction beams could have been better developed.
5. The Hitlerjugend might well have moved further away from the area, as might also the elements of 101st Heavy Battalion's Tigers. Hitlerjugend division was already under orders to move south but had delayed as long as it could, in direct contravention of Hitler's orders to reinforce the Germans' final attempt to cut off Patton's columns to the south.

On the point of the narrow front chosen by Simmonds, some of the critics have failed to notice the implications of a wider front. On Simmonds' right was the precipitous valley of the Laize in the area of Bretteville-sur-Laize, with the almost impossible country of Bois d'Alençon and Bois de l'Obelisque, two vast wooded areas with defiles, beyond. Bretteville in its ravine was such a tank trap that the Canadians troops who occupied it immediately requested permission to pull their tanks back to the heights above. On Simmonds' left, to the east of Saint-Aignan, was one of the most extensive panoramas even for that part of Normandy, a region still occupied by the enemy. The moment a Polish armoured squadron showed itself on that side of Saint-Aignan it was decimated, in the precise sense of the word. The only possible widening of the front of any significance would have been a major advance by the left-hand corps, a British corps but still under command of the Canadian army. Crerar did not envisage this.

It is difficult to study the details of 8 August without feeling some sympathy with Simmonds. His biographer, in quoting another (English) historian on the failure to cancel the American bombing attack, reveals also a failure of support for Simmonds in command:

> That he should have been overruled is quite clear, but equally clearly it would have taken an army commander with the *coup d'oeil* and stature of a Dempsey or Patton to do it. Crerar simply did not know as much as Simmonds, which in effect left the 2 Corps commander without any of the usual counsel, help, and coercion that he might have received from an army headquarters. He could not have been more alone.[14]

Another critic then carries the responsibility back from Crerar to Montgomery, suggesting that he might have used the 7th Armoured Division to reinforce the Canadian push towards Falaise:

> Whatever mistakes may have been committed during this series of battles, the most serious by Montgomery was failing to take advantage of the opportunity to reinforce the Canadians and thus bolster the advance on Falaise. Time was critical if the trap were to be sprung successfully. Montgomery's Operations Officer, General Belchem, has admitted that his C.-in-C. had forces available to reinforce them but did not do so.[15]

One might add to that observation the query as to why Montgomery and Dempsey continued to hammer away at the shoulder of the horseshoe trap when it was the two wings which needed to be closed on the enemy? By 8 August the Allied front resembled a horseshoe with one long flange and one short one. The long wing was represented by Patton's roaming columns, the short wing by Totalize. All classic lessons from Cannae (Carthaginians v. Romans, 216 BC) to Isandhlwana (Zulus v. British, 1879) suggested that in an enveloping movement the greatest power and mobility needed to be on the wings. It might be necessary to keep some pressure on the encircled centre to prevent a saving retreat, but it was the wings which were vital to the total success of the enterprise. At the time of Totalize a number of the best, or most complete, British divisions, including the 11th and Guards Armoured Divisions, as well as the 7th, were not made available on the short wing. Perhaps too much priority was given to maintaining pressure on the endangered German centre. It has also been pointed out that the congested Normandy beachhead inhibited fast movement of large groups of troops from one wing to another, as in Goodwood. On the other hand, one of the results of Goodwood itself was to open more options for movement of troops behind the lines.

It has been observed frequently that Montgomery was suffering from a lack of infantry reinforcements and had therefore to vary his strategy accordingly.

Estes has dissented from that point of view, noting that there were considerable numbers of trained infantry, many in well-established battalions, still available in Britain.[16] Given Montgomery's good understanding with Brooke, it is doubtful if a reasonable further reinforcement would have been denied him, although this seems to be the assumption of some writers. The Germans certainly calculated that the Canadian 2nd Corps already possessed enough strength to overwhelm the meagre German forces in front of Falaise. Simmonds himself was quickly aware that his wealth of numbers was not reflected in speed or potency of attack. Crerar could have widened the front to outflank the already overstretched defenders around Robertmesnil. Montgomery could have reinforced Simmonds directly or given Crerar the instructions and forces to widen the attack. Some commentators refer to a fear on the part of the British that such reinforcement would cause resentment on the part of the sensitive Canadians. At the time the Canadians seemed delighted to have the 51st Highland Division seconded to them, and it is doubtful whether the very professional Simmonds would have resented an addition of power to ensure the complete attainment of his objectives and the total justification of his novel concepts.

A further area of debate related to Totalize concerns the choice between a short and a long encirclement. The 1st Canadian Army diary during Totalize described the intention of the short hook in rather light-hearted words:

> The current plan is for the Canadians and Yanks to meet at Falaise, enclosing the German Seventh Army in a pocket and destroying it. Should this be a one hundred per cent success, the war is over. The rest will be a motor tour into Germany. It has not been laid on who is to take Falaise . . . the Canadians are driving down from the North, the Yanks are coming up to Argentan from the South.[17]

Montgomery's original intention was for a larger encirclement of the German forces by British and Canadian armies, from the north, and Americans, from the south, meeting along the banks of the Seine. Montgomery's head of operations and planning explained the change of plan:

> Montgomery's preoccupation was to accelerate the Allied thrust to the Seine in keeping with his broad encirclement plan. . . . But Bradley suggested that the suicidal Mortain attack by the Germans offered an opportunity for an 'inner encirclement' of the enemy. If Third US Army could send a Corps north from Le Mans to Argentan and on towards Falaise, to meet 2 Canadian Corps and the Polish Armoured Division driving south, the German troops comprising the remnants of the Mortain counter-attack could be rounded up. Montgomery agreed at once to Bradley's suggestion. . . . The gap was not, however, closed as quickly as had been intended.[18]

Apart from the delays suffered by the Canadian army coming down from the north, there was also a reluctance on the part of the commanders to risk serious 'friendly fire' problems by allowing the north-driving Americans to approach a rendezvous too fast. Falaise was eventually taken but the weight of German retreat and counter-attack had swung the epicentre of trap closure further east. The eventual encirclement could be described as 'short-and-a-half'. This still left open the possibility of a strong northern force reaching the Seine and moving down to meet Patton's main force coming from the opposite direction, well beyond the Falaise-Chambois area and trapping even more enemy troops. Instead the 51st Highland Division and 7th Armoured Division to the north were used more as a kind of mobile firm base rather than an encircling force. Meanwhile other useful British divisions were still retained at the top of the horseshoe when they might have been rushed into a secondary long encirclement movement.

All these hindsight options do not detract from the fact that a very substantial victory was won in Normandy, within Montgomery's general time-frame and enabling an almost bloodless Allied liberation of most of northern France and Belgium. Belchem also observes that at least nine German divisions were still active and battleworthy outside the pocket area and a too impetuous Allied rush to the Seine could have produced disasters.[19]

Returning to Phase 1 of Operation Totalize, it is useful to look at a particular aspect of the German counter-attack on 8 August. Some German accounts claim this, if not as a victory, then at least as a reverse for the Allies, which it certainly was. However, it was not the specific counter-attack itself which was a victory. The objective of the attack was to recapture Saint-Aignan and pass through to occupy the woods at Garcelles-Secqueville. In the end the attack did not move the main Northamptonshire Yeomanry line back from its 08.00 location, and the FDLs of the 1st Black Watch were not penetrated. On the other side of the main road, the Sherbrookes, the Royal Regiment of Canada and others continued to move forward. Only in the greater strategic sense, when compared to expectations, was this a reverse for the Allies.

Concentrating on the German advance towards Saint-Aignan/Gaumesnil, this is seen to be a failed German attack for a very interesting reason. The usual roles in Normandy, of Goodwood, Epsom, Cobra, and so on, had been reversed. Instead of the Allies being the vulnerable attackers they had placed themselves in a position of the advantaged defenders, with German armour constrained to attack. Although the Germans knew the ground, both the Northamptonshire Yeomanry and the Sherbrookes had found their way into good defensive positions in woods and orchards. The destruction of Wittmann's Tiger Troop is the best example of this. Some commentators have noted that, in Normandy, the Germans tended to appear to be better defenders than attackers. This was a reflection of the merits and demerits of the Tiger tank, as well as the Hummel SP, invincible weapons when offered a tasty morsel of Shermans at 2,000 yd range, but given to a rather dinosaurian approach when hunting well-hidden enemy in the jungles of Normandy.

Regiments do tend to develop characteristics, and the Yeomanry attitude was well summed up by one of its youngest soldiers on the day, Bruce Dickson, gunner to Capt Bill Fox: 'I think we scored by having a hunting tradition which permeated down the ranks. Also, the squadron was like a family. For me, having been brought up in an orphanage, the squadron was the first real family I had lived in. The NCOs cared about the "rookies" like me – Troop Sgt Dick Bates was just like an uncle.'

One theme which arises particularly in the Totalize interim, when compared with, say, the Gulf War, is the entire question of 'friendly fire' and post-traumatic counselling. On the Canadian side Bill McAndrew and Terry Copp have studied 'Battle Exhaustion' but it may be that a fascinating treatise could yet be written, drawing on the experiences of surviving veterans who have contributed to this present book, on 1939–45 post-traumatic rehabilitation. The author's wife, Jai, remembers vividly a return visit by Northamptonshire Yeomanry veterans (with wives) in 1984. One eighty-year-old ex-tanker burst into tears, confessing that until that moment he had never been able to deal with all the memories and horrors and personal guilt locked away in his subconscious mind for forty years. Yet discussion at a more recent veterans' reunion tended to suggest that perhaps the imperative to sort out one's own psychiatric problems after the war, without the benefit of counselling, 'made a better man'. It is a matter of record that when a Gulf War general went to speak to the troops after four days in action, the question most asked was 'When are we going home?'[20] Is that a symptom of a 'softer' generation?

It has already been said that this book responds to the relative lack of attention which military historians have given to Phase 1 of Totalize, or to the tendency to pass quickly over the extraordinary achievement of Phase 1 because of later, highly comprehensible disappointments. It would be appropriate therefore to make a final statement, both from the author's own essentially worm's eye view and also drawing upon critics of far greater military authority.

While a major reversal was never likely – that is, of the order of the Allies being forced back to the beachhead perimeter of D + 1 – the Germans might have been able to turn Totalize into a serious catastrophe of delays much more significant that those which are touted by so many critics. If, for instance, 1st Northamptonshire Yeomanry and 1st Black Watch had not stood fast at Saint-Aignan, and the German counter-stroke had burst through Saint-Aignan along the local high contour rim, the Polish advance would have been stymied and the entire operation could have gone lame. With more luck and discretion Wittmann's troop could have stampeded along the east of the main road. With twenty or thirty Mark IVs emerging triumphant out of le Petit Ravin and two efficient HQ 'Escort' companies swinging in an arc further right, the exposed left (eastern) flank of Totalize could have been rolled back almost to the start line, with the 88 mm guns always commanding the open fields of fire from the highest ground. The massed columns of the new Polish and Canadian Armoured Divisions could not have been eliminated by the available German forces, but several days of chaos could have been engendered.

Invoking the opinion of persons with more formal military skills, the first witness to be called is one of the participating COs, the then Lt-Col Derek Lang, who eventually rose to command the Highland Division and achieve full general's rank. He says, referring to Totalize, 'I cannot see how it can be recorded as a failure. The night action by armour and armour carrying infantry was a brilliant conception'.[21] Panzer Meyer himself agreed on more than one occasion with words such as, 'Around noon of 8th August the attacks had generally reached the objectives laid down for Phase 1 . . . the superior Canadian and British forces had achieved a great success'.[22]

In something of a panic Field Marshal von Kluge reported, 'We have to risk everything. A breakthrough has occurred near Caen, the like of which we have never seen.'[23] An early interviewer and commentator stated, 'there is little doubt that, if the Canadian and Polish armoured divisions had been more experienced and aggressive, the Totalize offensive would have been completely successful'.[24] Another participating British soldier called Totalize 'one of the most original and daring operations of the campaign in Europe' and quoted success after the Night March as 'it had been so far complete'.[25] The Argylls recorded that 'this new technique of penetrating deeply into the enemy positions and by-passing certain strong-points on the way met with great success'.[26]

The Canadian originators had no need for modesty about Phase 1 and could say 'the attacking formations, both Canadian and British, had achieved remarkable success. The concept of placing the infantry in Kangaroos had been brilliant, and attacking by night, supported by tanks, had proved well worth the risk.'[27] On a more partisan level, British infantry was, for once, most complimentary to the tanks, a Black Watch CO commenting on the 'excellent navigation on the part of the Northants Yeomanry' and 'the magnificent fire support given by the Yeomanry' and, when the counter-attack materialized, 'the Northants Yeomanry, however, moved forward of our FDLs, and did magnificent work against the Boche tanks, knocking out Tigers and Mark IVs.'[28]

The CO of 144 RAC, added his own gloss:

> Intercepted messages showed the consternation felt by enemy commanders . . . when armour was able to penetrate their forward defences at night. . . . At the expense of comparatively few casualties we were able to seize a key position well inside the enemy's defensive system. This forced him to counter-attack on the afternoon of 8th August . . . which was unsuccessful and cost him a considerable number of tanks.[29]

Some commentaries have tended to minimize German losses during the actual 8 August counter-attack, and to include in the statistics losses incurred by the British tanks during the Night March. It is perhaps relevant at this point to reiterate that, on 9 August, 1st Northamptonshire Yeomanry and 144 RAC were in reserve on their previous day positions. Commanders were therefore able to walk the battlefield and identify specific enemy armoured vehicles which had been knocked out during the counter-attack. In addition, the enemy vehicles thus counted could not be recovered by their owners, whereas about half of the Northants vehicles knocked out on 8 August were recovered and repaired. The same would apply to 144 RAC, 27 CAR and other Allies.

A final word comes from the official War Office report which, in typical terse and almost parsimonious civil 'service-ese', states that 'the operation is an example of a successful night action by tanks and infantry working in close co-operation'.[30]

This saga of heroics and 'Weltschmerz' is not yet complete. Military histories must record the horrifying statistics of combatant casualties and

Comrades for ever. RAF graves below (Torrans/Hill crew) and Yeomanry above – all Totalize casualties.

material losses. What sometimes passes unstated is the disruption and long-term cost to civilian life. In the general area of Caen, Falaise and St Lo, local civilians paid an inordinate price in lives and property so that the rest of France and Belgium (with the exception of certain ports) could be liberated quickly and at relatively little cost. Civilians were killed by the thousands in the holocaust of Caen and by one and twos when mistakenly emerging into the open in the middle of a brief skirmish in a village street or around a farm.

In Normandy many servicemen were revolted by the stench of rotting cattle killed in the battles. Many were even more horrified when called on to act as temporary vets and shoot maimed animals. And the dead animals were the life's work of generations of peasants. As were the demolished orchards and shattered buildings. Bourguebus had a population of about 200 inhabitants but, after Totalize, there remained habitable only the present-day bakery, a house opposite and one farm. La Hogue was totally destroyed. When the inhabitants returned in September they found seventeen or eighteen burned-out tanks between Bourguebus and Tilly (less than 1,000 yd).

Germain Cardon at Bourguebus and Roger Cardon at Tilly had ploughed their land, sweating behind the plodding horses. They had sown their seed and, in a sunny month of August, might have expected a golden harvest. Those cornfields were set on fire and men were burned or asphyxiated in

The same field, Saint-Aignan. Tank men of 'C', 1st Northamptonshire Yeomanry, celebrate on 9 August 1944 with a captured battle flag (above), but in 1994 (below) no sugar beet will grow on the spot where the Todd/Marchant tank brewed. (Photo, Rex Jackson)

them. When the Cardons returned there were patches of corn still standing, but they were infested with rotting human bodies and the dangerous detritus of battle, the very soil sterilized for posterity where tanks had burned.

Friendly fire was tragic but accepted as 'part of the game' by the front-line soldiers. Friendly fire was totally tragic for three men evacuated from Bourguebus on 20 July 1944. Michel Guillot, Roger Othon and André Quesnel were all killed by machine-guns fired from a low-flying Allied aircraft. In the brutal exchanges of war there may be some victors but there are very few winners. May the price of Victory not be forgotten!

Notes & References

Where a person is quoted or cited in the text without a numbered note the information is drawn from a personal statement, verbal or written, to the author by the person concerned, for which the author is most grateful, or from War Diaries, etc., of units concerned.

Chapter headings: Xenophon quotations are from the Rex Warner translation, in *Xenophon, The Persian Expedition*, Penguin, 1949.

Chapter 1. The Night is Not for Sleeping

1 See above. All further references without numbered notes are from personal statements to the author, or from unit records.
2 Florentin, *The Battle of the Falaise Gap.*
3 Lothian & Border Yeomanry (L & B) next day reports in Tank Museum Library, Bovington.
4 Jolly, 'Operation Totalize', *RAC Journal*, vol. 2, 1948.
5 L & B.
6 An application was made on behalf of Simonds for the Kangaroo to be registered as his 'invention' but this was refused by the Inter-Departmental Committee of Awards as it was deemed to have been improvised as part of his normal military duties (Stacey, 1960).
7 Hammerton, *Achtung! Minen!*
8 Florentin, *The Battle of the Falaise Gap.*
9 Birt, *XXII Dragoons*
10 Tout, *Tank!*
11 Birt, *XXII Dragoons.*
12 L & B.
13 Tout, *Tank!*
14 Whitehouse, *Fear is the Foe.*
15 Statement by Col Gevert Haslob.
16 Statement by Maj George Isecke.
17 Graham, *The Price of Command.*
18 Williamson, *Loyalty is my Honour.*
19 L & B.
20 Ibid.
21 Taylor, Tommy Cooker, unpublished text.
22 Tout, *Tanks, Advance!*
23 Tout, *Tank!*
24 L & B.
25 Birt, *XXII Dragoons*
26 L & B.
27 Personal memoirs of Brig G.L.W. Andrews, CBE, DSO.
28 Tout, *Tank!*
29 L & B.
30 Stacey, *The Victory Campaign.*
31 L & B.
32 Jolly, 'Operation Totalize'.
33 L & B.
34 Ibid.
35 Hammerton, *Achtung! Minen!*

Chapter 2. The Unassailable Fortress

1 Belchem, *Victory in Normandy.*
2 Roy, *1944 – The Canadians in Normandy.*
3 Graham, *The Price of Command.*
4 D'Este, *Decision in Normandy.*
5 Maczek, *Avec mes Blindées.*
6 Wallace, *Dragons of Steel.*
7 Graham, *The Price of Command.*
8 Stacey, *The Victory Campaign.*
9 Hastings, *Overlord.*
10 D'Este, *Decision in Normandy.*
11 Jones, K., *Sixty-four Days of a Normandy Summer.*
12 Roy, *1944 – The Canadians in Normandy.*
13 Reynolds, *Steel Inferno.*
14 Agte, *Michael Wittmann.*
15 Hastings, *Overlord.*
16 Isecke, George, personal statement, 1997.
17 Florentin, *The Battle of the Falaise Gap.*
18 Belchem, *Victory in Normandy.*
19 Hastings, *Overlord.*
20 Chant, *Battle Tanks of World War II.*

21 Maczek, *Avec mes Blindées*, and Diemel, personal statement, 1997.
22 Cordingley, *In the Eye of the Storm*.
23 Florentin, *The Battle of the Falaise Gap*.
24 D'Este, *Decision in Normandy*.
25 Williamson, *Loyalty is my Honour*.
26 Decker, Karl-Heinz, personal statement, 1997.
27 Hooper, Dr John, 1997.
28 Graham, *The Price of Command*.
29 Hastings, *Overlord*.
30 D'Este, *Decision in Normandy*.
31 Irving, *The War between the Generals*.
32 Ibid.
33 Ibid.
34 Hamilton, *Montgomery: Master of the Battlefield*.
35 Graham, *The Price of Command*.
36 Belchem, *Victory in Normandy*.
37 Mitcham, *Hitler's Field Marshals*.
38 Ibid.
39 Middlesbrook & Everitt, *The Bomber Command War Diaries*.
40 Richards, *The Hardest Victory*.
41 Roy, *1944 – The Canadians in Normandy*.
42 Cottell, Len, personal statement, 1997.

Chapter 3. Canadian Wizardry

1 Jolly, 144 RAC Notes, Bovington.
2 Grahame, *The Price of Command*.
3 Canadian *Armed Forces News*, 1.2.51.
4 Stacey, *The Victory Campaign*.
5 Birt, *XXII Dragoons*.
6 Hastings, *Overlord*.
7 English, *The Casting of an Army*.
8 Birt, *XXII Dragoons*.
9 This section follows Stacey, *The Victory Campaign*, and war diaries.
10 Delaforce, *Wessex Wyverns*.
11 Hastings, *Overlord*.
12 D'Este, *Decision in Normandy*.
13 Stacey, *The Victory Campaign*.
14 Based on REME reports.
15 Air Plan as distributed to ground forces (in Polish archives).
16 Based on Stacey and Harris' own recollections.
17 Hastings, *Bomber Command*.
18 Len Cottell, personal statement, 1997.
19 This explains the tragedy of the stricken US air leader whose bombs fell when the plane was hit by anti-aircraft fire, causing
the entire group to drop its bombs as normal practice (on own troops).
20 Photos in Air Photo Library, Dept of Geography, University of Keele.
21 Grahame, *The Price of Command*.
22 Maczek, *Avec mes Blindées*.
23 Other writers are strangely silent on the matter of the captured Canadian order.

Chapter 4. The Left Hook

NB. As in Chapter 1, all references without numbered notes are from personal statements to the author or from unit records.

1 Birt, *XXII Dragoons*.
2 Roy, *1944 – The Canadians in Normandy*.
3 Tout, *To Hell with Tanks!*
4 Birt, *XXII Dragoons*.
5 History of The Loyal Regiment.
6 Salmond, *The History of the 51st Highland Division, 1939–45*.
7 Jolly, 'Operation Totalize', *RAC Journal*, 1948.
8 Cameron, *History of the 7th Argylls*.
9 Deeming, W., personal statement.
10 Robertson, C., personal statement.
11 Stacey, *The Victory Campaign*.
12 Extract from 'Moose Squadron' bulletin.
13 Cameron, *History of the 7th Argylls*.
14 War Office, *Current Reports from Overseas, 30 September 1944*, covers the entire course of 1st Northamptonshire Yeomanry's Night March (Unit not identified).
15 Based on author's surveys on the ground.
16 Tout, *Tank!*
17 Hooper, J., unpublished text.
18 Birt, *XXII Dragoons*.
19 Whitehouse, *Fear is the Foe*.
20 Cameron, *History of the 7th Argylls*.
21 Jolly, 'Operation Totalize'.
22 Tout, *Tank!*
23 Personal memoirs of Brig J. Hopwood, DSO.
24 Wilmot, *The Struggle for Europe*.
25 History of the 79th Division.

Chapter 5. The Straight Right

1 Brig S.V. Radley-Walters, letter 9 October 1997.
2 Florentin, *The Battle of the Falaise Gap*.
3 L & B, see chapter 1, note 3 above.
4 Stacey, *The Victory Campaign*.
5 Keegan, *Six Armies in Normandy*.
6 L & B, Maj Watson.

7   Radley-Walters, letter 9 October 1997.
8   L & B, Lt Boreham.
9   Syd Johnson, letter 27 September 1997.
10 Denis Hughes, letter 6 October 1997.
11 Radley-Walters, letter 9 October 1997.
12 L & B.
13 L & B.
14 L & B.
15 Radley-Walters, letter 9 October 1997.
16 This section depends mainly on Stacey, *The Victory Campaign*, and Roy, *1944 – The Canadians in Normandy*.
17 Roy, *1944 – The Canadians in Normandy*, has a particularly good account.
18 Ibid.
19 Gen Sir Derek Lang, KCB, DSO, MC, DL, letters 1997.
20 Brig G.L.W. Andrews, CBE, DSO, personal recollections.
21 Borthwick, *Battalion*.
22 Tout, *To Hell with Tanks!*

Chapter 6. Counterpunch at Saint-Aignan

1   Chronology follows 1st Northamptonshire Yeomanry history, war diaries of participating units and personal recollections.
2   Whitehouse, *Fear is the Foe*.
3   Author checked RAF photos of area for 4, 8 and 9 August 1944.
4   Map held at Polish Institute, London.
5   Meyer, *History of 12th SS Panzer Division – Hitlerjugend*.
6   Hastings, in Introduction to Shulman, *Defeat in the West*.
7   Williamson, *The SS: Hitler's Instrument of Terror*.
8   Meyer, *History of 12th SS Panzer Division – Hitlerjugend*.
9   Brig J.A. Hopwood, DSO, diary, from J.A.R. Anderson, OBE, MC.
10 Neville, *The 1st Northamptonshire Yeomanry in NW Europe*.
11 Salmond, *The History of the 51st Highland Division, 1939–45*.

Chapter 7. A Points Victory

1   Birt, *XXII Dragoons*.
2   Stacey, *The Victory Campaign*.
3   Quoted by Stacey, *The Victory Campaign*.
4   Hammerton, *Achtung! Minen!*
5   Meyer, *History of the 12th SS Panzer Division – Hitlerjugend*.
6   Irving, *The War between the Generals*.
7   Stacey, *The Victory Campaign*.
8   Tout, *Tanks, Advance!*
9   Mieczkowski, *Monuments and Memorials . . .*
10 Conversation – Mieczkowski *et al.*, Polish Institute, 7.8.97.
11 Hammerton, *Achtung! Minen!*
12 Birt, *XXII Dragoons*.
13 Stewart, letter to parents, 1944.
14 Mieczkowski, letter 23.10.97.
15 See note 10 above.
16 Lucas and Barker, *The Killing Ground*.
17 Maczek, *Avec mes Blindées*.
18 From Stacey, *The Victory Campaign*, and Roy, *1944 – The Canadians in Normandy*.
19 Ibid.
20 Keegan, *Six Armies in Normandy*.
21 Birt, *XXII Dragoons*.
22 Whitehouse, *Fear is the Foe*.
23 Florentin, *The Battle of the Falaise Gap*.
24 Griffith-Jones, personal account, 1997.
25 Torrans, personal account, 1997.
26 Niewinowski memoirs (Polish Institute).
27 Stacey, *The Victory Campaign*.
28 Canadian Armed Forces release, 1951.
29 Obituary, *Daily Telegraph*, 13.12.94.

Chapter 8. The Opponent's Corner

1   Shulman, *Defeat in the West*.
2   Isecke, letter 15.8.97.
3   This review based on Williamson, *The SS: Hitler's instrument of Terror*; Hubert Meyer, *History of 12th SS Panzer Division – Hitlerjugend*; and Reynolds, *Steel Inferno*.
4   Haslob, letter August 1997.
5   Ibid.
6   Lucas and Barker, *The Killing Ground*.
7   89th Divisional Report written by Col Neitzel.
8   Haslob, as note 4 above.
9   Shulman, *Defeat in the West*.
10 For Wittmann see Agte, *Michael Wittmann and . . .*, Simpson, *Tiger Ace*, and articles by Taylor, 'Michael Wittmann's Last Battle', *After the Battle*, No. 48; and Jones, 'Michael Wittman', *Military Illustrated*, 48.
11 Keegan, *Six Armies in Normandy*.
12 See especially Taylor, note 10 above.

13 Isecke, see note 2 above.
14 Smith, letter 23.9.97.
15 Taylor, 'Michael Wittmann's last Battle'.
16 Williamson, *Loyalty is my Honour*.
17 Decker, conversations, 1997.
18 Reynolds, *Steel Inferno*.
19 Translation by J. and T. Suchcitz, in progress, of 1945 *1sz Dywizja Pancerna w Walce*, compilation by officers of 1st Polish Armoured Division's history.
20 Tout, *To Hell with Tanks!*
21 Obituary in NY Association Magazine, 1997.
22 Reynolds, *Steel Inferno*, pp. 24–37, and Hastings, *Overlord*, pp. 170–95.
23 2nd Army Intelligence Summary, No. 200.
24 Military Operational Research Unit Report, No. 23.
25 Irving, *Hitler's War*.
26 Hammerton, *Achtung! Minen!*
27 Irving, *Hitler's War*.
28 Shulman, *Defeat in the West*.
29 Wilmot, *The Struggle for Europe*.
30 Ibid.
31 Shulman, *Defeat in the West*.
32 Haslob, see note 4 above.
33 Irving, *The War between the Generals*.
34 See note 19 above.
35 Decker, conversations 1997.
36 Williamson, *Loyalty is my Honour*.

13 Maczek, *Avec mes Blindées*.
14 Saunders, letter August 1997.
15 Gillate, tape recorded memoirs 1997.
16 Maczek, *Avec mes Blindées*.
17 Griffith, *Battle Tactics of the Western Front*.
18 Reynolds, *Steel Inferno*.
19 D'Este, *Decision in Normandy*.
20 Jones, *Sixty-four Days of a Normandy Summer*.
21 Roy, *1944 – The Canadians in Normandy*.
22 Hastings, *Overlord*.
23 *The Sunday Times* Insight Team, *The Falklands War*.
24 Briars, letter 25.1.92.
25 Hastings, *Bomber Command*.
26 Grey, letter October 1997.
27 Graham, *The Price of Command*.
28 Gelb, *Ike and Monty-Generals at War*.
29 Jones, *Sixty-four Days of a Normandy Summer*.
30 Mitcham, *Hitler's Field Marshals*.
31 Keegan, *Churchill's Generals*.
32 Andrews, personal memoirs.
33 Gillate, see note 15 above.
34 Roy, *1944 – The Canadians in Normandy*.
35 Taylor, Tommy Cooker, unpublished text.
36 Hastings, *Overlord*.

Chapter 9. The Champion Dethroned

1 Liddell Hart, *History of the First World War*. For First World War tanks see also David Fletcher, *Tanks and Trenches*, and *Landships: British Tanks in the First World War*.
2 Glover, *Battlefields of Northern France*.
3 Stacey, *The Victory Campaign*.
4 Liddell Hart, *History of the First World War*.
5 Chant, *Battle Tanks of World War II*.
6 Jones, *Sixty-four Days of a Normandy Summer*.
7 Kay Summersby in Hastings, *Overlord*.
8 Gelb, *Ike and Monty – Generals at War*.
9 Ross in Hastings, *Overlord*.
10 Spittles, tape recorded memories (Bovington Museum).
11 Unit daily returns.
12 Mosely, *A Tankie's Tale* (NY Association magazine).

Chapter 10. The Verdict

1 McKee, *Caen, Anvil of Victory*.
2 Grahame, *The Price of Command*.
3 Kit/Saint-Michel, *Overlord – 6th June 1944 – Freedom*.
4 Belchem, *Victory in Normandy*.
5 Gelb, *Ike and Monty – Generals at War*.
6 Irving, *The War between the Generals*.
7 Hastings, *Overlord*.
8 D'Este, *Decision in Normandy*, cites Roberts – an absurd idea to retain 51st Highland Division in a purely defensive position – and O'Connor – his idea for armoured infantry carriers vetoed.
9 Maczek, *Avec mes Blindées*.
10 Shulman, *Defeat in the West*.
11 Isecke, letter 15.8.97.
12 Reynolds, letter 27.8.97.
13 Lothian & Border next day reports.
14 English, *The Casting of an Army*.
15 D'Este, *Decision in Normandy*.
16 Ibid.
17 McKee, *Caen, Anvil of Victory*.

18 Belchem, *Victory in Normandy.*
19 Ibid.
20 Lt-Gen Sir Peter de la Billière.
21 Lang, letter 19.8.97.
22 Hubert Meyer, *History of 12th SS Panzer Division – Hitlerjugend.*
23 Shulman quoting 7th Army telephone log.
24 Wilmot, *The Struggle for Europe.*
25 Birt, *XXII Dragoons.*
26 Cameron, *History of 7th Argylls.*
27 Roy, *1944 – The Canadians in Normandy.*
28 Hopwood, J., personal memoirs.
29 Jolly, 'Operation Totalize', *RAC Journal,* 2 (1948).
30 War Office, *Current Reports from Overseas,* 30.9.44.

Bibliography: Sources & Further Reading

For written work not in the public domain, see Acknowledgements.

Abbott, John, '1st NY, St. Aignan', *Military Illustrated*, No. 69, Feb. 1994.

Agte, Patrick, *Michael Wittmann and the Tiger Commanders of the Leibstandarte*, J.J. Fedorowicz Publishing Inc., 1960.

Belchem, David, *Victory in Normandy*, Chatto & Windus, 1981.

Birt, Raymond, *XXII Dragoons 1760–1945*, Gale & Polden, 1950.

Borthwick, Alastair, *Battalion (History of the 5th Seaforths)*, Baton Wicks, 1994 (originally as *Sans Peur*, 1946).

Bradley, Omar, *A General's Life*, Simon & Schuster, 1983.

Cameron, Ian C., *The History of the 7th Argylls*, Nelson, 1946.

Chant, Christopher, *An Illustrated Data Guide to Battle Tanks of World War II*, Tiger Books International, 1997.

Cordingley, Patrick, *In the Eye of the Storm*, Coronet, 1996.

Craven, W.F. *et al.*, *The Army Air Forces in World War II, Vol. 3 – Europe*, University of Chicago Press, 1951.

Delaforce, Patrick, *The Fighting Wessex Wyverns*, Sutton, 1994.

D'Este, Carlo, *Decision in Normandy*, Collins, 1983.

English, John, *The Canadian Army and the Normandy Campaign, A Study of Failure in High Command*, Praeger, 1991.

Fletcher, David, *Landships: British Tanks in the First World War*, HMSO, 1984.

— *Tanks and Trenches*, Sutton, 1994.

Florentin, Eddy, *The Battle of the Falaise Gap*, Elek, 1965.

Forty, George, *German Tanks of World War Two in Action*, Blandford, 1988.

— *Tank Commanders – Knights of the Modern Age*, Firebird, 1993.

Gelb, Norman, *Ike and Monty – Generals at War*, Constable, 1994.

Glover, Michael, *Battlefields of Northern France*, Guild Publishing, 1987.

Graham, Dominick, *The Price of Command (A Biography of General Guy Simonds)*, Stoddart Publishing Co. Ltd, 1993.

Griffith, Paddy, *Battle Tactics of the Western Front*, Yale, 1994.

Hammerton, Ian C., *Achtung! Minen!*, The Book Guild, 1991.

Hammilton, Nigel, *Monty*, Hamish Hamilton, 1986.

Harris, Sir Arthur, *Bomber Offensive*, Collins, 1947.

Hastings, Max, *Overlord–D-Day and the Battle for Normandy*, Michael Joseph, 1984.

— *Bomber Command*, Macmillan, 1993.

Hunnicut, Richard, *SHERMAN – A History of the American Medium Tank*, Taurus Enterprises, 1978.

Irving, David, *Hitler's War*, Focal Point, 1991.

— *The War between the Generals*, Allen Lane, 1981.

Jolly, A., 'Operation Totalize, An Unorthodox Battle and its Lessons', *RAC Journal*, Vol. 2, 1948.

Jones, Gregory T., 'Michael Wittmann', *Military Illustrated*, No. 48, May 1992.

Jones, Keith, *Sixty-four Days of a Normandy Summer*, Robert Hale, 1990.

Keegan, John, *GUDERIAN*, Ballantine Books, 1973.

— *Six Armies in Normandy*, Penguin, 1982.

— *Churchill's Generals*, Warner, 1991.

Lamb, Richard, *Montgomery in Europe*, Buchan & Enright, 1983.

Lefevre, Eric, *Panzers in Normandy – Then and Now*, Battle of Britain Prints, 1983.

Liddell Hart, B.H., *History of the First World War*, Cassell & Co., 1930/70.

— *The Other Side of the Hill*, Cassell & Co., 1951.

Lothian & Border Yeomanry, Next Day Reports (9.8.44), Bovington Tank Museum Library, 1944.

Lucas, J. & Barker, J., *The Killing Ground*, Batsford, 1978.

McKee, Alexander, *Caen – Anvil of Victory*, Pan, 1964/6.

Macksey, Kenneth, *Tank Force – Allied Armour in World War Two*, Ballantine Books, 1970.

Maczek, Stanislaw(s), *Avec mes Blindées*, Presses de la Cité, 1967.

Maule, Henry, *Caen*, David & Charles, 1976.

Messenger, Charles, *Hitler's Gladiator (Dietrich)*, Brassey's, 1988.

Meyer, Hubert, *History of 12th SS Panzer Division – Hitlerjugend*, J.J. Fedorowicz Publishing Inc., 1994.

Middlebrook, M. & Everitt, C., *The Bomber Command Diaries*, Penguin, 1990.

Mieczkowski, Zbigniew (ed.), *Monuments and War Memorials on the Battlefields of the Polish Armoured Division*, Veritas, 1989.

Mitcham, Samuel W., Jr., *Hitler's Field Marshals*, Heinemann, 1988.

Neitzel, Colonel, *89th ID in den Kaempfen an der Invasionsfront . . . (1. Teil zum 15.8.1944)*, Bundesarchiv ZA 1/775-B-425, 1944.

Neville, *The First Northamptonshire Yeomanry in Northwest Europe*, Meyer, 1946.

Northamptonshire Yeomanry Assocation, *Annual Report and Magazine*, various years.

Reynolds, Michael, *Steel Inferno – 1 SS Panzer Corps in Normandy*, Spellmount, 1997.

Richards, Denis, *The Hardest Victory*, Hodder & Stoughton, 1994.

Roy, Reginald, *1944 – The Canadians in Normandy*, Macmillan of Canada, 1984.

Salmond, J.B., *The History of the 51st Highland Division, 1939–1945*, Blackwood, 1953.

Shulman, Milton, *Defeat in the West*, Secker & Warburg, 1947/Pan, 1988.

Simpson, Gary L., *Tiger Ace (Wittmann)*, Schiffer, 1994.

Speidel, Hans, *Invasion 1944*, Chicago, 1950.

Spittles, Reg, Recollections of 2nd Northamptonshire Yeomanry, taped, Bovington Tank Museum.

Stracey, C.P., *The Victory Campaign (Official History of the Canadian Army in Second World War)*, The Queen's Printer, 1960.

Suchcitz, Andrew & Teresa (trans.), *1st Polish Armoured Division in Battle* (1st Dywizja Pancerna w Walce, 1945), in preparation, 1998.

Sunday Times Insight Team, *The Falklands War*, Sphere, 1982.

Taylor, Les (Spud), 'Michael Wittmann's Last Battle', *After the Battle*, 48.

Tedder, Lord, *With Prejudice*, Cassell & Co., 1966.

Terraine, John, *The Right of the Line: The RAF in the European War, 1939–45*, Hodder & Stoughton, 1985.

Tout, Ken, *Tank!*, Robert Hale, 1985/94.

— *Tanks, Advance!*, Robert Hale, 1987.

— *To Hell with Tanks!*, Robert Hale, 1992.

Wallace, John F., *Dragons of Steel: Canadian Armour in two World Wars*, The General Store Publishing House, 1995.

War Office, *Current Reports from Overseas*, No. 57, 30.9.44.

Whitehouse, Stan, and Bennett, George, *Fear is the Foe*, Robert Hale, 1995.

Williamson, Gordon, *Loyalty is my Honour*, Brown Books, 1995.

— *The SS: Hitler's Instrument of Terror*, Sidgwick & Jackson, 1995.

Wilmot, Chester, *The Struggle for Europe*, Collins, 1952.

Xenophon (trans. Warner, Rex), *The Persian Expedition*, Penguin, 1949.

Acknowlegements

I have been most fortunate to have a considerable number of surviving eye-witnesses willing to help in the preparation of a review of Operation Totalize Phase 1. In particular, I am lucky to be in touch with five field officers who carried out pivotal roles of tactical importance at the time and who have been most gracious in their information and advice. They are the 1st Northamptonshire Yeomanry navigator, now Lt-Col The Rt Hon The Lord Boardman, MC, TD, DL; the squadron leader of 'A', 27 CAR (The Sherbrooke Fusiliers), Brig-Gen S.V. Radley-Walters; the COs of 5th Camerons and 2nd Seaforths, respectively Gen Sir Derek Lang, KCB, DSO, MC, DL, and Brig G.L.W. Andrews, CBE, DSO; and the adjutant of 12th SS Panzer Regiment, Maj Georg Isecke.

I may have avoided many errors resulting from my own false impressions by having access to two members of the Totalize crew, 3 Baker, on which I was the gunner. Both Rex Jackson, MM, and Stan Hicken have been most assiduous in analysing memories and helping actively with research. Another one-time sharer of a dug-out refuge under a Sherman at night, Bruce Dickson, has also been most willing, including spending time searching for RAF photos of the appropriate dates – very complicated work among hundreds of thousands of, as yet, not adequately archived negatives.

In this kind of research the response of persons managing archives is crucial to the achievement of deadlines. My first port of call had to be the library of the Bovington Tank Museum, seeking the continuing advice of that great tank expert, David Fletcher. Long-range help came from the Canadian Directorate of History and Heritage (Dr Yves Tremblay), the Polish Institute in London (Andrew Suchcitz), the Bundesarchiv (Frau Kuhl), Auskunfte Deutsche Militargeschichte (Dr Ekkehart Guth), Militargeschichtliches Forschungsamt (Hauptmann Hagemann), and the Verband Deutscher Soldaten e. V. (Patrick Agte).

Ian Carter at the Imperial War Museum and Mrs Beech at the RAF photo archive in Keele University, as also David Fletcher, solved a number of photo problems.

A special word of thanks is due to those who have so selflessly allowed me to use some of their own unpublished work. Excellent writers and reporters all, they include Brig 'Geordie' Andrews, Len Cottell, Dr John Hooper, Bill Mosely, Les 'Spud' Taylor, while Robert Anderson provided me with some of Brig John Hopwood's memoirs. Teresa Suchcitz thought to advise me of the new translation which she and her husband are making of the Polish history and sent me the relevant pages. Don Gillate loaned me his fascinating taped memoirs of 'Goodwood'.

Obviously my old comrades of 1st Northamptonshire Regiment were foremost in contributing – among the 1944 officers still surviving: 'Bing' Crosby, Tony Faulkner, Wyn Griffith-Jones and Jim Owen, MC. From turrets and driving cabs were heard the voices, or came the helping hands, of Ray Ager, Jim Alcock, Brian Carpenter, Mack Clague, Brian Coleman, Joe Crittenden, Gordon Dursley, Joe Ekins, Bill Higham, Mike Hunt, Jimmy Kerr, Lou Lakin, Fred Musgove, Jack Pentelow, Charlie Rogers, Peter Smith, John Stenner, Percy Sumner, Wally Tarrant, Herbert Wilkins and others who have shared memories over the years.

Voices from nearby units included Wilf Mylan (1st Northants at Brigade HQ), E. Howley (144 RAC), Bill Deeming (148 RAC/later 1st Northants), and Keith Jones, A.E. Saunders and Reg Spittles, all of 2NY. Other 51st HD assistance was offered by Robert Anderson, John Cutland, John McGregor, Tom Renouf, Charlie Robertson, D.A. Rowan-Hamilton, Angus Stewart and Stan Whitehouse. Ian Hammerton and the Revd W. Ray Birt represented XXII Dragoons and P.R. Shurmur, CLY.

Totalize was a Canadian concept and from that country I was guided by Bill McAndrew, John F. Wallace, MC, and Douglas Grey, as also Alan Muller, USA. In a memory session at the Polish Institute and subsequently, much advice was forthcoming from Ryszard Dembinski, Zbigniew Mieczkowski, J.W. Suchcitz and Witold Diemel. French help over the years has been freely given by Eddy Florentin; M. Hoste and M. Dupuy Mayor and Alderman of Bourguebus; and Mme Desetable (Mayor), M. Bellenger (Deputy) and M. Dan (farmer) of Saint-Aignan-de-Cramesnil.

As at the start of Totalize, the RAF responded right on target – namely, Danny Boon, Ralph Briars, Len Cottell, Roy Grey, Denis Hughes, DFM, Syd Johnson, DFC, W.R. (Bill) Morris, Robbie Robson and Alan Watkins (The Aircrew Association).

Apart from the organizations mentioned, individual German responses were appreciated from Karl-Heinz Decker, Lt-Col Gevert Haslob, Georg Isecke, Hubert Meyer (GSO1 12th SS Panzer Division) and Manfred and Hazel Toon-Thorn, Hazel having set the ball rolling in Germany for me.

Of a more modern generation thanks go to Maj-Gen (Retd) M.F. Reynolds, CB, Winston G. Ramsey (editor of *After the Battle*), Frank Paulin (Keele University, translations), Roy. G. Mitchell, Ken Wharton (loans of books), Melvyn Marchant (a son of 1st Northamptonshire Yeomanry) and Euan Withersby (a young student of military history). I would also pay tribute to those writers quoted in this book whose researches have been wider and more profound than mine and without whom the panorama of military history would be very bleak and uninteresting.

It was my privilege and good fortune to have a number of conversations with the late David Bevan MC, squadron leader of 'C', 1st Northants, when he was able to enlighten me as to higher command reasons for what had often seemed unreasonable to a mere turret gunner. His drawings, while sitting on his turret, still evoke fragrant or tragic memories. I must also acknowledge the guidance of Jonathan Falconer and Sue Thomas, at Sutton Publishing. My wife, Jai, merits thanks and apologies for suffering the household chaos caused by researching a book; she has also been the instigator of journeys back to the slopes and villages where it all happened, and is always a much appreciated adviser. Thank you all! Deepest apologies to anybody I forgot.

Index

References in *italic* refer to photographs

African Campaign 36, 53, 55, 57, 70, 98, 153
Ager, Tpr R. 18, 41, 101
Agte, Patrick 26, 129
Alway, Lt-Col B.M. 72
Amiens, battle (1918) 38, 49, 141
Amtracs 151
Anderson, Capt R. 105
Anderson, Cpl 20
Anderson, Lt-Col J. 72
Andrews, Lt-Col G.L.W. 13, 27, 81 *et seq*,
    121, 136, 153
Anzio 40
Argentan 163
Argentines 151
Arbour, CSM A. 17, 18, 80
Armour, Cpl 151
Arras, battle (1940) 139
Atkinson, Lt 101
atrocities/behaviour 30, 100, 117, 124,
    136 *et seq*
Australians 55, 73, 96, 141

Bahlo, SS L/Cpl 131
Bailey, L/Cpl S. 92
Banneville-la-Campagne cemetery 156, *167*
Bannon, Tpr M. 61
Barnes, Sgt 84
Bates, Sgt D. 165
Bayeux 11, 40
Beauvais, Mr B. 117, *119*
Beauvoir 73
Belchem, Maj-Gen D. 22, 27, 162
Bell, Flg Off 58
Beval Farm 143
Bevan, Maj D.G. 55, *65*, 94, 99, *99*, 100,
    103, 132
Billy 48
Birt, Revd W.R. 11, 36, 37, 105
Blaydon, Flt Sgt 58
Boal, Lt 11
Boardman, Capt T.G. 7, 14, 17, 19, 50 *et seq*,
    62, 77, 89, 93, 101, 112, 118, 121, 129,
    132, 156
Bocage 21, 25, 28, 137, 144, 147
Bois d'Alençon/l'Obelisque 161
Booker, Cpl F. 65

Boorman, Tpr *39*
Booth, Brig E.L. 115
Boreham, Lt W.J. 12, 20, 75
Bourg-Achard 120
Bourguebus/Ridge 2, 21, 25, 53, 58, 62, 74,
    126, 144, 147, 158, 167
Bousfield, Capt 16
Bowden, Cpl E. 59, 92
Bower, L/Cpl J. 59
Boyd, Lt N. *77*
Boyd, L/Cpl 16
Bradford, Cpl 12, 20
Bradford, Lt-Col 101
Bradley, Capt D. *77*
Bradley, Gen O. 163
Bras 23, 43, 55
Brassey, Maj P. 56, 87, 132
Bretteville-la-Rabet 115, 124
Bretteville-sur-Laize 46, 68, 114, 126, 129,
    161
Brettevillette 143
Briars, Ralph 152
Broadhurst, AVM 46
Brooke, Gen Sir A. 32, 142, 163
Brown, AVM 46
Brown, Lt E.S. 96, *99*
Buck, Tpr J. 18, 98
Burgess, Maj J.W. 78
Burn, Lt A.R. 10, 14, 15, 76
Burnett, Sgt 15
Butcher, Maj-Gen 158

Caen 4, 23, 47, 88, 107, 111, 127, 144, 152,
    167
Caen–Falaise Road/Sector 2, 21, 27, 32,
    39 *et seq*, 69 *et seq*, 86, 113, 117, 123 *et seq*
Caillouet 43, 73, 78 *et seq*, 105
Calcar 121
Cambrai, battle 55, 140, 148
Campbell, Sgt 58
Cannae, battle 162
Capocci, Tpr L. *167*
Cardon, Germain and Roger 167
Carpenter, Tpr B. 9, 16, 19, 50
Cassells, Brig J. 57, 79, 81 *et seq*, 101
Cathcart, Lt-Col 56
Caughran, Sgt 58
Cauvicourt 45, 110, 115

Chambois 104, 119, 160
Christiansen, Lt-Col 32, 70
Churchill tank 27, 141
Churchill, Winston 31, *36*, 39
Cintheaux 6, 74, 114, 129, 130, 156, 157, 160
Clague, Sgt M. 101
Clark, L/Cpl 98
Clifford, Maj 55
Clift, Lt-Col F.A. 17, 79
Clos St Denis 59
Coakley, Lt D. 64, 98, 156
Coates, Cpl 12
COBRA, *see* Operation
Cochrane, Capt 53
Coleman, Tpr B. 9
Coningham, AVM 46
Conteville 48, 101, 120, 128, 129
Copp, Terry 165
Cordingley, Maj-Gen P. 151
Cormelles 23, 43, 50, 55, 58, 82, 105
Cracow 108
Cramesnil 23, 43, 63, 66, 70, 82, 105, 160
Crerar, Lt-Gen H.D.G. 31, 37, 46, 49, 70,
    104, 121, 152, 157, 158, 162
Creully 8
Crittenden, Tpr J. 16, 41, 87, 92, 103, 141
Crocker, Lt-Gen J.T. 32, 46
Cromwell tank 27, *111*, 139, 146
Crosby, Capt J. 52, 87, 148
Cumming-Bruce, Lt-Col 101
Cunningham, Brig B. 32, 70
Cuthbertson, Tpr C. 97
Cutland, Lt J. 52

deception 30, 45, 48
Decker, SS Cpl K.-H. 6, 29, 133, 134, *135*,
    136, 138
Deeming, L/Cpl W. 1, 3, 12, 45, 84, 150
De Guingand, Maj-Gen Sir F.W. 158
Deimel, Witold 28
Dempsey, Lt-Gen Sir M.C. 32, *36*, 40, 133,
    162
Dickson, Tpr B. 95, 102, 164
Dietrich, SS Gen S. 32, 135, 136
Dollinger, SS Lt 129, 131
Dowdor, Maj R. 111
Duff, Sgt G. 63
Duncan, Capt G. 41
Dunkirk 32, 109
Dursley, L/Cpl G. 20, 117, 137
Dwight, L/Cpl A. 96

Eberbach, Gen 33, 127, 133
Eisenhower, Gen I. 31, 34, 141, 153, 158
Ekins, Tpr J. 41, 54, 89, *90*, 121, 131, 141
el Alamein 153

el Hamma 36
Ensor, Sgt 69
EPSOM, *see* Operation
Esson, Sgt D. 5, 18
Estrees-la-Campagne 46, 112, 115, 129
Evin, Dr 117, *119*

Falaise (Gap) 24, 43, 92, 104, 116, 119, 128,
    137, 157, 158, 160, 163, 167
Falklands War 151
Farnham, SQMS *99*
Faulkner, Lt A.W. 9, *62*, 93, 96, *99*, 112
Ferguson, Col 58
Fergusn, Maj C.W. 17, 80
Ferrier, Cpl 14, 20, 100
Finney, Sgt 92
'Firefly' tank 16, 27, 41, 54, 87, *114*, 141,
    150
flail tanks 3, *10*, 20, 70, 76, 160
Flers, Somme 140
Fleury 105
Florentin, Eddy 2, 4
Fontenay-le-Marmion 2, 17, 73, 79 *et seq*,
    105, 126, 151, 159
Forster, Lt-Col D. 19, 52, 62, 64, 87, 121
Foulkes, Maj-Gen C. 23, 32, 42, 44, 70, 121
Fox, Capt W. 95, 99, *99*, 164
Frankham, Capt 97
'friendly fire' 17, 19, 65, 69, 76, 88, 97,
    106 *et seq*, 152, 161, 163, 165, 169
Frost, Tpr B. 5

Galland, Gen A. 135
Garcelles-Secqueville 56, 66, 91, 101, 130,
    164
Gaumesnil 23, 43, 68, 73 *et seq*, 105, 113
Gazelle 161
Geneva Convention, *see* atrocities
Gibbs, Cpl F. 133
Gibson, L/Cpl 65
Giles, Cpl T. 91, 93
Gillard, Tpr 11
Gillate, Don 146
Ginns, Sgt J. *42*
Goering, FM H. 124, 134
GOODWOOD, *see* Operation
Goose Green, battle 151
Gordon, Lt-Col M. 72, 77, 106, 114
Gordon, Sgt 89
Gouvix 106
Grant, Brig M.C. 40
Greece 130
Gregson, Capt 56
Grey, Roy 152
Griffiths-Jones, Lt W. 14, *14*, 20, *29*, 60, 100,
    105, 117, 137

Grimbosq 123, 129
Grint, Tpr R. 15, 61
Guderian, FM 33
Guillot, Michel 169
Gulf War 28, 151, 165
Gully, The, *see* Petit Ravin

Haig, FM Earl 30
Halpenny, Lt-Col 105
Hammerton, Lt I. 4, 5, 12, 20, 107, 110, 134
Hargest, Brig 149
Harris, ACM Sir A. 46, 57
Hartford, Plt Off 58
Haskard, Lt J. *99*
Haslob, Lt-Col G. 126, *127*, 136, 138
Hautmesnil 114
Hastings, Max 38, 154, 158
Hawkins, WO 58
Heaven, Lt W. 87, 93, *99*
Heinrichs, Lt-Gen C. 126, 138
Heurich, SS Capt F. 130
Hicken, Tpr S. 4, 8, 50, *56*, 86, 93 *et seq*, 99, 106, 113, 121, 137
High Wood, battle 148, 151
Higham, Tpr W. 1, 59, 92
Hill, Flt Lt 57, 117, *118*, *119*, *167*
Himmler, H. 124
Hitler, A. 6, 25, 29, 32, 48, 124, 133, 134, 136
Hobart, Maj-Gen Sir P.C.S. 43, 139
Hoeflinger, SS Lt 129
Hodges, Gen C.H. 133, 137
Holton, Tpr 7
Hood, L/Cpl R. 94
Hopwood, Lt-Col J. 19, 55, 64, 66, 97, 98, 121, 166
Hoth, Gen 33
Hoult, L/Cpl H. 94
Howard, Cpl 14
Howley, Tpr E. 53
Hubert Folie 54, 74, 82, 103, 146
Huebner, Maj-Gen H. 137
Hughes, Flt Eng D. 73
Hukens, Capt J. 56
Hulme, Sgt S. 96
Hummel (Bumblebee) SP *29*, 164
Humphrey, Capt W. *77*
Hunt, L/Cpl M.C. 97

Ifs 23, 43, 50, 55, 69, 105, 158
Iriohn, SS Lt 129
Isandhlwana, battle 162
Iseke, SS Adjt G. 6, 124, 132, 138, 160
Italian Campaign 35, 40

Jack, Sgt K. 101

Jackson, Tpr R. 4, 8, 50, *56*, 86, 93, 95, 99, 103, 121, 137
James, Lt 89
Jarvis, Pte 6
Jay, Sgt 65
Jelley, RSM G. 100, 103, 108
Jolly, Lt-Col A. 3, 19, 35, 54, 56, 60, 65, 166
Johnson, Sgt 97, 98
Johnson, Sqn Ldr S. 73
Jones, Lt K. 25
Jones, Lt-Col T.S. 17, 72, 78
Jurgensen, SS Maj 124

Kangaroos 4, 5, 13, 19, 39 *et seq*, 56, 66, 78, 79, 84, 121, 149, 161, 166
Kasserine, battle 141
Keegan, RSM 108
Keitel, FM 33, 134, 153
Keller, Maj-Gen R. 32, 42, 70, 107
Kerr, L/Cpl J. 14, 61
King, WO 58
Kirkwood, Cpl 75
Kisters, SS Lt 129
Kitchener, FM Lord 30
Kitching, Maj-Gen G. 32, 42, 48, 70, 105, 113, 120, 159
Knightsbridge, battle 139
Koller, Gen 134
Korean War 121
Koszutski, Lt-Col 111
Kranski, Lt-Col J.W. 111

La Dronniere 23, 68
La Hogue 4, 160, 167
La Jalousie 68, 73, 74
Laize, River 126, 161
Lakin, L/Cpl L. 100
Lang, Lt-Col D.L. 81, 82, 121, 165
Le Havre 21, 117
Le Mans 163
Leigh-Mallory, AVM 46
Liddell Hart 141, 147
Lisieux 120
Llewellyn, Capt 52, 88
Lorguichon 4, 23, 44, 63, 65, 68, 82
Lovibond, Maj T. 56, 60
Lwow 108, 121

McAndrew, Dr W. 165
McAnalay, Lt J. 19
McColl, Lt R.S. 93, 94, *99*, 100
McElwee, Capt A. 66
Maciejowski, Lt-Col J. 111
MacLachan, Lt-Col G.M. 72
McLean, Cpl 52
McManus, Maj 80

MacMillan, Wg Cdr 73
Maczek, Gen S. 24, 28, 42, 48, 108, *109*, 110, 113, 122, 147, 158, 160
Majewski, Col T. 111
Manley, Sqn Ldr H.G. 73
Mann, Brig C. 46, 152
Marchant, L/Cpl E. 94, *95*, *168*
Mareth Line 35
Mark IV tank 27, 89
Martin, Tpr J. 94
Matilda tank 141
May-sur-Orne 2, 23, 73, 79, 105, 126, 159
Mayer, Cpl A. 137
Meiklejohn, Lt-Col 56
Melville, Lt J. 12, 16, 75
Meyer, Hubert 138
Meyer, SS Maj-Gen Kurt ('Panzer') 26, 86, 91, 114, 123 *et seq*, 138, 152, 160, 165
Mieckzkowski, Z. 108, 121
Milner, Tpr *39*
Mitchell, Tpr 52
Monkman, Tpr 96
Mont des Renes 84
Mont Pincon 38
Montgomery, Gen Sir B. 12, 21, 24, 30, 31, *36*, 37 *et seq*, 55, 70, 104, *109*, 110, 115, 142, 144, 152, 157, 162
Morris, Flg Off W.R. 10
Mortain 136, 163
Moulin de Voide 73
Munk, Jan 29
Murray, Brig 57, 101
Murray, Capt G. 83, 84
Musgrove, Sgt F. 101
'Mushty' 88
Mylan, Cpl W. 53, 85

Neal, L/Cpl 59
Neville, Capt R.F. 68
Newman, Lt P.S. 7
New Zealand/ers 36, 55
Niewmowski, Lt J. 121
Noires Terres, Les 59
Norway 6, 48, 80, 126
Noyers-Bocage 147

O'Connor, Lt-Gen Sir R. 40, 145, 158
Oliver, Brig 54, 101
Omaha Beach 137
Operation COBRA 104, 144, 156, 164
Operation EPSOM 28, 143, 164
Operation GOODWOOD 5, 25, 26, 28, 31, 40, 47, 52, 53, 104, 124, 139, 144 *et seq*, 153, 156, 158, 162, 164
Operation SPRING 23, 24
Operation TRACTABLE 104, 119, 152, 157

Orne, River 23, 38, 54, 123, 126
Osbourn, Capt B. 56
Othon, Roger 169
Oudalle 117

Panther tank 27, *142*
Panzerfaust 9, 27, 60, 63, 113, 134
Paris 21, 144
Passchendaele, battle 5
Patton, Gen G. 2, 24, 25, 32, 136, 153, 161, 162
Pelly, Lt 15
Pentelow, L/Cpl J. 4, 64, 98
Petch, Lt-Col 32, 70
Petit Ravin, le (The Gully) 48, 68, 86, 91 *et seq*, 112, 129, 137, 161
Pickering, Capt 56
Pickert, Luft Gen 135
Poussy-la-Campagne 120, 128
Preston, Tpr J. 96
Prinz, SS Maj 124
Pryde, L/Cpl D. *39*
Pye, Tpr G. 96

Quail, Tpr K. 51
Quarries, the 16, 73, 78, 114
Quesnay/Woods 24, 160
Quesnel, Andre 169

Rabe, Capt Dr 100, 130, 132
Radley-Walters, Maj S.V. 69 *et seq*, *77*, 106, 113, 114, 121, 129, 131, 132, 133, 156
Rathbone, Capt M.S. *99*
Rawlins, Tpr A. 137
Reid, Maj R. 60
Reid, Tpr H. *42*
Rennie Maj-Gen T.G. 43, 44, 55, 100, 121, 140
Renny, Lt-Col 101
Renouf, Sgt T. 150
Resistance, French 117, *118*, *119*, 136, 167
Reynolds, Maj-Gen M.F. 161
Rhine, River 120, 138
Richardson, Brig 46, 58
Robertmesnil 45, 67, 86 *et seq*, 112, 163
Roberts, Maj-Gen G.P.B. 158
Roberts, Tpr E.H. 2, 7
Robertson, Lt C. 35, 50, 54, 66, 107
Rocquancourt 17, 70, 74 *et seq*, 126
Rodger, Elliot 35
Roesler, Col 126
Rogers, Cpl C. 96, 126, 128
Rolland, Lt H. 3, 75
Rommel, FM E. 33
Rose, Lt B. 134
Rossman, Col 126

Rowan-Hamilton, Capt D.A. 60
Runcie, Lt-Col J. 17, 80
Russian Front/Army 25, 30, 33, 109, 130,
134, 139
Rutledge, Tpr 18
Ryan, Sgt B. 59, 64, 93

Saint-Aignan-de-Cramesnil 2, 20, 23, 30, 43,
48, 59 *et seq*, 78, 82, 86 *et seq*, 105, 110,
111, 120, 123, 128, 150, 157, 161, 164,
168
Saint-Andre-sur-Orne 23, 81
Saint-Lo 167
Saint-Martin-de-Fontenay 23
Saint-Pierre-sur-Dives 120
Saint-Sylvain 45, 110, 112
Saunders, Maj A.E. 146
Scheuermann, Lt W. 6, 136
Schild, Emile 117, *119*
Schoerner, FM 153
Scobbie, Tpr A. *146*
Scott, Brig H.B. 43, 44, 50, 53, 71, 84, 118
Scully, Tpr 16
Secqueville-la-Campagne/woods 2, 4, 82,
101, 126
Seddon, Lt 57
Seine, River 120, 144, 163
Sherman tank 9, 27, 45, *56*, *111*, *114*, 133,
146
Shorthouse, Pte S. 63
Shulman, Milton 123, 128, 138
Shuter, Maj 56
Sicily 35, 54
Sikera, Lt R. 113
Sikorski, Gen/'Tourists' 109, 121
Simonds, Lt-Gen G.G. 1, 4, 6, 12, 24,
30 *et seq*, 35 *et seq*, *36*, 44, 53, 70, 104, 105,
114, 115, 120, 140, 144, 148, 151, 157
Simonds, Peter 116
Skelton, Maj G. 50, 55, 92, 132
Smith, Sgt P. 65, 98, 132
Smith, Tpr G. 93
Snowdon, Cpl K. *56*, 86, 94, 99, 100
Soignolles 24, 160
Soliers 58, 154
Somme, battle 5, 30, 140, 148
Spencer, Earls 53
Spencer, Tpr 7
Spittles, Cpl R. 21
SPRING, *see* Operation
SS (Schutzstaffel) 124
Stalingrad 2
Stanley, Cpl J. 87, 88
Stearns, Capt 151
Stefanowicz, Lt-Col 111
Stenner, Tpr J. 5, 87, 93, 97, 98

Stewart, Capt A. 110
Strachan, VC, Lt 140
Suchcitz, J.W. 157
Sumner, L/Cpl P. 1, 100
Sutch, Tpr J. 9, 96
Sutherland, Tpr 7
Symes, L/Cpl S. 15, 61

T 34 tank (Soviet) 139, 141
Tarrant, Tpr W. 87
Taylor, Peter J. 53
Taylor, Tpr L. 7
Tedder, ACM 31, 34
Thompson, Lt C. *77*
Thompson, Sgt R. 88
Thorn, Tpr *39*
Tiger tank 9, 26, 27, 134, 164
Tilly-la-Campagne 13, 24, 63, 82 *et seq*, 104,
118, 128, 136, 138, 151, 159, 167
Tobruk, battle 54
Todd, Capt K. 17, 55, 62, 64, 94, *95*, *168*
Torrans, W/Op J. 57, 117, *118*, *119*, *167*
Tout, Jai 165
TRACTABLE, *see* Operation
Troteval 73, 79
Tucker, Tpr T. *56*
Turton, SSM S. *99*

Urville 46

Valentine tank 141
Verrieres/Ridge 2, 23, 70, 72
Vietnam War 151
Vigors, Maj R. de C. 19
Villers-Bocage 29, 130, 134, 137, 139, 142
Von Kalm, Maj 128
Von Kluge, FM H. 33, 136, 153, 165
Von Runstedt, FM G. 33
Von Watter, Maj-Gen F. 140

Wagner, QM Gen 134
Waldmuller, SS Maj H. 26, 96, 97, 129, 130,
132
Walewska, Lech 122
Walford, Lt-Col J. 81, 84
Walker, Flg Off B.D. 58
Walker, Tpr 18
Wareing, Sqn Ldr 57
Warlimont, Gen 32
Washington DC 142
Wasilewski, Maj J. 111
Watt, Pte J. *106*
Wellbelove, Tpr E. 90, 93
Welsh, Cpl 11
Whelan, Tpr 16
Wheway, Capt 11, 12, 60

Whitehouse, Pte S. 6, 13, 63, 88, 150
Wiggin, Maj 40
Wilkins, Sgt C. *39*
Wilkinson, Tpr C. 66
Wilson, Flt Lt 58
Wilson, Lt A. 151
Witt, SS Maj-Gen F. 126
Wittmann, SS Maj M. 7, 26, 77, 113, 124, *131*, 129 *et seq*, 142, 157, 164
Worthington, Lt-Col D.G./Force 115, 129, 139, 157, 159
Wunsche, SS Maj M. 30, 38, 123, 129
Wykeham, Maj P. 56, 88, 98
Wyman, Brig 44, 71

Xenophon 139

Young, Brig H.A. 79, 80
Yugoslavs 48

Zgorzelski, Lt-Col 111

Units Mentioned

Allied
SHAEF 153
21st Army Group 152

British
Corps:
I Corps 32
III Corps 120
XII Corps 38
Divisions:
Airborne –
6th 149
Armoured –
Guards 145, 162
7th 149, 154, 162
11th 53, 70, 144, 162
79th 43, 57, 72, 139
Infantry –
15th (Scottish) 143
43rd (Wessex) 38, 149
49th (S. Yorks) 149
51st (Highland) 5, 13, 20, 35, 38, 43, 44, 50 *et seq*, 70, 78, 110, 120, 140, 149, 163
53rd (Welsh) 149, 150
59th (Staffordshire) 38, 120, 123, 147
Brigades:
Armoured –
7th (Gulf War) 151
29th 145
32nd Guards 149
33rd 38, 43, 44, 50 *et seq*, 85, 118, 120, 149, 157

Infantry –
9 149
152 (Highland Division) 54, 57, 79, 81, 101
153 (Highland Division) 54, 57, 101
154 (Highland Division) 54, 101
Regiments (armoured & infantry):
7th Argyll & Sutherland Highlanders 6, 44, 52, 56 *et seq*, 71, 98, 166
1st Black Watch 6, 13, 19, 44, 55 *et seq*, 71, 86, 93, 97, 98, 101, 105, 111, 150, 164
5th Black Watch 100, 101, 107, 150
7th Black Watch 35, 44, 54, 56 *et seq*, 84, 91, 107, 149
5th Cameron Highlanders 80, 81 *et seq*, 121
2nd Derbyshire Yeomanry 57
XXII Dragoons 3, 11, 36, 44, 52, 55, 60, 105, 109, 116
8th East Lancashire 53
1st East Riding Yeomanry 120
2nd Gloucesters 149
1st Gordon Highlanders 101, *159*
5/7th Gordon Highlanders 101
1st Highland Light Infantry 150
1st Lothian & Border Yeomanry 2, 7, 10, 12, 19, 44, 68, 71
9th Loyal 54
1/7th Middlesex 101
1st Northamptonshire Yeomanry 2 *et seq*, *3*, 23, *39*, *42*, 44, 51 *et seq*, 56, *62*, 71, 74, 77, 86 *et seq*, 102, 108, 111, 117, 120, 129, 130, 147, 164, *168*
2nd Northamptonshire Yeomanry 21, 25, 53, 143, 145, 150
Oxs & Bucks Light Infantry 150
1/6th Queen's 149
8th The Rifle Brigade 146
144 Royal Armoured Corps 3, 11, 19, 35, 44, 53 *et seq*, 71, 74, 78, 86, 91, 98, 101, 111, 120, 130, 150, 166
148 Royal Armoured Corps 1, 3, 44, 53 *et seq*, 84, 91, 108, 118, 120, 149, 150
4th Royal Tank Regiment 54
Scots Dragoon Guards (Gulf) 151
2nd Seaforth Highlanders 13, 17, 27, 81
5th Seaforth Highlanders 81, 83
2nd South Wales Borderers 149
Staffordshire (Gulf) 151
Tyneside Scottish 150
Royal Armoured Corps 149
Royal Artillery 4, 13, 43, 55, 57, 58, 92, 97, 127, 152
344 Ind. Searchlight, RA 115
Royal Corps of Military Police 44, 58
Royal Corps of Signals 45
Royal Engineers, 79 & 80 Assault 43, 44, 52, 56, 81, 101

Royal Electrical and Mechanical Engineers 40, 65
Royal Tank Corps (1916–18) 149
Royal Tank Regiment 149
Royal Navy 30
Royal Air Force:
general 10, 30
Bomber Command/bombers 2, 10, 17, 33, 38, 46, 57, 73, 80
83 Group 46, 152
84 Group 46
Pathfinder Group 11, 47, 73
419 (Moose) Squadron 58
550 Squadron 73
582 (PFF) Squadron 57, 73, 152, *167*
OBOE/GH 11, 33, 47
Air Photography 48, 91

Canadian
Army:
First Canadian 32, 120, 121, 163
Corps:
2nd Canadian 17, 26, 36 *et seq*, 120, 157, 163
Divisions:
Armoured –
4th Canadian 42, 105, 113 *et seq*, 120
5th Canadian 35
Infantry –
1st Canadian 35
2nd Canadian 23, 42
3rd Canadian 42, 107, 157
Brigades:
Armoured –
2nd Canadian 69 *et seq*
4th Canadian 115
Infantry –
4th Canadian 69 *et seq*
6th Canadian 79
Regiments (armoured & infantry):
Algonquin 115
6th Anti-tank 72
Argyll & Sutherland of Canada 114
Calgary Highlanders 50, 114
1st Canadian Armoured Carrier 41
10 Canadian Armoured Regiment = CAR (Fort Garry Horse) 72 *et seq*, 140
22 CAR (Grenadier Guards of Canada) 105
27 CAR (Sherbrooke Fusiliers) 69 *et seq*, *77*, 113, 129, 130, 164, 166
28 CAR (British Columbia) 115
8 Canadian Reconnaissance 18, 44, 72 *et seq*
Canadian Royal Artillery (*see also* RA) 13, 107
Canadian Royal Engineers 72, 74
Canadian REME 40
Essex Scottish 17, 72 *et seq*

1st Hussars 80, 114
Lake Superior (Motor) 105
Masionneuve, Le Regiment de 114
Mount Royal Les Fusiliers 17, 81
North Shore (New Brunswick) 107
QO Cameron Highlanders of Canada 17, 80, 85
Royal Hamilton Light Infantry 72 *et seq*, 85
Royal Regiment of Canada 72 *et seq*, 113, 164
South Alberta 114
South Saskatchewan 17, 79 *et seq*
Toronto Scottish 72, 78
123 LAD, REME 41
Royal Canadian Signals 116

German
Army:
Wehrmacht general 124, 136
Panzer Group West 25
Fifth Panzer Army 135
Seventh Army 116, 163
Corps:
1st SS Panzer 25
III Luftwaffe Flak 26, 114, 135
LXXXVI 25
Divisions:
Armoured/SS –
1st SS Panzer (LAH) 7, 125, 127, 129
2nd SS Panzer (Das Reich) 125
12th SS Panzer (Hitlerjugend) 6, 26, 32, 48, 70, 78, 94, 98, 119, 123 *et seq*, 143, 154, 161
23rd SS Panzer (Bosnia) 125
2nd Panzer 108
21st Panzer 25
Infantry –
89th (Horseshoe) 6, 11, 13, 26, 48, 59, 69, 79, 123 *et seq*, *127*
271   126
272   48, 84, 123 *et seq*
Regiments (armoured & infantry):
1 SS Pz Grenadier 26
12 SS Pz Regiment 6, 124
I Panzer 124
II Panzer 124
12 SS Pz Artillery 26
12 SS Pz Flak 26
25 PZ Grenadier *135*
101 SS Heavy Tank 26, 124, 129 *et seq*, *131*, 161
83 Werfer 26, 123
89 Fusilier 126, 128
189 Artillery 126
Grenadier 1055 126 *et seq*
Grenadier 1056 126 *et seq*
KG Waldmuller *see* Waldmuller

KG Wunsche *see* Wunsche
Luftwaffe 54, 107, 133, 134 *et seq*

Polish
Division:
1st Armoured 12, 38, 42, 70, 88, 93, 96, 102,
  105, 108 *et seq*, *111*, *114*, 119, 128, 153,
  158, 161
Brigade:
10th (Armoured) Cavalry 108, 110
Regiments:
1st Armoured 111
2nd Armoured 108, 111 *et seq*
8th Rifle 110
10th Dragoons 28, 110, 111

10th Mounted Rifles 110
24th Lancers 111 *et seq*, 161
in German Army 102

United States
Army:
US Army general/operations 2, 6, 22, 24, 39,
  104, 110, 119, 144, 148, 159, 163
Third US Army (*see also* Patton) 163
Division:
30 US Infantry 148
USAAF:
general 48, 88, 105, 128, 152
8th USAAF 107
9th USAAF 46, 107